THE POLITICS OF GLAMOUR

DAVID F. PRINDLE

THE POLITICS OF GLAMOUR

Ideology and Democracy in the Screen Actors Guild

The University of Wisconsin Press

The University of Wisconsin Press
114 North Murray Street
Madison, Wisconsin 53715

The University of Wisconsin Press, Ltd.
1 Gower Street
London WC1E 6HA, England

Chapter 8 is based upon material that has appeared previously in *Social Science Quarterly*, 69 (Sept. 1988) as "Labor Union Ideology in the Screen Actors Guild."

Library of Congress Cataloging-in-Publication Data
Prindle, David F. (David Forrest), 1948–
The politics of glamour.
Bibliography: pp. 221–246.
Includes index.
1. Screen Actors Guild—History.   2. Trade-unions—
Motion picture industry—United States—History.
3. Motion picture industry—United States—History.
I. Title.   II. Title: Democracy in the
Screen Actors Guild.
PN 1993.5.U6P75   1988   331.88'1179143028'0973   88-40194
ISBN 0-299-11810-X

For Angalene, who makes it all worthwhile

CONTENTS

ABBREVIATIONS

AAAA	Associated Actors and Artistes of America
AFA	American Federation of Actors
AFL	American Federation of Labor
AF(T)RA	American Federation of (Television and) Radio Artists
AGVA	American Guild of Variety Artists
AMPTP	Alliance of Motion Picture and Television Producers
AWAG	Actors Working for an Actors' Guild
CAC	Concerned Actors Committee
CAM	Caucus of Artists for Merger
CIO	Congress of Industrial Organizations
CSU	Conference of Studio Unions
FMPC	Federation of Motion Picture Crafts
GGRC	Guild Government Review Committee
HCUA	House Committee on Un-American Activities
HICCASP	Hollywood Independent Citizens Committee of the Arts, Sciences, and Professions
HUAC	"House Un-American Activities Committee" (colloquial name for HCUA)
IATSE	International Alliance of Theatrical and Stage Employes
IBEW	International Brotherhood of Electrical Workers
LACLC	Los Angeles Central Labor Council
MCA	Music Corporation of America
MGM	Metro-Goldwyn-Mayer
MPA	Motion Picture Alliance (for the Preservation of American Ideals)
NIRA	National Industrial Recovery Act
NLRA	National Labor Relations Act
NLRB	National Labor Relations Board

ABBREVIATIONS

NRA	National Recovery Administration
SAG	Screen Actors Guild
SEG	Screen Extras Guild
SPU	Screen Players Union
SWG	Screen Writers Guild
TVA	Television Authority
USTG	United Studio Technicians Guild

ACKNOWLEDGMENTS

I have conceived and implemented the research on which this book is based, and I am responsible for it. Nevertheless, at every point in my labors I was assisted by people who gave freely of their time, expertise, good nature, and trust. Without their help the book would never have been written.

I am, first of all, grateful to my family and friends in the South Bay area of Los Angeles. My parents, Vivian and Elliott Prindle, my brother Ken and his wife, Marilyn, my sister Vicki Dennis and her husband, George, and my friends William A. Rennie and Deborah Rennie were my support group for two summers and several shorter trips spent conducting interviews and pursuing documents. They allowed me and my family to sleep in their extra rooms, lent me their cars, fed me, took my phone messages, and generally assisted me far beyond the requirements of family hospitality. Someday I hope to be able to repay their generosity.

In addition, my sister Robin Defenbaugh and her husband, Lyle, my grandmother, Charlotte Prindle, and my uncle, Marshall Prindle, although they live away from the area of my research, found less direct ways to assist me.

When I first began this study I thought it might be a good idea to learn something about the way actors are educated. Professor Marian Hampton of the University of Texas Department of Drama allowed me to sit in on one of her sophomore acting classes for an entire semester, which was both a useful and entertaining experience. I owe her one. The students in the class not only put up with my incongruous presence, but cheerfully answered my questions about their backgrounds and aspirations. I wish success to all of them. They are Paula Baker, David Davalos, Ginny Davis, Dee Dawson, Desi Doyen, Marc Garza, Clair Hamilton, Elyse Luck, Leslie Redden, Christopher Steinmetz, Missy Thibodeaux, and Sandra Volls.

Actors William Schallert and Robert Easton took time off from their busy schedules to read the entire manuscript in second draft, and supply me with high-minded and meticulous critiques. They saved me from many errors of fact and interpretation. My colleague Robert Hardgrave at the University of Texas, Dan Cornfield at Vanderbilt, and Ron Gottesman of the University of Southern California read parts of early drafts of the manuscript and made helpful comments. Since I did not always take the advice of these gentlemen, they cannot be blamed for the remaining imperfections in the book.

My research assistant Catherine del Castillo spent months discovering, analyzing, and summarizing academic notions of the psychology of actors, and further months ferreting out obscure information on the personal background of some specific performers. Without her help I would probably still be spending my days in the basement of the Perry-Castaneda Library, reading through the obituaries in long-forgotten issues of *Variety*.

Similarly, Mary Beeman, who is both a graduate student in the University of Texas Government Department and an attorney, devoted a semester to investigating the legal and Constitutional issues surrounding HUAC and the blacklist. Her clearly written summary and analysis saved me from having to delve too deeply into an area where I lack training.

John Bitsche and Maurice Franklin, undergraduate computer science majors at the University of Texas, crunched my raw interview data into the statistical tables that form the basis for the discussion in chapter 8.

In 1986 William Livingston, vice-president for academic affairs at the University of Texas, helped me to get a $1,000 grant from the University Research Institute, which enabled me and my family to get through that summer in California without ending up in debtor's prison. I thank him.

The book would obviously have turned out differently had it not been for the many people, mostly actors, who allowed me to interview them at considerable length on the history and politics of the guild. I discuss the setting of the interviews, and list those who talked to me, in the Sources section of this book.

David Robb of *Daily Variety* not only gave me the benefit of his knowledge of Hollywood labor through personal discussions, but lent me some precious documents which I don't think I could have acquired anywhere else. I hope he approves of the use to which I put them. One of Robb's colleagues, who prefers not to be named, also spent a lunchtime with me early in my quest, and got me started in the right direction.

Many other people helped along the way, always with surprising good cheer and never with a hope of reward. I cannot thank them all in detail, but I will nevertheless remember them. They are Woolsey Ackerman, Leith Adams, Richard Adcock, Amy Boardman, Eric Boardman, Don Carleton, Larry Ceplair, Ned Comstock, Carol Cullen, Diana Denman, Randy Hodgson, Bob Knutson, Les Kurtz, Carol Lanning, Mort Lewis, Jayne Loader, Marti Martin, Harry Medved, Peter Ordeshook, Tony Phipps, Frank Riley, Dennis Stephens, Howard Suber, Mitch Tuchman, and Robert Vianello.

Last, my wife, Angalene, put up with having her family uprooted and moved to southern California two summers in a row, for what must have seemed at first like a rather crackpot project. That we are still married is testimony to her patience. She has earned the dedication at the beginning of this book.

THE POLITICS OF GLAMOUR

It's the stuff that dreams are made of.

Humphrey Bogart to Ward Bond, *The Maltese Falcon*, screenplay by
John Huston

Chapter One

A UNION OF SCREEN ACTORS

This book is a case study of ideology and democracy within a labor
union called the Screen Actors Guild (SAG).

The guild is a labor union composed of actors who have performed
in feature motion pictures, television series, television commercials,
and industrial and educational films. As is the case with other unions,
it is an organization that bargains with management in the collective
name of its sixty thousand members to improve their wages, hours,
and working conditions. As with other unions, it is successful because
it is able to credibly threaten to withhold enough workers, by striking,
to shut down the electronic entertainment industry. As with other
unions, it both attempts to protect its members from arbitrary treatment by management and to raise their aggregate income by restrict-
ing management's access to the supply of labor.[1]

Despite these fundamental similarities, however, the guild is different from other unions. Like only a very few labor organizations—the
other entertainment and sports unions—it can boast dozens of members who are both very rich and world-famous. Because of the glamour
that emanates from most successful screen actors, in any conflict with
management guild members have immediate access to the mass media
to tell their side of the story, which alters the context of negotiations.
Moreover, unlike the case in most unions, any dispute within the guild
is likely to wind up not only in the headlines of Hollywood trade papers, but on the evening television news. The celebrity of some of its

3

members thus infuses SAG with nearly unique power, and guarantees that its internal life has a distinctive tone.

The Screen Actors Guild can therefore be studied both as a typical example of labor unions and as one that is utterly unlike the others.

A Union . . .

For at least the past century, American labor union activists have been engaged in an argument about the ultimate goals their movement should pursue, and the strategy with which it should pursue them. Its history is thus partly the story of a series of internal conflicts, none of which have been resolved. By the 1950s, most individual unions had declared themselves as supporting the more conservative side of each issue, and had either suppressed or expelled activists who pushed contrary points of view. They have thus brought an uneasy peace to the movement as a whole. Some individual unions, however, have never been able to suppress dissent, and have had to adjust to a state of permanent internal strife. The Screen Actors Guild is one of these.

The most basic philosophical issue faced by a partisan of labor is whether the American system of private ownership and control of the means of production is just and efficient, or whether it should be replaced by socialism. A subsidiary issue, for those who favor government ownership, is whether the transition to that new system must be peaceful, or whether violence is justified. Differences of opinion over this issue divide Socialists, who prefer evolution, from Communists, who endorse revolution.

Once capitalism is accepted as a fact, the major question becomes whether the labor movement will be relatively more, or relatively less, militant in its relations with management. Some activists view management as the enemy, and believe that only a vigilant and confrontational work force can hope to protect itself from exploitation. This group is usually ready to strike to force its will upon the bosses. In this book I refer to labor activists who lean in this ideological direction as *progressives* or *leftists*. Socialists and Communists are extreme leftists. At the other philosophical pole, some workers see management and labor as partners cooperating for mutual benefit. In their view, reason and good faith will allow negotiators to work out accommodations that are profitable to both sides. They abhor striking. I call those who lean to this opinion *conservatives* or *rightists*. At the extreme of this side are unionists who actually oppose the whole existence of unions.

These opposed ideological positions imply other differences. Leftists see workers as struggling against not only management but also a hostile legal and political system. They believe that a single union, isolated and alone, is usually in a weak position. The way to fight the system is therefore to forge alliances outside their own backyard, first with the national labor movement and ultimately with a workers' political party. Serious progressives yearn for the "one big union" that no corporation or government would dare defy. Their attention is therefore focused at least as much outside their union as within it.

On the other hand, conservatives accept the system in which the union operates, and consequently see no value in outside labor and political activities. They believe that bargaining with management is the beginning and end of the functions of their union.

Because few people of any persuasion can boast a completely consistent set of beliefs, there are not many union activists whose set of ideas places them entirely at one philosophical pole or another. I have described two ideal types of ideologues. In actual fact, participants in the Screen Actors Guild, like union activists elsewhere, tend to be arrayed along an ideological spectrum with a very few found at the pure extremes, and most clustering closer to the muddled middle. For purposes of simplicity, through most of this book I portray the ideological divisions in the guild as being clearer than they historically have been. In chapter 8, however, I explore some of the complexities of ideology.

In the early decades of the labor movement, progressive and conservative ideologies tended to be associated with different types of unions. In general (and greatly simplifying), craft workers—electricians, carpenters, plumbers—were in a more favored position in relation to management. Because of the skilled nature of their occupation, they were difficult to replace; this lent credibility to a threat to strike, and rendered management more agreeable. Their relatively secure situation led them to view the social system in general, and their employer in particular, without fear. The consequence was conservatism. Traditionally, the national organization that represented local craft unions was the American Federation of Labor (AFL).[2]

On the other hand, unskilled workers in industries such as mining, steel, and automobile manufacturing were typically in a much less powerful position in relation to management. As interchangeable parts in a manufacturing process, they were readily replaced; it was therefore easy to break their strikes. Being in a vulnerable position, they naturally regarded management as an antagonist, and yearned for outside alliances to bolster their strength. All this encouraged a leftist perspective.[3]

The desire of industrial organizers to enroll every worker in a particular industry could easily collide with the intentions of craft unionists to recruit members of specific trades which cross industries. The early history of American labor, therefore, was rife with disputes between, say, the Carpenters, who wanted to add to their membership just the skilled workers who turned out wood used in the construction industry, and the Amalgamated Wood Workers, who wanted to organize everyone employed in an industry dealing with wood. As a result, the story of organized labor is not only a chronicle of the struggle between management and workers, but also of the often equally rancorous conflict between the AFL and its industrial-union rivals, first the Industrial Workers of the World (IWW), and later, in the 1930s, the Congress of Industrial Organizations (CIO). Since technological and business evolution was constantly altering the workplace, disputes between these two types of unions were for decades a frequent part of the American economy. This was as true in Hollywood as in any other town.[4]

For the first half of this century, the fight between craft (AFL) and industrial (first IWW, then CIO) unions was the major arena for the national struggle between rightists and leftists. As we shall see, however, industrial unions never gained much influence in Hollywood, so ideological disputes tended to be fought out within and between members of the AFL. Moreover, as the labor movement changed to adapt to the evolving national economy after World War II, and especially after the AFL and the CIO merged in 1955, the ideological battle became less easy to assign to a structural context. It is now much harder everywhere to distinguish between "craft" and "industrial" unions, and more difficult to predict where a particular philosophy will predominate. One of the tasks of this book is to explore the personal and occupational background of variations in ideology within the screen actors' union, and to thereby be able to say something about the origins of these philosophical differences in general.[5]

Disagreements of broad perspective are not the only kind of conflicts within the ranks of labor, however. Almost equally disruptive have been battles between individual unions or groups of unions over *jurisdiction*.

At their core, unions deal with clearly demarcated jobs. No one, for example, would confuse the work electricians do with the tasks performed by railroad porters. But at the margin, jobs are not so easily defined, and might logically be assigned to any of several unions. Should beer-truck drivers belong to the brewers' or to the truck-drivers' organization? Will the builders of motion-picture sets be assigned to the carpenters' or to the stagehands' union? The answers to such questions are ambiguous, and are more likely to be answered with power than with argument.

Because it is obvious that conflict over jurisdiction could dissipate labor's energies in futile internal squabbling, one of the prime purposes of the "international" organization has always been to head off and resolve such disputes. From the moment jurisdictional arguments first appeared in the 1870s, therefore, national labor leaders sought to find ways to resolve them amicably. Under the "principle of exclusive jurisdiction" adopted in the 1880s, the AFL declared that "it is detrimental to the interests of labor to have more than one organization in any trade."[6] Since that time one of the prime benefits to any union of belonging to the parent organization is that it is thereby less subject to jurisdictional poaching by other members.

However, such protection, imperfect as it is, applies only to established unions dealing with settled job areas. When several unions are attempting to move into an unorganized city, or when technological change creates new and different jobs, jurisdictional strife is inevitable.

Because Los Angeles in the 1930s and 1940s was the least organized large city in America, and because the motion picture industry was using a rapidly evolving technology, Hollywood was a union battleground during those decades. The Screen Actors Guild found itself not only having to struggle with the film producers, but equally forced to maneuver among the contending battalions of labor.

Even if unions are frequently at odds over goals, tactics, and jurisdiction, one question of organization on which they are typically united is that of endorsing the principle of democracy within unions, while denying it in practice.

Every American labor organization is, on paper, governed by individuals who are responsible to the rank-and-file members. Unions have written constitutions which guarantee regular election of officers, clauses protecting the rights of the minority from harassment, and other accoutrements of democracy.[7]

In fact, however, George Bernard Shaw's observation in *The Apple*

Cart decades ago that "no king is as safe in office as a trade union official" is as true today as when he wrote it.[8] Many years of academic research into union government have confirmed the typical picture of government by a self-perpetuating oligarchy, that is, by a political machine. The ruling group is typically impervious to attack because of its control of information to the members, its domination of the union administration, the members' paucity of political skill, and the lack of legitimacy accorded to workers who seem to want to weaken the leadership in the face of the enemy (management).[9]

The great exception to this monotonous oligarchy is the printers' organization, the International Typographical Union (ITU), which has for over sixty years maintained a vigorous internal two-party system.[10] The parties advocate policies that roughly correspond to what I have just labeled the progressive and conservative philosophies. Several academic studies have uncovered various episodes of successful rebellion in American and British unions, in which unusual stupidity, arrogance, or brutality by the ruling group led to its electoral downfall. But these episodes were temporary; the ITU is the only union that has regularized rule by its ordinary members,[11] except for the Screen Actors Guild and its sister performers' unions. From its founding in 1933, a struggle between progressive and conservative actors in SAG was constant but muted, with the conservatives generally dominating. In 1971, however, leftists openly challenged the ruling group, and, in 1973, overthrew it. The conflict between the two philosophies simmered thereafter until 1981, when it burst out into a riot of democracy. In the ensuing six years, the competing parties became institutionalized, so that they now have well-recognized leaders, slates of candidates, and policy platforms. SAG is therefore a fine laboratory in which to study the conflict between the two tendencies in the American labor movement.

In following philosophical arguments as they developed in the guild over the course of five decades, however, we must remember that we are not watching a typical labor union. Actors are not like other workers, and so their politics are different. To understand this, it is necessary to think about actors, and their place in that complex of electronic entertainment known as Hollywood.

. . . *Of Actors*

"Concerning *acting*, there is no doubt about the nature of the underlying basic partial instinct: it is *exhibitionism.* . . . Persons who are fixated on this partial instinct are regularly persons who need this specific type of pleasure for the purpose of counteracting inner fears."[12] So wrote Otto Fenichel, one of the heirs to the Freudian mantle, in 1946. Fifteen years later, Ronald Taft summarized his empirical study of seventy-four actors and actresses with the words, "The over-riding picture that emerges is of a comparatively undercontrolled, disorganized personality who is quick to panic. He is sensitive to his environment and interested in artistic activities and social relations without really empathizing with other people."[13]

These two psychological portraits illustrate the unflattering view of actors that is common in modern society. Followers of the theatrical profession are portrayed as trying to find in the love of the audience what they lack in their own characters. Their narcissism is an overcompensation for inner emptiness, their orientation to the crowd a camouflage for their inability to deal with other humans one at a time.[14]

Nor have actors as a group been much respected within their own industry. Anthropologist Hortense Powdermaker's synthesis of Hollywood's view of actors during the studio system of the 1930s and 1940s is perhaps extreme, but nevertheless representative: they were seen as "children who do not know what is good for them, immature, irresponsible, completely self-centered, egotistical, exhibitionistic, nitwits, and utterly stupid."[15]

This attitude is not new. As Mendel Kohansky demonstrates in his book *The Disreputable Profession*, the modern consignment of acting to the realm of pathology merely continues the contempt and fear that performers have traditionally evoked from the respectable institutions of society. For much of Western history, actors' alleged impiety, personal affectation, and sexual license have made them the object of ridicule, condemnation, and occasionally legal prohibition.[16] The rise of many actors in the twentieth century to the status of celebrity has not destroyed the ancient prejudice, merely deflected it into the channels of academic put-downs, of which Fenichel's and Taft's are examples.

I don't know whether or not actors in general are narcissistic and vapid. But I am certain that those who participate in the governance of the Screen Actors Guild are not the self-obsessed dummies portrayed in academic writing. Working in guild government, which largely consists of serving as an officer or member of the board of directors, is not the stuff that dreams are made of. It is difficult, tedious labor, demanding intelligence, judgment, and self-discipline. The board and officers meet at least twice a month to conduct guild business: disbursing the $12 million annual budget, overseeing contract negotiations, analyzing information on the development of the industry, debating the value of merging with other unions, and much more. Though actors can be faulted for the verbosity they bring to the boardroom, there is no doubting the basic maturity of their behavior there.

Nor are guild activists compensated for their contributions of time and energy. It has from the beginning been SAG policy not to pay its officers a salary. This distinguishes it immediately from every other labor organization (excepting the other entertainment unions). Moreover, those involved cannot expect a boost to their careers from their years of service, for it is their unanimous observation that activism in SAG never helps an actor with prospective employers.

In other words, participants in Screen Actors Guild government are good citizens, serving their union out of a sense of responsibility.

If narcissism is not a relevant attribute of guild activists, other aspects of the actor's life are important to understanding the history of their union. Chief among these is unemployment.

Except for those very few performers who have the good fortune to be featured in a long-running television series, jobs for even the stars are discontinuous and precarious. In the first place, there are simply too many actors for the available parts. Unlike the case in a more normal, uncharismatic industry such as, say, coal mining or cab driving, the labor supply in motion picture production does not, over time, adjust to the jobs available. The profession's glamour and its much-publicized colossal salaries for the top stars have always lured thousands more hopefuls to Hollywood than can ever make a living there. Many of these hang around on the fringes of employment for years, waiting tables or parking cars to stay alive while they attend hundreds of auditions. The mob of aspirants thus created makes every other actor insecure, for even those with a distinguished record can never be certain that they might not be replaced by some talented newcomer willing to work longer hours for lesser pay.

In the second place, even disregarding the overabundance of actors, their careers are terrifyingly precarious. A certain face or body type may go out of style; an agent may offend a powerful person; producers may decide a particular actor is "overexposed;" through no fault of his own an actor may appear in a series of box-office flops and be blamed for their failure; an actress may discover that despite her talents she has grown "too old" for the available female parts; or for many other reasons even a respected, well-known player may suddenly be unable to find work. It is not only possible in theory. Every actor knows stories of stars who have suddenly, inexplicably, dropped into a professional void. It is part of the mythology of Hollywood.

This awareness of the uncertainty of their professional standing permeates actors' attitudes toward their lives, their industry, and their union. As former SAG president William Schallert describes the situation, "Making a living as an actor is like trying to cross a rapidly rushing river by stepping from one slowly sinking rock to another."[17] To this metaphorical description, former vice-president Joseph Ruskin adds a more concrete warning: "I hope you recognize that actors live in fear."[18]

Fear, indeed. Officially, at any given moment, about 85 percent of SAG members are out of work, and two-thirds earn less than $2,000 a year from their announced profession.[19] The unofficial situation is not nearly as bad as these figures make it seem, because at least half of the Hollywood branch's twenty-five thousand members are not really actors. Many nonactors have joined because, for example, they happened to become caught up in a "real people" television commercial while shopping in a supermarket one day, thereby earning the right to acquire a SAG card. Still, the situation is bad enough. If unemployment among actual, career-oriented actors is only 20 percent, it is still horrendous from the perspective of almost any other profession. Nor can realistic observers hope that prospects will improve with new technology or an upturn in the national economy, for it has been this way through boom, bust, war, and depression for over seventy years. The entire guild membership thus consists of workers who are likely at any particular time not to be working, and who face the quite real possibility of never working again. This is the primeval situation with which SAG officers must live, and it conditions everything they do and say.

One of the major functions of a union—providing its members with job security—is therefore forbidden to the Screen Actors Guild. The fact that actors live in fear has had profound consequences for the guild's history. In particular, the blacklisting episode of the 1940s and 1950s still weighs like a nightmare on the collective memory of actors. It forms the background against which SAG members discuss union policy, and offers a lens through which they view contemporary events. When president Ed Asner's "Lou Grant" television series was canceled in 1982 after his leftist politics were publicized, for example, actors overwhelmingly assumed that this was another instance of blacklisting. Whatever the facts (and they are arguable), actors perceived the episode through a prism of paranoia. It became just another example to add to the mythology of insecurity.

Another phenomenon that distinguishes an actors' union from others is that the conditions of their work vary markedly. A professional actor may, over the course of a career, work in four major types of jobs: theatrical, industrial, or educational films; television series; television commercials; and live stage. Theater players have their own union, of course (Actors Equity), but most successful performers have experience in at least two of the four media, and therefore belong to more than one union.

As every text on the subject is quick to point out, stage acting is fundamentally different from screen acting. The performance of a play is a continuous episode, unfolding in a logical sequence from first scene to last. The actors thus always know where they are in the dramatic action, and understand how their particular lines at one point relate to the overall purpose of the plot. Similarly, the members of the cast rely upon and support one another, for a play is an ensemble effort, and an individual failure spoils the overall effect. Further, the nature of live drama is that it is repeated every day at a certain time, which means that once rehearsals are over and opening night past, the actor spends only a few hours a day at the theater. Additionally, because stage actors must reach an audience sitting some distance away, they cultivate resonant voices and expansive gestures. Finally, on the stage the players have to adapt their performances anew to each night's crowd, and therefore must be constantly sensitive to the reactions of the audience.

Acting for the screen is utterly different. Films (and, to a somewhat lesser extent, television series and commercials) are shot with scenes out of sequence, to be reassembled in proper order in the cutting room. Actors are therefore presented, during a workday, with a jumble of scenes that may bear no obvious relation to one another; they may never, in fact, be informed of the overall tone or purpose of the story. For the same reason, the members of the cast need not be so cooperative, for they depend far less on a group effort to carry the overall dramatic message. Film acting is thus an individual, not an ensemble, profession. Moreover, because filming lasts weeks or months, with no obvious pauses, the workdays of the participants are indefinite, which in practice can easily lead to sixteen-hour days. In addition, because the camera is capable of giving the audience minute close-ups of actors, it requires understatement and subtlety. Finally, the camera does not function as an audience, so film actors must respond to their own inner cues, or to their director, in fashioning a performance.[20]

Screen and theater actors, then, are performing two different jobs. The first is far more individualistic, and far less cooperative, than the second. One of the questions I address is whether these differences in professional experience translate into differences in ideological outlook.

Another aspect of actors' lives that has important consequences for their union is that a few of them are stars, but most of them are not. Since about the time of World War I, motion-picture (and now, television) producers have assumed that the presence of one or several popular names in a cast enhances the box-office appeal of any film.[21] There is, I should point out, little to support this view. Movies with top stars in strong roles not uncommonly flop (*Annie, The Formula, Ishtar*); movies with a cast of unknowns occasionally make hundreds of millions of dollars (*American Graffiti, Star Wars, Crocodile Dundee*). The academic studies that have tried to measure the impact of stardom on ticket sales have been inconclusive.[22]

But whether or not stars can sell a picture (or a television series) is not important. What counts is that producers believe that they do. Fifty years ago studio executives thought themselves dependent on stars to sell films, which gave SAG's threat to withdraw all the actors at once real clout. Today, the different way that movies (and, again, TV series) are financed gives the big-name actors even more influence. A large percentage of the movies financed by studios, and TV series financed by networks, are first "packaged" by an agent, who puts together a writer, a director, and an actor, and offers them as a group project to the producers. Nothing helps get a project launched like a team of big-name "talent" as its underpinning. When the Screen Actors Guild goes on strike, the stars temporarily withdraw not only from actual work in front of the camera, but also from this process of deal-making. Without stars, there is no package; without a package, there is no financing; without financing, there is no movie or series.[23]

Minus the stars, the guild's authority over all professional performing talent would still make it a powerful organization. As the producers learned during SAG's TV commercials strike in 1979 when they tried to make commercials with amateur performers, the guild controls an unsubstitutable resource even in its unknown members. Nevertheless, because of the stars' position astride the financial system of Hollywood, and because of the producers' almost superstitious faith in the box-office appeal of name actors, the guild's ability to call out the stars enormously enhances its weight in any negotiation.

The irony is that the stars need the guild far less than do ordinary actors. Although some SAG contract provisions, such as those pertaining to safety, benefit all players, many more help only the ordinary performer. Before starting on a project, stars would have had their agents negotiate a work agreement much more favorable to themselves than is the standard SAG contract. They would have high salaries, favorable working conditions, and partial artistic control whether or not there was a Screen Actors Guild. It is the ordinary supporting cast member who is powerless, and thus needs the protection of a labor union.

The guild is therefore in the uncomfortable position of relying on its stars to lend support to a collective-bargaining process that mainly benefits its rank-and-file members. This is a problem that cannot be overcome. Although each performer offers a unique face, voice, and bundle of talents, in a structural sense the great mass of screen actors are undifferentiated laborers, and should be in an industrial union like the CIO. But the stars, as irreplaceable artists, would be more appropriately ensconced in a craft union like the AFL. Such a thing is impossible, of course, even were it not true that some actors become stars, and others fall from the ranks of stardom. And so, whereas most labor organizations represent one side of the movement or the other, the Screen Actors Guild is fated to be permanently a member of both.

It would be convenient at this point if I could announce that the ideological cleavage in the guild is simply reflective of the political differences between the progressive rank-and-file and the conservative stars. Such is not the case, however. For reasons to be explored in later chapters, many of the most successful actors adopt a leftist posture, and speak as if they viewed themselves as common laborers. Similarly, perhaps because they aspire to stardom, or perhaps because they vote on other than philosophical grounds, a generous proportion of SAG's ordinary members can be counted on to support conservative candidates. Although the ideologies underlying SAG politics are clear, therefore, the interests represented by them are obscure. Part of the task of this book is to clarify the forces at work.

It is in this peculiar union, then, that the struggle for the soul of the American labor movement, a struggle a century old, continues. The history of the guild is, of course, far more complex and inconsistent than this account makes it sound. Unions are not self-sufficient, and must react to technical, economic, and political forces outside themselves. The Screen Actors Guild, like any other union, has had to do its share of adjusting to history. But the fundamental conflicts within unionism infuse the arguments that accompany all its maneuvering. It is to these actual events that we now turn.

This is the West. When the legend becomes a fact, print the legend.

Carleton Young to fellow newspapermen, *The Man Who Shot Liberty Valance*, screenplay by James Warner Bellah and Willis Goldbeck

Chapter Two

ACTION

The year 1933 was not turning out to be a good one for the American motion picture industry. Although Hollywood was the most important movie-making center in the world, its financial underpinnings were buckling.[1] In 1929, the last year of national prosperity, an average of 80 million Americans had attended movies every week, paying $720 million that year to do so. Now, in the spring, the trough of the depression, 20 million fewer customers were clicking through the turnstiles each week, and gross receipts were down by a third. By midsummer, about five thousand of the sixteen thousand regularly operated theaters in the United States would be closed. Real-estate losses were mounting.[2]

A decade before, such a contraction might have been borne. But now, the financial structure of the movie companies prevented retrenchment. The arrival of sound in 1927 had forced them to take out large loans for the purchase of the new technology. Moreover, during the boom years before 1929 they had built lavish studios and acquired theater chains at inflated prices. When the bottom fell out of the motion-picture market, the companies were left with the loan payments of prosperity, but the income of depression.

In January 1933, Paramount and Radio-Keith-Orpheum (RKO), two of the dominant studios, declared their theater chains bankrupt and went into receivership. Of the others, only Metro-Goldwyn-Mayer (MGM) was relatively healthy. 20th Century-Fox, Warner Brothers, Universal, and Columbia also teetered on the edge of insolvency.[3]

16

So it was that when the new president, Franklin Roosevelt, signed legislation on 9 March that closed every bank in the country, the reaction in Hollywood was swift and severe. Universal immediately suspended all its contracts. Fox notified its employees that it could not pay their salaries. The rumor swept the industry that the studios would shut down.[4]

The moguls announced, however, that they had discovered a way to stave off disaster. Employees would simply be asked to take a 50 percent cut in wages. Five days later the Academy of Motion Picture Arts and Sciences (now famous as distributor of the Academy Awards, but then the producers' company union) changed this across-the-board plan to a formula: those earning less than $50 a week would be exempt from the salary waiver; those earning between $50 and $75 would lose 25 percent; those earning between $75 and $100 would sacrifice 35 percent; and only those topping $100 would forfeit half their income. The cuts were to last for eight weeks.[5]

Although some of the studio bosses, experts at providing melodrama to an audience, literally cried when they informed their workers of the need for this sacrifice, they were unconvincing.[6] A labor movement among artists in Hollywood had been struggling to be born for years, and the pay cuts of March 1933 were the catalyst that turned potential into reality. The birth and youth of the Screen Writers Guild (SWG), which was founded 6 April, has been extensively chronicled by historians.[7] But for the actors also, the events of that month began a chain of action that took them through negotiation, political maneuver, violence, and other nonartistic realms, to emerge six years later triumphant, as probably the most powerful and cohesive labor union in Hollywood.

Stage Door

When the sound era hit Hollywood, it mandated enormous changes not only in equipment but also in creative talent. In terms of script preparation, it meant that stories could no longer be told as a series of visual images; they now required dialogue. The industry therefore began to hire New York playwrights, whose skill, obviously, was in giving the actors interesting words to say. And in regard to those actors, it meant that they had to be able to say the words. Nasal twangs, regional inflections, sloppy locutions, and grating voices had been perfectly acceptable when films were silent. But actors in the talkies had to speak clearly, richly, and with a neutral delivery. Those who could not, learned how, or retired. Clara Bow, for example, had been a tremendous success in the silents, despite her dingbat Brooklyn accent. When she opened her mouth in a talkie, however, audiences laughed, and her career was soon over.[8]

On the other hand, stage actors, every one in possession of a trained speaking voice, were suddenly in demand. There had always been players with theatrical experience in Hollywood, of course, but the late 1920s saw the beginnings of a mass migration from Broadway to Los Angeles that has never stopped. The movies simply paid more money than the theater. As a result, with a few exceptions such as Katherine Cornell, the competent actors of New York stepped on the westbound train and went off to try to supplement their fame with some fortune.

Some of the veterans of that era offer this change in the population of the acting cadre as an explanation for the rise of the Screen Actors Guild. Their argument is that it was the newly arrived stage actors who founded the guild, often against the opposition of the old silent actors. They say that the conditions of working in films were so much worse than those of working in the theater that they shocked the newcomers into resistance. Chief among their objections to the demands of their new jobs were those about hours.

Lyle Talbot remembers, "In the theater, we were used to working during the play—going to the theater at five o'clock, and we were usually finished at eleven o'clock. We did the play, and that was it. But in Hollywood, hours meant nothing. . . . We would work twelve to fourteen hours, and get called back the next morning."[9] "I've worked until midnight and at four o'clock in the morning been called back to makeup at seven o'clock," recollects Leon Ames.[10] Robert Montgomery recalls a film in which "we were actually on the set and working for over thirty-five hours without a break."[11] Barbara McCandless McLean explains that "the typical day was up at 5 A. M., travel and arrive in the studios by 7 A. M. for two hours of makeup, hairdressing and wardrobe, and ready on the set by 9 A. M. Sometimes we worked until midnight, and the strain was almost beyond endurance."[12]

There were also other objections, less important but cumulatively maddening. Sometimes the directors would not allow a lunch break until three or four in the afternoon. Often, on location, bathroom facilities were inadequate. Frequently, especially on location, there was little concern for safety. Although the new arrivals were not about to give up the money that the movies offered, they grew more and more disgruntled about their working conditions.

There was, in addition, another way in which the experience of the stage actors differed from that of the silent-film actors who had survived the transition to the new Hollywood. They were members of Actors Equity. This labor union had been founded in New York, and won the right to represent actors on Broadway in 1919. It negotiated contracts that regulated the wages, hours, and working conditions of stage actors, and took their side when they had complaints against management.[13] In the 1920s, when the town was prosperous and there were fewer actors with stage experience, Equity had tried and failed to organize Hollywood.[14] Now, in a different era, runs the argument, the grumblings of the ex-Broadway players began to take the form of discussion of the possibility of forming a new union.

If it is correct to maintain that it was the newly arrived stage performers who were so discontented as to form a labor union, it is logical to assume that the members of the profession who opposed it came from the long-established silent film players. There were certainly actors who were against the creation of SAG; some of these came to early meetings to argue against the organization. Ralph Bellamy, a stage actor who joined SAG shortly after its founding, remembers more than one of his friends insisting, "MGM and Louis B. Mayer have been very good to me. I'm not going to do this to him!"[15] Leon Ames recalls Edmund Breeze walking up to Ralph Morgan and intoning, "You guys are crazy; you're going to get us all thrown out of the industry. What the hell is the matter with you?"[16] It might well be that the argument within the ranks was a community struggle between the survivors of a former era and the new arrivals.

This is a wonderful explanation for the rise of the Screen Actors Guild—neat, plausible, and in line with academic theories about social conflict. I wish I could report that an examination of the backgrounds of those who founded and those who opposed the new labor union establishes that the founders were, indeed, recently arrived stage artists, and that the resisters were long-established silent players. As table 2.1 illustrates, however, there is no evidence supporting such a theory. On the average, the founders actually began their film careers a bit earlier than did the resisters; this collapses the newcomers-versus-old-timers contention. Almost all of the players in both categories had live theater experience; this destroys the stage-versus-screen argument. Because many of the people cataloged in table 2.1 were relatively obscure, few records exist on their personal and professional backgrounds. Otherwise we might, through detailed examination, discover some other facet of their experience which might explain, at least statistically, their difference in philosophies. As it is, we must be content with the knowledge that stage experience played a significant role in the guild founders' labor activism, and that they faced significant opposition to that activism from within their own profession.[17]

At any rate, the arena of conversation was the Masquer's Club on Sycamore just off Hollywood Boulevard. This was a private club founded by silent film actor Antonio Moreno. It did not officially restrict its membership to actors, but most of those who belonged did in fact follow that vocation. The clubby shoptalk of the Masquer's all-male clientele naturally included a good deal of griping. As the depression deepened, the griping evolved into organizing efforts, and in late 1932 a group of around twenty-five actors began to meet weekly at one another's homes. They continued these gatherings through the winter of 1933, and when their employers announced the 50 percent pay cut, decided that the time had come to form a labor union.[18]

In the half-century since the heroic days of the founding, a legend has grown that it was primarily to help the extras—players without speaking lines, who are hired mainly to create crowd scenes—that the actors organized.[19] On the contrary, although the plight of the extras was real enough, it did not inspire the formation of the actors' union. Talbot, who was present for many of the discussions at the Masquer's Club and joined the guild shortly after its first official meeting, does not remember once hearing anyone talk about extras. "In the first place, I don't think we knew too much about whether they had problems or not."[20] They didn't know if the extras had problems because they didn't know any extras. In Hollywood, unlike Broadway, there tended to be a class system among performers. "There was this star, who doesn't speak to the supporting player, and the supporting player who doesn't speak to the bit player, and the bit player, who will have nothing to do with the extras."[21] In its first weeks the guild was a union of supporting players uniting to solve their own problems.

The early assemblies in the spring of 1933 were not publicized, but the studio bosses found out about them anyway. They sent private de-

Table 2.1. Backgrounds of Pro- and Anti-Union Screen Actors,
Early 1930s

First Screen Actors Guild Board of Directors, 1933		
Name	Year of First Film	Stage Experience
Leon Ames	1932	Yes
Clay Clement	1914	Yes
James Gleason	1922	Yes
Lucille Gleason	1929	Yes
Boris Karloff	1919	Yes
Claude King	1920	Yes
Noel Madison	1930 Median Year:	Yes
Ralph Morgan	1923 1922½	Yes
Alan Mowbray	1931	Yes
Bradley Page	1934	No
Ivan Simpson	1915	Yes
Alden Gay Thomson	a	Yes
Kenneth Thomson	1926	Yes
Richard Tucker	1913	Yes
Arthur Vinton	1931	Yes
Morgan Wallace	1920	Yes
Anti-SAG Screen Actors[b]		
Elizabeth Allen	1931	Yes
Arthur Aylesworth	1932	No
Wallace Beery	1913	Yes
Lionel Barrymore	1911	Yes
Alice Brady	1914	Yes
Edmund Breeze	1923	Yes
George Brent	1931	Yes
James Burtis	1930	No
Harvey Clark	1922	No
Ricardo Cortez	1923 Median Year:	Yes
Cecil Cunningham	1930 1924	Yes
Roy D'Arcy	1919	Yes
Al Hill	1927	Yes
DeWitt Jennings	1915	Yes
Ian Keith	1924	Yes
Dorothy Lee	1929	Yes
Eric Linden	1931	Yes
Lucien Littlefield	1913	No
Edwin Maxwell	1927	Yes
William Mong	1910	Yes
Conrad Nagel	1919	Yes
Jack Oakie	1927	Yes
Reginald Owen	1929	Yes
Nat Pendleton	1924	Yes
Rosalind Russell	1934	Yes
Robert Warwick	1914	Yes
Harry Worth	1920	Yes

[a] Alden Gay Thomson was married to Kenneth Thomson.
[b] Names gathered from the memories of the founders, added to those suspended by Actors Equity for not joining SAG.

tectives to spy on those who came and went from the houses, and indirectly threatened the careers of the malcontents. These threats were not idle. Many of the conspirators experienced great difficulty finding work for the next two years. But the meetings continued.[22]

A Star Is Born

When they began to move toward establishing a formal organization, the actors asked members of the new Screen Writers Guild to recommend an attorney. Laurence Beilenson, the SWG's lawyer, agreed to act in that capacity for the actors also. In late June 1933, at a meeting chaired by Ralph Morgan at Ken Thomson's house, with eighteen actors and Beilenson in attendance, the actors decided to turn their informal group into a legal entity. The day after the meeting, James Gleason and Alan Mowbray paid an incorporation fee out of their own pockets. Beilenson filed the papers on 30 June.[23]

From the initial meeting it was apparent that this would not be an ordinary labor union. In the first place, the choice of "guild" as opposed to "union" was no whim. Many of those present, despite their activism, were socially and politically conservative, and would have been uncomfortable in any group that featured "union" in its title. (In other words, the founders were not "progressive" labor activists as I have defined the term.) Conscious of this, Ivan Simpson suggested that they follow the example of the writers in picking a name that harked back to medieval associations of artisans. So it became the Screen Actors Guild.[24] The symbolic importance of the title would not be lost on succeeding generations of actors.

There were also more tangible peculiarities. Lawyer Beilenson knew, with everyone in the room, that the infant SAG would not survive unless it could induce stars to join. The stars, being rich (and this being prior to the New Deal's laws protecting labor unions), would be reluctant to become members of an organization through which they might become individually liable for collective action. He therefore advised the assembly that the guild should be a corporation, a legal form that would insulate its members from financial responsibility. While other unions were generally composed of a mosaic of locals, with national power therefore highly dispersed, the Screen Actors Guild would be a centralized organization with power entirely concentrated in its board of directors.[25]

In detail, also, the original bylaws set apart the guild as unusual. The membership had to approve a strike by a 75 percent vote, as opposed to the customary simple majority. A small percentage of the members could demand the initiative, referendum, and recall. All the people on the board, and all the officers, would be directly chosen in an election in which every senior (nonextra) member would be eligible to vote. This contrasted with the customary union practice in which officers are chosen by a convention of delegates from the locals. In other words, lack of militancy and unusually democratic government were structural features of SAG from its inception.[26]

In addition, there was another provision in the bylaws which has ever since given guild government a distinctive cast. Whereas the officers of most other unions are salaried, SAG's were to volunteer their time. The professional labor official, who looks upon his officer's job as his livelihood, and consequently has a strong incentive to hold on to it by whatever means, cannot arise in the Screen Actors Guild. This tends to make government more democratic. On the other hand, it also tended to restrict access to the boardroom, at least in the first few decades, to those who could afford the time: stars and near-stars. In the beginning, SAG officers habitually paid many of their expenses themselves. When Kathleen Nolan, a nonstar, was elected president in the 1970s, however, she quickly found herself in trouble over her use of the presidential expense account.

Once they had become an official organization, the members of the founding group had to create a board of directors. At the first corporate meeting, on 12 July, they drew numbers out of a hat to apportion the first "union cards" in sequential order. Richard Tucker received number one. When, shortly thereafter, they elected Ralph Morgan president, Tucker and Morgan exchanged numbers, so that the chief executive would be first among equals. Leon Ames, holding card number fifteen, was awarded the title of treasurer, and assigned to collect the monthly dues.[27]

The next two months were not spectacular. A few more character actors joined, and two very big stars, James Cagney and Robert Montgomery, sometimes attended meetings. But by September the fledgling union had grown to only fifty-four members, and they, despite Ames's best efforts, seldom paid their dues. (On 7 August the organization's bank balance had stood at $381.50). Faced with opposition from within and without, and lacking star members to lend credibility to their cause, the prospective labor leaders were in no position to impose their will on the motion picture industry. It would take another dramatic injustice like the 50 percent pay cut (since withdrawn by the producers) to make their fellows receptive to their plan. They waited for the moguls to blunder.[28]

Meanwhile, the National Industrial Recovery Act (NIRA) had been passed in Washington on 16 June. This was the New Deal's first, very ambitious attempt to establish national economic control. The National Recovery Administration (NRA) had been created to administer the NIRA, and was busy writing a series of comprehensive codes which attempted to regulate supply, demand, labor, management, and prices in every important industry in the country.

In the writing of the film code, actors, writers, and directors were supposed to be represented by the secretary of the Motion Picture Academy, Lester Cowan. The actors also knew, however, that Eddie Loeb, of the law firm representing the producers' association, had been active in its formation, as had J. T. Reed, a producer and the current president of the academy. Many of the more sophisticated among them were therefore highly suspicious of the process of codewriting, and were not content to wait and see what it would look like.[29]

Through his own contacts, Laurence Beilenson managed to obtain a copy of the proposed motion picture code in September, and distributed it widely. These tentative regulations caused a sensation. In Beilenson's words, "The code was really written by the producers, and it was a monstrosity." Among its provisions, three especially dismayed actors. First, after a performer's seven-year contract expired, his studio would still have the right of first refusal on his services. This amounted, of course, to professional slavery. Second, no actor could earn more than $100,000 per year. There were no limits on the compensation available to the bosses. Third, agents were to be licensed by the studios. In effect, they would be working for management, rather than for their avowed clients.[30]

As the 50 percent pay cut had been the affront that led to the guild's formation, the producer-dominated NRA code was the outrage that turned it into a vigorous organization. At a meeting at Frank Morgan's house on 4 October, twenty-one prominent actors, including Montgomery, Cagney, Fredric March, Groucho Marx, Adolphe Menjou, Gary Cooper, Jeanette MacDonald, Paul Muni, and George Raft resigned in writing from the academy. Ralph Morgan stepped down as

SAG president, Eddie Cantor (who was not physically present but had sent a written application for membership) taking his place. This was part of the founders' strategy to harness the glamour of celebrity on the guild's behalf. Cantor was not only a big name with the public, but was known to be friendly with Roosevelt. As part of the same strategy, Montgomery, March, and Menjou were elected vice-presidents. The guild finally had the star-power that would give it clout.[31]

Four days later the actors and writers sponsored a mass meeting at the El Capitan theater. Out of this gathering came a telegram to Roosevelt attacking the producers and protesting the code. The president responded by inviting Eddie Cantor to visit him during his vacation in Warm Springs, Georgia. Cantor, accompanied by writers Fannie Hurst and Robert Sherwood, found FDR sympathetic, and left him with a legal brief, written by Beilenson, pleading their side of the case.[32]

Cantor's visit had the desired effect. When the motion-picture code (the longest, incidentally, of the more than six hundred written under the NIRA) was promulgated on 27 November, Roosevelt had suspended all the provisions obnoxious to actors.[33]

This was a great victory, and had several consequences. The academy was branded a traitorous management tool, and lost all credibility as a spokesman for the artistic community. The Screen Actors Guild, although it still could count fewer than a hundred members, had become the actor's semiofficial representative. Though still cozy with the producers, the Roosevelt administration was at least listening to the writers and actors. From November, the guild's survival and influence were assured.

But this was not enough. The moguls still refused to recognize SAG (or, for that matter, the SWG) as the legal collective bargaining agent for performers. Their apparent strategy was simply to stall until the guilds went away. And so the tiny actors' union embarked upon a campaign to force the rulers of Hollywood to recognize it as an equal. This quest lasted four years, and was rich in complication. The part of it that really mattered, however, occurred in the spring of 1937.

Crossfire

Long before the artists got serious about unionizing, Hollywood's craftspeople were the object of fights between rival labor organizations. The stagehands—scenery builders, sound and lighting technicians, makeup artists, set erectors, and dozens more—were skilled blue-collar workers, and, as such, ideal members of an AFL-type union. But it was not at all clear which of two types of craft unions would enroll them.

The International Alliance of Theatrical Stage Employes (IATSE, often shortened to IA) had grown up in the latter nineteenth century representing stagehands in the legitimate theater. The IA was an odd sort of AFL member. By representing stage workers as a group, its membership spanned a large number of different skills. While it catered to crafts, therefore, it combined them in a horizontal aggregation more like an industrial union. As a consequence it was constantly feuding with other unions whose jurisdiction crossed into the theater from outside.

In its early years the IA had frequently run into competition from the construction unions—fighting with the International Brotherhood of Electrical Workers (IBEW), for example, over who should have authority over the people operating the stagelight switchboard. And as soon as the IA had begun to follow a seemingly natural path of expansion into the infant motion picture industry in 1908, its jurisdictional conflicts had become all the more intense.[34]

The movies were far more technological than the theater. For example, whereas theaters use house lights which are comparatively simple and are rarely changed, the filming of a motion picture often demands the creation of an intricate wiring system for a diverse set of lights. With each new film, and perhaps even for each scene, the lights, and hence the wiring, might have to be modified. In short, movie-making requires electricians. As a result, squabbling between the IA and the IBEW was almost a tradition in Hollywood by the 1930s.[35]

As with the Electricians, so also with the Painters, Carpenters, and Machinists. The stagehands could expand only by competing for jurisdiction with the building-trades unions. From about the time of World War I, therefore, the Hollywood labor scene was the story not only of the relationship between the IA and the producers, which was sometimes touchy, but also of the relationship between the IA and the construction unions, which was frequently murderous. A truce had been arranged under the Studio Basic Agreement of 1926, but that had collapsed in the early 1930s. In the confusion that followed, the IA had used its authority over projectionists, who could starve the industry of cash by refusing to show films in the theaters, to pressure the producers into backing its jurisdictional claims. In January 1936, it reentered the Studio Basic Agreement, winning the first closed shop in Hollywood history. By the spring of the following year, however, it was being challenged anew by a coalition of rival unions calling themselves the Federation of Motion Picture Crafts (FMPC).[36]

If the events of that year were ever made into a movie, the IA would certainly be the villain. Early in the depression, George Browne, head of the IA in Chicago, had tried to set up soup kitchens for unemployed performers in that city. In so doing, he had accepted the help of Al Capone's organization. The relief was successful, but the mob had become a silent partner in Browne's local. When he was elected national president of the IATSE in 1934, Capone's men (although the don himself was by this time on his way to federal prison) rode along to power. Browne immediately appointed mobster William Bioff, ex-pimp and possibly a murderer, as his "personal representative" in Hollywood.[37]

As befitting a union run by gangsters, the IA was primarily a machine for extorting money. Its leaders denied its members any vote in their government, even at the local level. Thus immune from questioning, they had imposed a 2 percent levy on the wages of the workers in December 1935, and never accounted for the use of the funds. At the same time, Bioff was shaking down the studio bosses, accepting suitcases full of cash in return for guaranteeing a steady supply of docile workers. Over a million tax-free dollars flowed from Hollywood to Chicago.[38]

The IA's opponent, the FMPC, was a loose grouping of craft unions led by Charles Lessing of the Painters. The immediate cause of the conflict was the allegiance of the studio makeup artists. Although their brushes moved across faces rather than wood and metal, these craftspeople belonged to Lessing's union. The IA hoped to capture them, and thus encouraged the producers in their refusal to recognize the makeup artists as an independent union.[39]

Fearful of IA domination, a dozen other small, unrecognized unions had joined the Painters in forming the FMPC in 1932. In the ensuing five years, the situation seemed stalemated. On 12 April 1937, however, the U.S. Supreme Court upheld the constitutionality of the National Labor Relations Act, guaranteeing the right of workers to vote for their own representation. This set off a wave of organizing across the country, and gave impetus to the FMPC. On 30 April six thousand painters, plasterers, plumbers, cooks, hairstylists, and set designers, among others, walked out of the studios, demanding recognition. It was labor warfare, with the companies and the other unions caught in the crossfire.[40]

Although the basis of the struggle between the stagehands and the FMPC was plainly jurisdiction, it had another dimension as well. The IATSE, the conservative, despotically governed, suspected mob-affiliated union, had nothing to offer anyone with any idealism. And so the FMPC attracted the sympathies of all the leftists in Los Angeles. Some of these were union progressives, some Socialists, some Communists. As red-baiting was not yet fashionable, attacks on the radicalism of some of the FMPC leaders did not become part of the public rhetoric of the strike. Nevertheless, the radicals were there, in the Screen Actors Guild as elsewhere, pushing for support of the FMPC. Their vocal advocacy of its cause formed part of the subtext of SAG's internal politics, and their reaction to the outcome of the strike reverberated for years in Hollywood.[41]

Meanwhile, as the motion picture industry had revived and prospered, SAG had been treading water for four years. Attempting to achieve recognition as the bargaining agent for actors, it had participated in talks with management under the auspices of the NRA, but these had produced only frustration. It had sponsored a variety of fund-raising meetings, dances, dinners, and fairs, which had yielded funds but no recognition. Its leaders had persuaded Actors Equity to recognize the guild as the legitimate representative for screen actors, but although this had greatly aided them within the labor movement, it was no help with the moguls. It had joined the AFL in 1936, but, again, this was not the ultimate goal.[42]

By late 1936, however, the guild's leaders felt that the time was approaching for a showdown. The three most important people in the organization at this time were president Robert Montgomery, Laurence Beilenson, and Ken Thomson, who had given up his acting career to fill a paid position as executive secretary. Beilenson, although still not (and never to be) employed full-time as counsel, had severed his connection with the Screen Writers Guild the previous year, and so was able to give concentrated attention to the needs of the actors.

Although publicly denying that they had any intention of urging a strike upon the actors, the guild's leaders began to prepare for just such an occurrence. They called weekly gatherings of perhaps fifty performers at one anothers' homes, and made speeches attacking the producers, sketching the benefits of unionism, and outlining the proposed plan of attack. At the end of each meeting, those invited were asked to submit written pledges of support for a strike. The presentations must have been effective, for the invited actors committed themselves almost unanimously. This process went on through the winter of 1937, so that by April SAG's leaders had received over a thousand pledges of support. As Leon Ames later described it, "We built a house with a fence around it, and when we were ready, we tore the fence down."[43]

In April, guild leaders again began to meet with representatives from the producers. Someone leaked to the press their demand for a union shop, averring that they would "not shrink from calling a strike" if the negotiations were to fail. But progress was not evident.[44]

Montgomery, Thomson, and Beilenson therefore began a masterful series of maneuvers designed to induce other unions to do their bidding, without requiring the guild to commit to anything. This was a campaign carried on partly behind the scenes, and partly in the full glare of publicity. In both areas, SAG's leaders proved themselves more than a match, in toughness and guile, for everyone else in town.[45]

While the FMPC was girding itself for battle, guild leaders made a tacit alliance with its dominant union, the Painters. Two days after the walkout, on 2 May, they held a mass meeting at the Hollywood Legion Stadium to consider striking. There was strong sentiment, especially among leftists, to join the fray on the side of the FMPC. The presiding officers announced, however, that this was an action that could only be taken after a three-quarters vote by the 1,200 senior guild members.[46]

All was not as it seemed at this mass meeting. In actuality SAG at this time could properly claim fewer than five hundred total members ("senior" actors plus "junior" extras), and most of those were behind in their dues. In Hollywood, however, a little exaggeration has never been held against anyone.[47]

Even more curious was the announcement about the "75 percent" rule. Since this requirement was in the bylaws, and well known to the leaders, and since at any rate they had already procured a strike authorization in the preceding months, the question naturally arises as to why the meeting had to be held at all. The answer, of course, is that it was staged not so much for the actors in attendance as for the audience outside. Its purpose was to simultaneously egg on the FMPC and frighten the producers. It was political theater.

On a more tangible level, the strike was growing violent. The IA had imported thugs from Chicago, who had been met, that first week of May, by goons of a more local vintage. For a few days the papers featured photographs of striking workers lying in hospital beds, telling their stories of ambush and assault.[48]

Not wanting the FMPC to become discouraged, the guild announced a $500 contribution, much publicized, to its strike fund on 5 May. Two days later SAG leaders disclosed that they had received a strike-authorization vote of 99 percent, and that they would certainly advise actors to refuse to come to the studios if the producers did not capitulate at the next scheduled meeting on Sunday, 9 May. To ice the cake, Aubrey Blair, the guild's business agent, announced that unnamed "top-bracket" stars favored standing firm with the FMPC.[49]

Things did not look good, at this point, for the IATSE. The Los Angeles Labor Council had just placed ten major studios on the "unfair" list, thus siding with the FMPC. Since the labor council was the local arm of the AFL, this meant that the parent body might condemn it also. If that happened, the IA would be stripped of legitimacy. Moreover, if the actors joined the strike, they might very well push the producers into recognizing the unions in the FMPC. Although Willie Bioff, by reason of his extortionate relationship with the producers, enjoyed both access and influence with them, he could not be sure that they would not desert him if the correlation of forces changed so drastically. Further, on 5 May the newly formed CIO had wired the FMPC that it would support the strike by picketing the films of the major studios. Since the CIO was not on good terms with the AFL, this opened the possibility that it might shortly ally with the FMPC, with incalculable results.[50]

And so, when Thomson, Montgomery, Franchot Tone, and guild business agent Aubrey Blair arrived at Louis B. Mayer's beach house for the climactic negotiating session on the morning of 9 May, they were perhaps not altogether surprised to find Willie Bioff in attendance. When the four presented their demands for recognition of the Screen Actors Guild, Mayer and the stagehands' leader left the room to confer briefly. Upon their return, Mayer announced that the producers would indeed accept the guild as bargaining representative for the actors. The four men promptly disavowed any intention to join the FMPC, and departed victorious.[51]

That night, the president announced to 5,600 jubilant actors at the

Hollywood Legion Stadium that they had won. As the *New York Times* reported, "When Mr. Montgomery completed his statement in the stadium virtually everyone leaped to his feet, cheering and applauding." He thanked the leaders of the stagehands for their support. According to the minutes of the meeting, IA vice-president Ralph Holmden then "assured the membership of the continued support of the IA at all times." A few leftists, furious at the desertion of the strikers, objected to the agreement, but they were ignored. Everyone went home to more private celebrations.[52]

The next morning, members of the FMPC woke up to discover themselves betrayed. In a rage, Charles Lessing told the local papers, "I've learned never to depend on an actor. . . . It was a sellout. The heat is on tomorrow. I'll break every star who passes through the picket lines." Later, he cooled down and decided that it would not be in his coalition's best interest to attack America's royalty as they went to work. And so the strike sputtered on through the summer. Eventually, the individual unions made separate agreements with the producers, and the FMPC evaporated. The IATSE reigned.[53]

Leftists, of course, were incensed at the guild's leadership. In the 1938 presidential election they united behind Melvyn Douglas, a well-known Hollywood liberal, in his campaign against Ralph Morgan, Montgomery's designated successor. Morgan's four-to-one victory gives a sense of the domination of the conservatives in the guild, then and in the following years. The progressives did not try again until after World War II.[54]

In the years since 1937, the story of the negotiation at Mayer's house, and of the deliriously happy meeting that followed, has been told and retold among actors, given in various versions to the press, printed in Screen Actors Guild publications, and repeated as history so many times that it has achieved the status of Hollywood legend. The FMPC is never mentioned in these accounts.

Crossfire: The Sequel

The day after the victory, on Monday, 10 May, Screen Actors Guild membership increased by over four hundred, as a line of actors waited outside its headquarters on Sunset Boulevard to apply for their union cards. The papers could not resist reporting that Jean Harlow and Greta Garbo stood in the crowd.[55]

In the official contract signed on 15 May, the producers agreed to regard the guild as the exclusive collective bargaining agent for all actors in the motion picture industry, and SAG leaders promised not to strike for the length of the contract. Scale payments were set at twenty-five dollars for a player hired by the day, and sixty-five dollars for one hired by the week. These were only minimums, and it was explicitly stated that any actor could negotiate a higher salary. There were rules regulating the employment of stunt men and extras, and governing such matters as overtime and location shooting. Each side was to appoint a committee to discuss problems in the event of complaints, and a machinery was set up to arbitrate matters that could not be settled in that way. Although the minimums have been hiked many times and many provisions have been added in the ensuing half-century, the pattern of this first contract has been the basis for those that have followed.[56]

Although the battle against the producers seemed to be over, however, the guild had not won the war. In June, an extra named Jane Tallant obtained an IA card and began working (scabbing the still-striking FMPC) as a makeup artist. It was contrary to SAG policy for one person to hog the available employment by working at two types of jobs. After a trial committee had looked into her offense, therefore, she was in August suspended from the guild for ninety days.[57]

There are several versions of what happened next, but although they differ in detail, they agree in substance. Robert Montgomery immediately received a phone call from Willie Bioff requesting, in untactful language, that Tallant be reinstated. Montgomery, whose debonair screen persona concealed a strong character, hung up on him. Thus began a second round of survival training for the guild.[58]

Shortly thereafter, someone slashed the tires of Montgomery's car. Beilenson and Thomson began getting death threats, relayed through third parties. Vice-president George Murphy received a communication that his children were going to have acid thrown in their faces. Soon one of the guild's employees, hired to check compliance with the new contract, discovered a bomb concealed under the hood of his automobile. These were Bioff's private activities. Publicly, he and George Browne announced to the press that the stagehands would absorb the actors, writers, and directors, and thereby come to monopolize all labor negotiation in Hollywood.[59]

For the next two years, two dramas unfolded side by side. In the first, the Screen Actors Guild and its allies tried to neutralize Willie Bioff as a person. In the second, the actors played union politics to keep out of the clutches of the IATSE as an organization.

The Bioff problem was of more immediate urgency. Some guild officers, and even some of their wives, began to carry guns. A few stunt men formed themselves into a committee of bodyguards, and for six months accompanied Robert Montgomery whenever he traveled in public. For his part, the president asked for and received an appropriation from the guild's board of directors to hire a "public relations man" to deal with problems arising from the IATSE situation. He turned this money over to SAG's chief counsel. Beilenson hired two Los Angeles newspapermen part-time, changed the job description of one of the guild's public-relations men in Chicago, and told the three of them to uncover whatever they could about the IA leader.[60]

As might be expected, the actors were not the only people in Hollywood who had become curious about Willie Bioff. During the summer of 1937 a group of stagehands who were angry about the lack of democracy within their union, and its leaders' cavalier expropriation of their wages, formed the "IA Progressives" to combat these evils. As SAG was putting its bloodhounds on the trail, the Progressives were hiring labor lawyer Carey McWilliams and a private detective agency for the same purpose.[61]

Working separately and together, the investigators discovered a $100,000 check in a Hollywood bank, payable to William Bioff and signed by Arthur Stebbins, nephew of Joseph M. Schenck, chairman of the board of 20th Century-Fox. Although they did not know it at the time, this was merely the latest installment in the $1,100,000 the producers had paid the IA leader for labor peace over the preceding few years. When the news hit the papers, however, it started a chain of investigations that eventually included the state legislature, county and federal grand juries, the United States Department of Labor, and the Internal Revenue Service. Whenever any of the employees of these agencies searched through the morgues of the Hearst papers or the *Los Angeles Times*, they discovered masses of material on Bioff's Chicago criminal record, thoughtfully placed there by the two newspapermen at Beilenson's behest. By the middle of 1938, Bioff was so busy trying to fend off the various investigations that he had no time to concern himself with devouring the Screen Actors Guild. A year later, when the pace of the investigations seemed to slacken and the guild was still being hard-pressed by the IA, its leaders began to feed information to newspaper columnists Victor Reisel and Westbrook Pegler. Their revelations made Willie Bioff a household name, and spurred the government to press its case.[62]

In 1941, Bioff, George Browne, and Joe Schenck went to prison for extortion and federal income-tax evasion. Fourteen years later, in Phoenix, somebody blew up Bioff with a car bomb.[63]

Removing the gangster from Hollywood was the easy part. The greater threat was from the IA as an organization, within the labor movement. The stagehands were very well connected. George Browne was a vice-president of the AFL, and was allied with Joseph Padway, chief counsel to president William Green (in 1940, Padway left the federation to become chief counsel to the IA). Faced with this stacked deck, the guild was forced to engage in a two-year dance of power within the AFL to try to remain independent.[64]

The original excuse for conflict, be it remembered, had been Jane Tallant and her two union cards. In early 1938 SAG took this problem to the Associated Actors and Artistes of America (AAAA, or the "four A's" in colloquial speech), a holding corporation of eleven performers' unions. All but one, the American Federation of Actors (AFA), a group of night club and vaudeville performers organizationally chummy with the IA, voted their support. The AAAA then expelled the AFA, which was promptly issued a charter by the stagehands.[65]

Being on the verge of absorbing one talent union, George Browne had become able to claim to represent workers on the business end of the camera. In June, therefore, he petitioned the AFL to revoke the charter of the Screen Actors Guild and other "so-called guilds, falsely parading as labor organizations," labeling them a "mockery on organized labor which creates dangerous resentments over their pretensions to be classed in the ranks of American labor."[66]

The next day, SAG formed an alliance with the as-yet-unrecognized Screen Writers Guild and Screen Directors Guild, issuing a statement urging writers to support the SWG in the upcoming National Labor Relations Board (NLRB) ratification election. They did, by more than four to one. Over the next year the guilds and the IA fired publicity salvos at each other and grappled within the labor movement, each trying to convince the public, various governments, and the AFL to take their own side.[67]

During this period, while the Screen Actors Guild had been focused on its own problems, the labor movement as a whole had been undergoing convulsions. Disagreements between the two philosophic wings of the AFL came to a head in 1936, when the parent organization suspended the CIO. The suspension changed to expulsion in 1938. Meanwhile, the two groupings had launched into a recruitment war centered especially on the largely nonunion West Coast. Beginning in 1937, blood ran in the streets of Portland, Seattle, San Francisco, and Los Angeles as mobs of Teamster-led AFL partisans battled the Longshoremen-led CIO. As was frequently the case in those years, the CIO appealed heavily to radicals, including within its ranks a number of Communists.[68]

Early in 1939, the IA Progressives, who had been getting nowhere in their efforts to reform that union, united with the Communist Party and the CIO to form the United Studio Technicians Guild (USTG). This organization was led by the Painters, and so the struggle, in addition to being AFL versus CIO and Communist versus Mafia, also had overtones of the traditional Hollywood construction versus theatrical unions. As the unfolding revelations about Bioff and Browne began to make the IA appear vulnerable, the leaders of the USTG decided to try to wrest control of the stagehands from the corrupt union. In July, they petitioned the NLRB to hold a certification election. The board agreed, and set 20 September 1939 as the date.[69]

From the perspective of hindsight, what followed looks like a rerun of 1937. Again, leaders of the Screen Actors Guild made a show of collaborating with the insurgents, even letting it be known that they themselves were ready to quit the AFL and join the CIO. Again, without actually promising anything, they leaked to the press that some of their members were giving the rebels financial aid. Again, they threatened to strike in sympathy with the IA's opponents, which would of course have disrupted the industry and possibly tipped the scales in their favor. (SAG now had a contract, of course, and a strike would have violated it. When a *Los Angeles Times* reporter pointed this out to Thomson and Morgan, they responded, "Actors have broken contracts before, and nothing happened. But we know we will be victorious. We are fighting for an ideal—honest unionism.")[70]

And just as they had two years earlier, SAG's leaders made a last-minute deal with the IA. In a written agreement, Browne promised to stop trying to incorporate the actors or extras, to refuse to accept the AFA, and to leave the AAAA in peace. Morgan and Thomson agreed to support him against the UTSG. Emerging from this meeting, they endorsed the IA in the upcoming election. Partly as a result of this, the stagehands won.[71]

Once again, the Left cried double-cross, and once again, nobody cared. The USTG followed the FMPC into the dustbin of history.[72]

By 1940, then, the leadership of the actors had outwitted and outfought both management and other workers, and emerged unchallenged as the strongest and most prestigious labor union in Hollywood. They had also demonstrated that theirs was a union of conservatives, and that they were quite ready to use the Left as a stalking-horse in any fight for power. This seemed easy to do in the 1930s. In the next decade, however, progressives were better organized and more determined. The next chapter of SAG's history would see the Left attempt to turn the tables and to use the guild itself as a stalking-horse.

Maybe there's only one revolution: The good guys against
the bad guys. The question is—who ARE the good guys?

Burt Lancaster to Robert Ryan, *The Professionals*, screenplay by
Richard Brooks

Chapter Three

REACTION

Having won its first battles for survival, the Screen Actors Guild settled
down to become an institution. Three months after the producers recognized the guild in May 1937, its leaders felt the need for some full-
time legal help. On Laurence Beilenson's recommendation, they hired
John Dales, a recent graduate of Stanford Law School, to be their "res-
ident counsel." Two years later, Dales became assistant to Ken Thomson. In 1943, he and Thomson switched jobs, so that the guild's executive secretary would be a lawyer. Dales would hold the position for
thirty years, providing the stability and institutional memory any organization needs. Beilenson continued to give SAG part-time advice
for three years after his return from military service in 1946.[1]

In a union run by movie stars, the clash of egos is going to be a
constant theme. Any executive secretary with the smallest neurosis, the
slightest tendency toward envy, or the most occasional abrasiveness
would be headed for a nasty and short career. But Dales, who never
intended to work with performers, soon discovered that he liked them.
For their part, the actors quickly came to the conclusion that he was
an ideal choice. A slightly built man with a gentle voice and self-effac-
ing manner, Dales seemed to be able to handle the union's administration without ever offending the artistic temperaments around him.
For its first generation, therefore, part of the guild's success can be
attributed to the harmony with which its staff worked with its officers.[2]

The main administrative work of the guild for several years after
1937 was enforcement of the contract. As with all such documents,
there was both evasion of its requirements and disagreement about its

meaning, and so some machinery had to be devised to resolve disputes and interpret ambiguities. SAG and the studios set up committees in which delegations from each side heard complaints and tried to agree on ways to end them; if that was impossible, they went to arbitration.[3]

It did not take long for the actors to discover that they were spending the great majority of their time in these committees dealing with the problems of extras. Whether the position of extras was one of inherent injustice, or whether extras as people were impossible to please, is not clear, but they complained constantly of mistreatment and cheating by the producers, and bad treatment by the guild's government. Part of this latter discontent was no doubt because they were not allowed to vote in SAG elections, since they outnumbered actors and would have been able to control the union's policies if they had had the franchise. SAG had won the right to represent all performers before the cameras in a National Labor Relations Board election in 1938, but as the forties progressed the din of dissatisfaction increased until the extras were ready for divorce.[4]

In early 1944 a rival group calling itself the Screen Players Union (SPU) arose, and persuaded the National Labor Relations Board to call another election to determine whether extras wanted to stay within the guild. They didn't, voting 1,451 to 456 for the SPU over SAG in December. The NLRB then not only removed the extras from the guild's representation, but compounded the insult by ordering that they could thenceforward speak on camera without joining SAG. In other words, the Board not only severed the extras from the guild but in the process awarded a large dollop of its jurisdiction over actors to the SPU. The Screen Players Union thus became a threat to the life of the Screen Actors Guild. Although SAG's leaders later managed to persuade the NLRB to return this lost jurisdiction, they had by that time become implacable enemies of the SPU.[5]

The key to destroying the upstart organization would be to block its entry into the Associated Actors and Artistes of America (the four A's), the holding corporation of AFL performers' unions. If it were not protected by the AFL umbrella, the SPU would be vulnerable to jurisdictional challenges and membership raids from rival unions. Very conveniently, soon after the December jurisdictional election a second extras' union appeared, which was founded by players who had not wanted to leave SAG in the first place, and which renounced any intention of seeking jurisdiction over speaking parts. This was called the

Screen Extras Guild (SEG). Both SEG and the SPU applied to the four A's for admission. With the guild exerting every bit of its influence within the parent organization, the choice was a foregone conclusion: SEG was admitted in July 1945.[6]

The next step would be for SEG to win the right to represent all extras. With another NLRB election looming, the two new unions began a contest to capture their allegiance. Or rather, it would be more correct to say that the Screen Actors Guild began a contest with the SPU, for the larger union virtually ran the campaign. Buck Harris, the guild's chief of public relations, also functioned in that capacity for SEG. Laurence Beilenson included both SAG and SEG among his law clients, and the guild "loaned" its small cousin more than $26,000 to see it through the fight. When the extras finally voted to affiliate with SEG in March 1946, the guild had managed to save just about all of its former control over screen performers except formal organizational authority.[7]

Viewed in isolation, the tussle over extras seems a small and obscure episode. Placed in historical context, however, it becomes crucially important. In the course of fighting what was to them a desperately important battle, the leadership of the Screen Actors Guild came to have strong prejudices about who in Hollywood was a friend and who was a foe. Any person or organization who supported them on the extras question would be a potential ally; anyone who endorsed the Screen Players Union would likely be their enemy. And because this contest became entangled in a much larger and more significant conflict, it had momentous consequences.

Crossfire III

Its president in prison, its connections to organized crime publicized to the world, its name a synonym for corruption and tyranny, the International Alliance of Theatrical Stage Employes was, by the beginning of World War II, reeling and vulnerable. The building-trades unions, vanquished in the Hollywood jurisdictional fights of the 1930s, saw a window of opportunity. No one of any respectability would come to the aid of the discredited IA; now was the time to seize back the workers they had lost. The Painters, Electricians, and Carpenters prepared for another war.[8]

The guiding force behind the new coalition of construction unions was Herbert K. Sorrell of the Painters. An ex-boxer and labor militant of considerable experience, he had been much involved in the FMPC in 1937, and had led the USTG in 1939. Two years later he directed the Cartoonists Guild (members of the Painters) in a bitter and successful strike against the Disney studios. In the wake of this action he had organized the Conference of Studio Unions (CSU), which at first included close allies of the Painters, like the Machinists, but later admitted the Carpenters, the IBEW, and a number of smaller unions.[9]

By all accounts, Sorrell was a leader of strength, resourcefulness, courage, and integrity. What people do not agree about is whether he was a Communist. Sorrell himself, while acknowledging that he was surrounded and influenced by members of the party, denies, in his unpublished memoirs, ever having joined it. As we will soon see, there is some reason to think that his memory was faulty on this point. Whatever Sorrell's personal affiliations, however, his coalition, the CSU, participated in the activities of a large number of Communist and Popular Front organizations, and frequently received their support in return.[10]

During the FMPC drive for recognition in 1937, a group of set decorators had obtained recognition from the producers as a separate union, not affiliated with the IATSE. Partly because they had other, larger problems, and partly because the decorators were not members of any grouping hostile to them, the stagehands' leaders tolerated this independence. In October 1943, however, the set decorators voted to join the Painters, and thereby, of course, the CSU. Here was a direct challenge. If the Painters could nibble off a bit of the jurisdiction of the weakened IA today, it would only encourage the Carpenters and the Electricians to think that they could gobble up bigger chunks tomorrow. Richard Walsh, the IA's new president, decided to fight.[11]

The stagehands, by virtue of their control over the projectionists, still exercised great influence with the studio bosses. The threat of darkening every screen in the country was, then as earlier, the foundation of the IA's power. For their part, the bosses were not eager to help the militant CSU expand at the expense of the more agreeable IA. Tacitly beginning an alliance that was later to become openly cooperative, the studios therefore stalled in negotiating a new contract with the set decorators; meanwhile, the IA organized its own local of decorators and applied for recognition. Despite efforts of the War Labor Board and the Department of Labor to resolve the dispute, it dragged on into

1945. On 12 March of that year, its patience exhausted, the CSU pulled 12,000 workers out on strike.[12]

Meanwhile, Walsh had asked one of his officers, Roy Brewer, to go to Hollywood as a troubleshooter to see what he could do about solving the jurisdictional problem. Brewer had been a projectionist in Nebraska, and in 1933, at the age of 23, had become the youngest head of a state federation of labor branch in the country. Added to this obvious evidence of ability was the fact that Brewer was untainted by any connection with Willie Bioff, which would help in a Hollywood that was extremely suspicious of the IA. He arrived in Los Angeles the day the strike began.[13]

Leftist historians have portrayed Brewer as a cynical manipulator, choosing to launch a campaign of red-baiting against the CSU because he knew that the IATSE could not win the argument on its merits. This is an abject misunderstanding. There is nothing cynical about Roy Brewer. He is a short, round man with a soft voice and a polite, almost shy demeanor, but his words carry the certitude of the righteous. Four decades later, he still believes passionately that all that is good and true in life is in imminent danger from an evil conspiracy on the Left. Further, he is a religious man, and he knows the devil when he sees him. He saw both the conspiracy and the devil in the person of Herb Sorrell.[14]

Some historians, argues Brewer, don't "really understand the capacity of the Communists to destroy things. . . . Things will not grow naturally with the Communists in the picture. . . . I don't mind opposition—I like opposition—because sometimes I'm wrong, but I don't want a guy telling me something that he isn't, especially when he's attached to an organization that's trying to destroy the world."[15]

Brewer did not come to Hollywood convinced that his union was facing more than just a jurisdictional fight. But soon after his arrival, he noticed some peculiar behavior in the Los Angeles Central Labor Council (LACLC). One of its executive board members was an IA business agent, while the president of the Council was a member of the Painters. On the first test vote, the business agent voted for the CSU, while the Painter supported the IA. The only way such an irrational lineup could be explained, Brewer thought, was if he assumed that some strong outside force was distorting the loyalties of the LACLC members.[16]

His friends in the Teamsters were glad to inform him of the nature of that outside force: the Communists, attempting to take over the Hollywood labor movement, had launched the strike to further their imperialist designs; they had already infiltrated some locals of the IA. Now, to believe this took a certain amount of creative thinking. As part of its all-out effort to defeat fascism, the Communist party in America had early in World War II resolved not to initiate or support anything, such as a strike, that would interfere with the smooth functioning of the national economy. Since the war was still going on when the CSU strike began, it is hard to see how anyone involved in it could have been under Communist discipline. But no matter—Brewer allowed himself to be convinced that the strike was part of a party plot against Hollywood in general and the IA in particular.[17]

Later, Brewer came up with a plausible explanation for the "premature" quality of the CSU strike: Sorrell had been a member of the party in the 1930s, but had withdrawn officially in 1940, striking a deal as he did so. He would follow the Communist line on everything outside his own union, and they would support him on whatever he did with that. Thus, although there was grumbling on the Left when the strike was launched, the Communists did not vigorously oppose it; a few months later when the party line changed, they swung in behind Sorrell.[18]

But it was not just the Communists. Early in the strike Brewer decided (and with good reason) that the Carpenters were planning to use the disruption it afforded as an excuse to raid the IA of every member who worked with wood. The two attacks, from a political party and from a rival union, quickly became fused in his mind, just as the vulnerability of his stagehands became indistinguishable from the plight of the free world. Consequently, within a month of his arrival in Hollywood Brewer had decided upon a historical interpretation of what was happening, and resolved upon a course of action: in order to save Western civilization in general and the IA in particular from subjugation by Communism, a holy war of extermination had to be waged against the CSU.[19]

Through four years, three separate strikes, dozens of press conferences, several lawsuits, many legislative hearings, and at least two pitched street battles, Brewer hammered at his theme. The CSU, of course, responded with a massive propaganda barrage of its own.

Newsletters, speeches, radio debates, leaflets, telegrams, rallies, marches, and pamphlets followed one upon another in a cascade. But Brewer's argument was the one that prevailed, probably because it was far easier to understand.

The public being not very well informed on current events, a campaign to persuade ordinary citizens must be simple in argument and strong in emotion. But the CSU partisans could never seem to make their case in a clear, uncomplicated way. Their publicity was full of intricate retracings of history, abstruse points of discussion, and detailed recounting of grievances. Nor could they settle on a single theme. Sometimes they emphasized the sordid history of the IA, sometimes the evident preference of the producers for the conservative stagehands over the radical CSU, sometimes the violence directed against their picket lines, sometimes the alleged internal democracy of the CSU as against the machine politics of the IA, sometimes the nonjurisdictional nature of their strike, and sometimes the suspected launching of an anti-union drive by employers. Meanwhile, for four years Brewer bludgeoned them with a never-varying attack: communism, communism, communism.[20]

Although he was aiming to convince the public in general of the virtue of his cause, there were particular groups to which Brewer gave special attention. Chief among these was the Screen Actors Guild, and especially after the third and longest strike began on 12 September 1946.[21]

According to the rules of the AFL, unions not involved in a labor dispute should respect the strikers' picket lines if the disagreement was between management and labor over benefits. If, however, the strike was the result of a jurisdictional dispute between unions, outsiders were not required to honor the picket lines. Therefore, if the actors believed that the CSU strikes were jurisdictional, they would continue to go to work, the studios would remain open, and the IA would be able to fill in the positions of the absent CSU workers with its own people. On the other hand, if the actors decided that the strikes were indeed over wages and hours, as every leftist in Hollywood was urging them to do, they would refuse to come to work, the studios would shut down, and the CSU might win. Shortly after the first strike began in March 1945, when the guild membership voted overwhelmingly to cross the CSU picket lines, the issue was drawn. For much of the next

four years, pro-CSU activists tried to persuade SAG to reverse this initial decision, and Brewer tried to reinforce it. The contest became a
battle for the hearts and minds of the screen actors.[22]

Although many of the ordinary members of the board of directors
favored the CSU in the first two years of the conflict, SAG's leadership
was always prejudiced against any organization led by Herb Sorrell.
This was because Sorrell committed the supreme blunder: he backed
the Screen Players Union against the Screen Extras Guild in the dispute over extras that was taking place at the same time. The CSU would
thus have had to have been clearly in the right, and the IATSE clearly
in the wrong, for SAG to have favored the CSU. Since nothing about
this period was clear, Sorrell's grouping was doomed never to be
friendly with the only organization that might have saved it.[23]

Inside Moves

As it had been in the past and would be in the future, the Screen Actors
Guild in the mid-1940s was split between ideological factions. Although
the conservatives dominated, there was an active progressive minority
on the board of directors as well as in the membership. One leftist,
Anne Revere, later recounted her memories of 1944:

> When I came on the Board, there was a minimal concern with the mem-
> bership. I remember my very first session with the Board. There was a
> great deal of questioning going on, and there was no response on the part
> of the Board to any of the questions. . . . When I started to speak, it was
> as though a cataclysm hit. All eyes were on me. There were some very
> clear problems that the membership did not have and a problem that the
> Board had—they kept complaining bitterly that no one ever came to the
> meetings and they couldn't understand why.[24]

In their autobiographies the conservatives remembered the same
period quite differently, of course. Theirs was a SAG leadership constantly in touch with the membership and eager to serve it in any way
possible. Just as they do today, progressives and conservatives recall the
board of directors in the 1940s as though they are describing two completely different institutions.[25]

The conservatives did not have to be talked into anticommunism by
Roy Brewer. George Murphy, who became president in 1944, and Robert Montgomery, who resumed the office in 1946, were already among
those who were alarmed about the manner in which party members
seemed to be able to employ tight discipline to exercise influence in

organizations out of proportion to their numbers. They were particularly concerned about the Communist penchant for showing up in a
solid group at sparsely attended meetings of a variety of organizations
and taking over because they happened to be a majority at the meeting,
although they were a tiny minority in the organization. As his last official act as president, George Murphy supported a change in the bylaws which made it impossible to alter guild policy through a vote at a
membership meeting alone; any resolution passed at such a gathering would now have to be ratified by all the actors in a mailed
referendum.[26]

Nevertheless, guild leaders were not Brewer's automatic allies. First,
having just barely escaped the clutches of the IATSE not long before,
and remembering very well Willie Bioff and his tactics, they were wary
of any blandishments from his successor. Second, they were aware of
the close relationship that the stagehands enjoyed with the studios,
which increased their suspicions about the IA's motives. Third, they
were not certain that the CSU was run by Communists. Fourth, they
were unclear as to whether the ongoing series of strikes were jurisdictional, as the IA maintained, or over benefits, as the CSU insisted.
Fifth, their primary interest was in seeing the various disputes resolved
so that people could go back to work, rather than in taking sides. As
a consequence, they would not be easy converts.[27]

As soon as he was oriented in Hollywood, however, Brewer began to
hold a series of talks with the guild leadership. At these meetings he
assured the actors that taking over their union had been entirely Willie
Bioff's idea, and that under Walsh's presidency they had no further
need to fear anything from the IATSE. Moreover, and most crucially,
he powerfully supported SEG against the SPU. As noted in the 20
August 1945 minutes of the board of directors, SAG "found itself in
the position of being unable to refuse" to aid the stagehands' union
"because of the unsolicited militant support which the IATSE has
given the SEG." Thus, although there was still a strong anti-IA prejudice on the board, on balance it gradually swung in behind Brewer
on the strike.[28]

Brewer also supplied evidence to back up his claims of Communist
infiltration. In February 1946 he produced a document that he
claimed was a photostatic copy of the receipt Herb Sorrell had signed
in the 1930s when he joined the Communist party. Although the signature read "Herbert Stewart," Brewer explained that for reasons of

security Communists were usually known within the party by pseu-
donyms, and that Stewart was Sorrell's mother's maiden name. Hesi-
tant to accept this strange story, the guild leaders borrowed the document and hired a handwriting expert to analyze the signature.
Amazingly enough, he reported that the handwriting did indeed belong to Sorrell. Two years later FBI professionals examined it and
came to the same conclusion. Here was something more than a mere
partisan accusation, and it had real effect.[29]

How did Roy Brewer, who did not arrive in Hollywood until 1945,
come to own a copy of a document that the secretive Communist party
had created in the 1930s? As Brewer tells it, the receipt was originally
in the possession of a radical CIO organizer named Jeff Kibre, who
was sent by the party to Hollywood to help the FMPC in 1937. In those
days the Los Angeles Police Department was so intensely antiradical
that it supported a "Red Squad" whose sole purpose was harassing CIO
organizers, Communists, and kindred undesirables. Sometime during
the FMPC strike in 1937, Kibre had been served with a subpoena (as
part of what investigation, no one now remembers). He did not respond. Given this excuse, the Red Squad went to his house, broke down
his front door, scooped up all the documents they could find, and took
them downtown to be photocopied. Some years later, an IATSE lawyer
who enjoyed close relations with the police department purchased a
number of the documents. This lawyer gave the "Herbert Stewart"
copy to Brewer.[30]

But it was not just the IA representative who persuaded the actors
that something was rotten in the CSU. The strike leaders' own behavior
supported the arguments against them. During the summer of 1945,
with the struggle against European fascism won and the war in the
Pacific within sight of victory, the Communist party, following direc-
tives from Moscow, adopted a new hard line. Swearing off cooperation
with liberals except on its own terms, it explicitly returned to a program of disruption and revolution. Over the next two years, as SAG's
leaders encountered mounting frustration in their attempts to mediate the strike, they became increasingly convinced that Sorrell's hidden purpose was simply to bring Hollywood to a chaotic halt.[31]

Hoping both to resolve the immediate issues and to persuade the
AFL to set up permanent arbitration machinery to prevent such problems in the future, in October 1946 SAG sent a delegation consisting
of Edward Arnold, Gene Kelly, Robert Montgomery, George Murphy,

Walter Pidgeon, Dick Powell, Ronald Reagan, Alexis Smith, Robert Taylor, and Jane Wyman to the labor organization's national convention in Chicago. There, Sorrell and Bill Hutcheson of the Carpenters were so uncooperative that the actors came home thoroughly disgusted with the CSU and its allies.[32]

Their last effort to restore peace came two weeks later. Laurence Beilenson chaired a meeting of the leaders of the various unions, at which they agreed on a formula to settle the strike. The next day the CSU and the Carpenters backed out of the agreement. This episode convinced the SAG mediators that Sorrell was not a free agent, but was instead under orders from outside. They issued a three-page "Report To the Motion Picture Industry," in which they proclaimed that "in view of the factual record, the Guild board reluctantly has been forced to the conclusion that certain of the leaders of the CSU do not want the strike settled."[33]

This swing of the guild into an anti-CSU stance occurred just as the Communist party was attempting, in familiar Leninist fashion, to seize control of the union's policy-making machinery so as to dominate its decisions on the strike. Sterling Hayden, who joined the party in June 1946, later testified that he was among ten actors who were assigned the task of attempting to influence SAG on the strike issue. The ten would caucus in advance of guild membership meetings and draw up an agenda to be followed if any one of them should be recognized to speak. The object was to coordinate their activity so that it appeared that the mass of actors favored the CSU. To this end, Hayden and the others also met with a larger group of fifty to seventy non-Communist, pro-CSU progressives to plan strategy for the meetings that were taking place regularly in the fall of that year.[34]

On 19 December 1946, as a result of a petition from about 350 of its members asking for "a fair presentation of the opinions of those members of the Guild who disagree with the Guild's present policy," on the strike, the leadership held a mass meeting at the Hollywood Legion Stadium. It is likely that among the 1,800 actors in attendance were all the able-bodied leftists who were then in town, from Communists and fellow travelers through Socialists and union radicals to ordinary liberals—every one supporting the CSU.[35]

Ronald Reagan gave a report on the Chicago delegation's conclusions. To the conservatives in attendance, it was an impressive performance—clear, simple, persuasive. According to Hedda Hopper, one-time actress and now one of Hollywood's most important news-paper columnists, "Without resorting to notes, he reeled off facts and figures with an ease that flabbergasted members of the audience." In John Dales's recollection, it was a "masterful" explanation, and prob-ably contributed to Reagan's attainment of the guild presidency three months later. Sterling Hayden, who left the party shortly thereafter, gave Reagan the credit for defeating its plan to control the guild. Hay-den characterized Reagan as "a one-man battalion against this thing. He was very vocal and clear-thinking on it. I don't think many people realized how complex it was. I know I didn't. There was very little head-way made."[36]

Radicals who kept the faith held another opinion. "Reagan was mak-ing speeches about how it was an unimportant jurisdictional beef," re-called Karen Morley years later. "He made long, fancy speeches about technicalities like which union was allowed to touch rubber." Alex-ander Knox remembered that "Reagan spoke very fast. He always did, so that he could talk out of both sides of his mouth at once." Katharine Hepburn, Edward G. Robinson, Hume Cronyn, and Paul Henreid all argued against the official position, maintaining that it was proprod-ucer and dangerous to actors. In the end, those at the meeting voted to endorse a resolution from the Los Angeles Interfaith Council urg-ing both sides in the strike to begin once again to talk to one another. Because it was the IA that had broken off negotiations, this resolution was in effect an endorsement of the CSU position.[37]

Because of the recent change in the SAG bylaws, the pro-CSU res-olution had to be submitted to a mailed referendum vote by the entire membership. In the envelope with the ballot, sent out in January 1947, the guild leadership listed three questions, the first being "Does the membership of the Guild go on record as affirming its confidence in its duly elected Board of Directors and approving its policies and ac-tions in the Hollywood strike?" It urged a "yes" vote on this question. To the next, "Shall the Board take under advisement the plan of the Inter-Faith Council, as read by Mr. Knox at the SAG membership meet-ing December 19, 1946 . . . ?" the officers urged a "no" vote. The third question was similarly phrased to stack the cards in favor of the lead-ership. Given choices presented this way, it is no surprise that the actors supported their officers on each question by huge majorities.[38]

Up to this point, the guild's leaders had had to endure a good deal of personal abuse, but had not been physically threatened. For months the CSU had been circulating handbills accusing vice-president Ronald Reagan and former presidents George Murphy and Edward Arnold of being stooges for the producers, and fascists to boot. Now, however, while the referendum was still out, someone began making anonymous threats on their lives. For a while, in scenes reminiscent of the Bioff era, they carried guns and employed bodyguards. According to Reagan biographer Anne Edwards, Reagan's wife, Jane Wyman, "told one close friend there had been more than one night that she had awakened to see him holding the gun, sitting in bed having thought that he had heard noises in the house." Nothing concrete came of these threats, but they reinforced the leadership's growing belief that Brewer's view of the world was the correct one.[39]

The Screen Actors Guild's refusal to endorse the CSU strike in any manner doomed it to failure, although, as with the labor battles of the 1930s, the actual struggle dragged on long after the outcome was no longer in doubt. When the CSU finally disintegrated in 1949, the IATSE was left in complete command of Hollywood crafts, and has not been seriously challenged by the construction unions in the decades since. Of greater importance, however, was the change wrought in the attitudes of the actors. Having undergone the trauma of the strike, and having observed, as they thought, the ruthlessness and cunning of the far Left in its drive for domination, guild officers had decided that one of their own priorities must become the eradication of subversion from Hollywood. By 1947 the Screen Actors Guild as an organization, and Ronald Reagan in particular, were ready to enlist in the anti-Communist crusade.[40]

On 10 March 1947 president Robert Montgomery, vice-presidents Franchot Tone and Dick Powell, and several members of the guild board of directors resigned. They had recently acquired production interests in films, and because this made them a part of management it created the unavoidable suspicion that their decisions as officers of a labor union would be tainted by conflict of interest. Third vice-president Reagan, who had no production interests, was promptly chosen president by the board.[41]

Reagan himself had once been a political liberal, and with his penchant for joining organizations had become involved in a number of Communist fronts. Before he reversed his course in mid-1946, he had even turned up in an internal Federal Bureau of Investigation memo listing people in the motion picture industry who "have records of

Communist activity and sympathies." Once he became president of SAG, however, it did not take long for him to demonstrate his change of heart. He and his wife, who was also a board member, contacted the FBI and requested an interview, explaining that "they might furnish information regarding the activities of some members of the Guild who they suspected were carrying on Communist Party work."[42]

On 10 April 1947 two FBI agents visited the Reagans at home. The SAG president told them about having quit an organization with the impressive title of the Hollywood Independent Citizens Committee of Arts, Sciences and Professions (HICCASP) because of his conviction that it was a Communist party front. He discussed his duties as SAG president, and he and Wyman provided the agents with, as they wrote in their report, "information regarding the activities of some members of the Guild who they suspected were carrying on Communist party work." The agents did not record their own reactions, but this report added to the information piling up in Washington about the good guys and the bad guys, information which would soon be put to use.[43]

Trouble In Paradise

Although Roy Brewer was the catalytic figure in the swing of Hollywood toward reaction, he was not its originator. In the 1930s and early 1940s the town had been home to a variety of left-wing political groups, who opposed nazism, racism, and capitalism, and supported Roosevelt, equality, and World War II. It was not until February 1944, however, that it spawned an important organization of the hard Right.

The Motion Picture Alliance for the Preservation of American Ideals (MPA), as it was called, grew out of the conviction shared by a number of prominent producers (Walt Disney), directors (Sam Wood), writers (Morrie Ryskind), and eventually actors (Gary Cooper) that Communism was metastasizing unhindered through the movie colony. "In our special field of motion pictures, we resent the growing impression that this industry is made up of, and dominated by, Communists, radicals, and crack-pots," it proclaimed in its "Statement of Principles" published as an ad in the trade journals. "Motion pictures are inescapably one of the world's great forces for influencing public thought. . . . We refuse to permit the effort of Communist, Fascist, and other totalitarian-minded groups to pervert this powerful medium into an instrument for the dissemination of un-American ideals and beliefs."

(Although the alliance thus included Fascists in its list of villains, it never reported finding any in Hollywood; it detected legions of Communists.) The MPA received much of its financial support from the rabidly anti–New Deal publisher William Randolph Hearst, which insured its survival but cost it dearly in the propaganda wars with the Left.[44]

In seeking to forge a coalition against Communism, and combat the accusations of its many critics that it was merely a cover for antilabor agitation, the MPA sought allies among Hollywood's unions. Within a month of its founding it had added officers of the Studio Plasterers, Studio Drivers, and IATSE to its executive committee. Soon after Brewer came to Los Angeles, he too joined, eventually becoming president.[45]

Before his arrival, however, the members of the MPA had already taken an action that would have profound consequences. In March, they mailed a letter to United States Senator Robert Reynolds of North Carolina, which he obligingly read into the *Congressional Record*. "Aliens of un-American ideology have infiltrated into the United States, here to take jobs in American industries and to spread European and Asiatic propaganda detrimental to American principles, institutions, and safety," it read. "Because of the flagrant manner in which the motion-picture industrialists of Hollywood have been coddling Communists . . . there has been organized in Hollywood the M. P. A. All decent Americans who had the courage to protest the manner in which the motion-picture industry was spreading un-American propaganda before the war have been smeared as either anti-Semitic or pro-Nazi."[46]

Some members of Congress had in the past shown interest in investigating Hollywood for a variety of political sins, and the House Committee on Un-American Activities (HUAC)* had opened hearings into the motion-picture industry several times. These attempts, however, had been very unsatisfactory from the point of view of the politicians, for two reasons. In the first place, the industry had presented a solidly hostile front to the committee, which prevented it from unearthing much sensational testimony. In the second place, Democrats were in control of both houses of Congress, and the members of that party were generally uninterested in exposing a Communist infiltra-

---

*Although "HCUA" would be technically correct, I follow the almost universal habit among journalists and historians in shortening the name to the pronounceable "HUAC" (for "House Un-American Activities Committee").

tion which would have occurred during their own incumbency. By writing their letter to Senator Reynolds, however, the members of the Motion Picture Alliance had sent a loud and clear, if implicit, message to the Communist-hunters that the next time they came to Hollywood they would find a divided town, with a faction willing to cooperate. It now would take only an electoral victory by the Republicans to change the balance in Congress so that they could take advantage of the MPA's invitation. History was on their side.[47]

The Searchers

For the first time in eighteen years, the Republican party won majority control of both houses of Congress in the November elections of 1946. In May of the next year, J. Parnell Thomas and John McDowell of the House Committee on Un-American Activities arrived in Hollywood and began to interview "friendly" witnesses ("friendly" was the term HUAC members used to describe people who cooperated with their investigations). A large proportion of this group could claim membership in the Motion Picture Alliance. Although the meetings were held in executive (secret) session, Thomas and McDowell followed congressional committees' time-honored practice of leaking sensational tidbits to the press. The curious citizen could therefore easily learn that the friendly witnesses had named a substantial number of Hollywood's artists—and especially of its screenwriters—as Communists. The HUAC members left town without holding open hearings, but it was obvious that this had been a mere preliminary sortie to help prepare for the serious assault to come.[48]

On 21 September the committee issued subpeonas to forty-three members of the Hollywood film industry, including the present and two former presidents of the Screen Actors Guild. A number of those summoned were members of the Motion Picture Alliance, and nineteen were Communists or former Communists.[49]

Although HUAC's members undoubtedly welcomed the willingness of the people in the MPA to tattle on their fellows, they did not really need that intelligence to be able to subpeona the actual Communists in the motion picture industry. The Los Angeles Police Department's Red Squad had thoroughly infiltrated the Hollywood branch of the party; for several years in the 1930s, its membership secretary had even been a policeman. In the years to come Senator Joseph McCarthy and his epigones would engage so freely in groundless accusation that a later generation would find it difficult to believe that American Communists had actually existed. They did, however, and the committee, which enjoyed good relations with the LAPD, knew who they were.[50]

For the subpeonaed members of the Motion Picture Alliance, the path ahead was clear. They would cooperate with the committee in every respect. For the nineteen "unfriendly" witnesses, the choices were more difficult but still relatively obvious. They would have to decide which of several possible means of defiance would place them in the least danger of going to jail and/or losing their jobs. The ten who were finally called had, after much agonizing, decided to adopt a curious combination of refusal to answer any questions about their affiliations and an attempt to answer "in my own way"—that is, reply to a question about their Communist membership with a speech about civil liberties.[51]

But for Robert Montgomery, George Murphy, and Ronald Reagan, who were staunchly anti-Communist but who had not invited HUAC to come bother their industry, the proper strategy was not at all evident. To agree too readily with committee suggestions that Hollywood was riddled with subversives would make themselves and other leaders of the industry look weak and incompetent, and might inspire congressional efforts to censor movies, take over studio administration, interfere with union activities, or otherwise meddle where the three certainly did not want them to. On the other hand, to deny that Communists had significant presence or influence in the city would both falsely represent their own experience and leave themselves vulnerable to suspicions that they were dupes or even fellow travelers. The trick would be to convince the committee members that the guild's officers believed that the Communist threat to Hollywood was indeed substantial, but that they and the present leaders of the industry had the situation well in hand.

And this is just what they did. Their testimony was so consistent that it could almost have been traded among the three of them without anyone noticing. Each praised the committee. Each dilated upon the evils of Communism. Each acknowledged that a devilishly clever but extremely tiny minority of SAG's membership also belonged to the party, and that this group had been maneuvering to take over the union. But, as each reported in some detail, this subversive splinter had been headed off, outsmarted, exposed, and altogether stifled. In

other words, although the committee was perfectly justified in being
alarmed about the inroads of Communism, it need not do anything
about it in the Screen Actors Guild. Reagan gave the most extended
version of this argument, but his was not in any essential different from
Montgomery's or Murphy's:

> Ninety-nine percent of us are pretty well aware of what is going on, and
> I think within the bounds of democratic rights . . . we have done a pretty
> good job in our business of keeping these people's activities curtailed. . . .
> We have exposed their lies when we came across them, we have opposed
> their propaganda, and I can certainly testify that in the case of the Screen
> Actors Guild we have been eminently successful in preventing them from,
> with their usual tactics, trying to run a majority of the organization with
> a well-organized minority.[52]

It worked. The committee members asked them some questions
about whether they had ever seen any un-American propaganda in
their own films (no), and whether they believed that the Communist
party should be outlawed (maybe), then praised their characters and
let them go. It was an important performance. Although individual
actors would be put through a great deal of trouble by HUAC in the
coming years, the Screen Actors Guild as an institution was not disturbed again.

This was of small comfort, of course, to the unfriendly witnesses—
the Hollywood Ten. Attempting to impose their own version of reality
on the committee in the last week of October, they were instead
dragged, sometimes shouting imprecations, from the witness stand.
On 24 November Congress voted to cite them for contempt. Hollywood sat back to await the outcome as their appeals began to wind
through the court system.[53]

The ten, however, would have to wait without jobs. The day after the
contempt vote, fifty top Hollywood executives, meeting at the Waldorf-
Astoria hotel in New York, not only fired them but adopted a declaration that no subversives would henceforward be given jobs in the
motion picture industry. For several years afterward no one else was
denied employment, partly because the legal appeals of the Hollywood
Ten were in the courts, and partly because there were no further
HUAC inquiries into motion pictures.[54]

By 1950, however, the ten had lost their appeals, and most had gone
to prison. The constitutional authority of HUAC to question citizens
about their political beliefs, the power of Congress to cite noncoop-
erators for contempt, and the legal right of producers to refrain from

employing morally suspect artists had been upheld by the courts. When the second round of hearings began in 1951, there was consequently no possibility that the present and former Communists who were called to testify would follow the strategy of the ten and simply defy the committee. Their remaining choices boiled down to two. If they answered every question, including those which commanded them to produce the names of their former comrades, they would be freed with a "thank you" and could expect to continue to work in Hollywood. If they refused to testify by citing the Constitution's Fifth Amendment privilege against self-incrimination, they need not fear imprisonment but would be immediately blacklisted. About three dozen artists chose the first alternative, over two hundred the latter.[55]

Frenzy

Hollywood's reaction to the HUAC hearings must be seen in the context of its own troubles. The first round in 1947 occurred at the beginning of the television-induced depression, to be discussed in chapter 4. The second round took place at the depths of that depression. Movie-making was already an extraordinarily insecure occupation, leading those serious observers who wrote about Hollywood to emphasize its atmosphere of anxiety. The worsening economic situation can only have heightened this pervasive fear, and made the producers hypersensitive to anything else which might further cut into their business, such as a threat to boycott or picket their pictures. And actors, following probably the most precarious of all Hollywood livelihoods, must have existed in a near-hysteria for years. Given this background, the willingness of the producers to sacrifice valued artists when subjected to the merest breath of a threat from self-appointed guardians of patriotism, and the failure of the actors' union to protest such sacrifices, become more understandable. Blacklisting became the offering of a panicked industry to the gods of convention.[56]

A blacklist, that is, a list of names circulated among employers to enable them to deny jobs to specific unwelcome persons, was illegal under California and federal law. For a variety of reasons, however, including the choice of legal strategy by the plaintiffs and the manner in which the courts interpreted the issue, the legal question in the lawsuits filed against the blacklist became: by refusing to employ a given set of persons, have the producers "interfered with a contractual or business relationship?" Given this definition of the issue, the peculiar nature of employment in the motion picture industry made it virtually impossible to establish in legal terms that a blacklist existed.[57]

Even before the tumult over Communism, the capriciousness of employment in the movies was legendary. Normally an actor, writer, or director could expect to be retained only film-to-film. Even those few who enjoyed contracts, such as five of the Hollywood Ten, knew that these contained option clauses allowing the studios to dump them at the end of any given six months. Hundreds of artists had thus outlived their usefulness to the producers and lost their jobs without politics having had anything to do with it. The situation was essentially the same in the infant television industry, based in New York. In deciding lawsuits filed against the system, the courts consequently ruled that the jobless had not proved that their sudden inability to find work was the result of a coordinated campaign by management. Apparently, as long as there was no public cooperation among the studios, they could keep suspected subversives out of the industry for as long as they pleased.[58]

There soon arose private individuals and organizations who were happy to compile names for television and motion picture producers, and thus relieve them of the necessity of overtly conspiring. In the latter months of 1947 three ex-FBI agents formed American Business Consultants and began publishing (for a fee) *Counterattack*, a list of names gathered from government reports, files of radical newspapers, programs of rallies, organization letterheads, and other official and unofficial documents. Three years later the same group put out *Red Channels*, a compilation of 151 people in the radio and television industries who, according to the authors, had at one time or another been associated with "Communist causes." Technically, this was a "graylist," with the term "blacklist" reserved for those who had not cooperated with HUAC. Television and movie producers were, however, reluctant to employ anyone whom someone somewhere had found politically objectionable, and avoided artists on graylists almost as ardently as those on the blacklist. The exact shade of unemployment, of course, made no difference to artists who lost their jobs.[59]

The first actor whose firing can be unambiguously blamed on the graylist is Jean Muir, who was dropped from the cast of the television series "The Aldrich Family" in the fall of 1950. Probably many others never got to a point from which they could be fired, because they were eliminated early from consideration.[60]

In the best free-enterprise tradition, the success of American Business Consultants inspired the formation of competitors. Wage Earners Committee and Aware, Inc. were soon busily mailing graylists to anyone who would buy them, and in addition offering to "clear" the names of victims who would come to their offices, grovel a little, and pay a few hundred dollars. Because many would not cooperate in this ritual of humiliation, agreeing with the smeared artist who stated that "I don't want to have anything to do with pigmies [*sic*] playing God," they remained unemployed.[61]

Red Channels, Counterattack, and their imitators were important primarily in New York, and in television. Hollywood was somewhat different. Dozens of artists who had signed petitions supporting the Hollywood Ten or attacking HUAC experienced a lessening of studio enthusiasm for their careers, beginning in 1948. It was, however, three years before the process of exclusion became institutionalized.[62]

When it became clear during HUAC's 1951 hearings that a significant number of people were going to escape both testimony and jail by pleading the Fifth Amendment, the American Legion decided that it would force the studios to punish them. It began to picket the films of the alleged subversives. Representatives of the film industry, terrified at the thought of empty theaters, immediately contacted the legion and offered to cooperate. Out of the meeting came a list, not just of the "Fifth Amendment Communists," but of about three hundred names of people whom the legionnaires found questionable—a combination of graylist and blacklist. The legion mailed a copy to each of the studio heads, who, because they were receiving the letter separately rather than as a group, were thus not violating the antiblacklist laws. Besides, they kept the existence of such a list secret. Most of the artists on this list were writers, but it also contained the names of several dozen actors.[63]

Most of the people involved with Hollywood graylisting on the industry side understood that it was a process that might involve serious mistakes. The various subversive-listers were sloppy in their methods, and sometimes, say, misidentified a face in a photograph in the *Daily Worker*, thereby blighting the career of a completely non-Communist actress. Or, for example, an otherwise apolitical actor might have signed a petition advocating civil rights for the Hollywood Ten at the urging of a friend, thus landing on someone's list. Or, a performer might have been involved with the Communist party many years before and repudiated it long ago, yet fall victim to *Counterattack*'s research. Or, there might be a confusion about similar-sounding names.[64]

As a consequence, a number of unquestioned anti-Communists became unofficial "clearance officers," to whom the innocent, repentant, or misunderstood might apply for intervention with the powers that be. Until he moved from Hollywood in 1953, Roy Brewer was the most important of these. If a conversation plus his own research convinced him that the artist either did not deserve to be on a list in the first place, or had genuinely mended his ways, Brewer would write a letter to the studios attesting to his political cleanliness. This was usually all that was necessary for professional resurrection.[65]

In the Screen Actors Guild, also, there were people available to help mislabeled or contrite performers restore themselves to the good graces of the industry. As SAG national executive secretary Jack Dales recalled in an unpublished interview with labor historian Mitch Tuchman, an actor might come to him and complain about being unable to find work. Dales would call the studio heads, find out what the "charge" was, then go and talk again to the actor, and ask how he could help. "Then we were beginning to find out that there were people on the list who shouldn't be there, who were simply there in error . . . and that became almost a career for Reagan, certainly, among others, in correcting this."[66]

Given the fact that he was spending so much time keeping people off the blacklist, Reagan's later denial that there was one seems to approach the status of a fib. (He was not alone—George Murphy and John Wayne also maintained there was no such thing.) Perhaps they could believe in such a falsehood because they insisted on the technical definition of a blacklist, which had been officially declared by the courts not to exist in Hollywood. Or perhaps they simply preferred not to remember their own participation in an activity which became unpopular afterward.[67]

Even in the 1940s and 1950s, of course, the guild's cooperation with HUAC, and its acquiescence in the graylists and blacklists, were not universally endorsed by its members. Dales remembers that "in those days it sounded perfectly proper, but there were people, of course, who didn't think so. They felt that freedom to think what you want and to join what you want was above all; we didn't at the time. We thought that this was a matter of patriotism and of propriety."[68]

On the other hand, those who thought that patriotism and propriety counseled not to cooperate in the blacklist ran an independent slate of candidates for the board of directors, and for the office of recording secretary, in the guild election of November 1947. Although Van Heflin and Larry Parks each captured a seat, the insurgents failed to make much of a dent in conservative control. This was the only election during the Communist-hunting period in which the Left mounted an electoral attack on SAG government. Its results demonstrated that there would be no internal restraints on the actions of the conservative leadership.[69]

This leadership stated its position in no uncertain terms when Academy Award–winning actress Gale Sondergaard appealed for help following her HUAC subpoena in 1951. Taking a full-page ad in the trade papers on 13 March, Sondergaard announced that she intended to avail herself of the Fifth Amendment, and continued, "I . . . appeal to the Board, to my fellow actors, to consider whether it will not be proper and necessary for it to make a public declaration that it will not tolerate any industry blacklist against any of its members who see fit to act upon a unanimous decision of the Supreme Court and avail themselves of the privilege against self-incrimination which is once more available for the purpose for which it was originally established—as a barrier to political and religious persecution."[70]

At a specially called meeting on 19 March, the board and officers discussed potential replies at some length. Anne Revere, who had herself been subpoenaed, agonized over the choices ahead of her (she finally took the Fifth and was banished from Hollywood). Ronald Reagan "pointed out that what Miss Sondergaard really asks in her letter is . . . for the Guild to assume responsibility for the results of her personal decisions and non-union activities." Ward Bond "pointed out that actors are dependent upon the good-will of the public." "The general consensus of opinion," read the minutes, "appeared to be that this was a perfect opportunity for stating SAG's stand in regard to member-actors under investigation by the Government." Therefore, the assembly voted, with two dissenting (but unnamed) voices, to issue a statement already composed by executive secretary John Dales, assistant secretary (and guild co-founder) Ken Thomson, and head of public relations Buck Harris.[71]

When it was published in the trade papers two days later, this statement could not have been cheering to Sondergaard. "The deadly seriousness of the international situation dictates the tone of our reply," it said. "Like the overwhelming majority of the American people, we believe that a 'clear and present danger' to our nation exists. The Guild board believes that all participants in the international Communist party conspiracy against our nation should be exposed for what they are—enemies of our country and of our form of government. . . . The Guild as a labor union will fight against any secret blacklist created by any group of employers. On the other hand, if any actor by his own actions outside of union activities has so offended American public opinion that he has made himself unsaleable at the boxoffice, the Guild cannot and would not want to force any employer to hire him."[72]

Sondergaard took the Fifth and did not see the inside of a motion-picture studio for twenty years.[73]

In 1948, the Screen Actors Guild membership had voted 1,307 to 157 in favor of a resolution requiring officers, directors, and committee members to sign individual affidavits swearing that they were not party members. After the Sondergaard episode, there remained one task for the guild to perform in order to dispel any suspicions that it coddled Communists. In March 1953, the board passed, and in August the membership approved, a bylaw requiring new professional actors to pledge that they were not members of the party and would not join it.[74]

The blacklists and graylists in their various guises lasted into the early 1960s. Partly, they succumbed to a waning of public concern over the issue of subversion. Partly, enforcement proved too difficult, as the increased numbers of independent producers after 1950 began at first to evade, then to ignore the ban on using certain highly regarded talents. The practice of graylisting in particular, however, was destroyed by a libel suit brought by liberal television personality John Henry Faulk in 1956. Aware, Inc. had launched a scurrilous and entirely unfounded attack on Faulk that year because it disapproved of his antiblacklisting activity in the American Federation of Radio and Television Artists, the TV artists' union. The case, which was finally decided in Faulk's favor in 1962, established the legal principles that accusation before a congressional committee did not prove any person a Communist, and that the reporting of such testimony, or any facts implying the subversive affiliations of anyone, constituted a libel per se. In other words, the court in effect declared the compiling of lists of suspicious persons illegal. With their input from professional busybodies thus cut off, the television and movie studios had no source of names of people to avoid, and blacklisting and graylisting withered away.[75]

The final casualty count of the anti-Communist frenzy among screen actors must remain inexact. By 1955, 106 writers, 36 actors, and 11 directors had been blacklisted for taking the Fifth Amendment before HUAC. Because the various graylists were semisecret, however, it is impossible to make an accurate further compilation. Perhaps a hundred SAG members discovered at one time or another that they could not get work for political reasons. Some of those talked to a "clearance officer" and were reestablished; some waited out the 1950s on Broadway or elsewhere and eventually returned to the screen; some dropped into obscurity; a few died of stress or committed suicide. For those individuals involved, of course, to be blacklisted was an emotionally searing experience that affected the rest of their lives. The greater impact, however, was on actors as a group.[76]

The Legacy

I had finished interviewing a formerly blacklisted actor about his experiences in the Screen Actors Guild in the 1970s. He had told me at the beginning of our talk that he did not wish to discuss his problems with HUAC and I had avoided the subject. We had, however, gotten along well in the conversation. As I was leaving and thanking him for his time, he suddenly said, with a slightly wistful expression, "You know, so-and-so died last week" (identifying a prominant actor who had informed). "He named me to the committee. I forgave him. I forgive each of them, one at a time—as they die." Although the tone of his remark was mostly one of sadness, as of a hurt remembered through the mists of time, there was still a note of hatred in his voice.

This is one small scene in one person's life, but in a sense it is indicative of the continuing horror that all actors feel when they remember the blacklist. They do not have to be old enough to have lived through it. In the quarter-century since it expired, it has not faded from the memory of the profession, but has attained the status of folklore, to be recounted again and again wherever actors gather to discuss their craft. Almost every one of the fifty-six actors I interviewed mentioned it spontaneously at some point. It is the devouring monster that stalks them in their nightmares, that they cannot run away from or insulate themselves against, no matter what their bank balance or status in the industry. If the blacklist had never existed, it would, in a sense, have been invented, for it objectifies the dread of unemployment that sits at the center of every actor's soul.

Because the process of getting or losing a job seems so entirely irrational to actors, they can never feel secure. No matter what their talent, experience, connections, fame, or clout in the industry, each one feels that *this* job is his last, that something horrible will happen tomorrow to erase his popularity, and close all casting offices to him.

Insecurity creates permanent nervous vigilance. To actors, the blacklist seems always on the verge of returning. They detect the advance guard of a resurgent McCarthyism everywhere. As a group, therefore, they react with near-hysteria to statements which, to a non-actor, appear to be normal political utterances. To suggest even obliquely that there might be Communists, by membership or philosophy, in the Screen Actors Guild is to create an instant emotional rejection. In such an atmosphere, thinking about certain issues is impossible.

The legacy of militant anti-Communism among actors is therefore militant anti–anti-Communism. The politics of the Screen Actors Guild in the 1980s is thus partly the politics of the 1940s and 1950s stood on its head. As we shall see, this forms an important part of the context in which SAG activists try to govern their union today.

Presidents and National Executive Secretaries of the Screen Actors Guild

Chester L. Migden
1973–1981
Executive Secretary

John L. Dales
1943–1973
Executive Secretary

Kenneth Thomson
1933–1943
Executive Secretary

Ralph Morgan
1933, 1938–1940

Eddie Cantor
1933–1935

Robert Montgomery
1935–1938, 1946–1947

64

Edward Arnold
1940–1942

James Cagney
1942–1944

George Murphy
1944–1946

Ronald Reagan
1947–1952, 1959–1960

Walter Pidgeon
1952–1957

Leon Ames
1957–1958

Howard Keel
1958–1959

George Chandler
1960–1963

Dana Andrews
1963–1965

Charlton Heston
1965–1971

John Gavin
1971–1973

Dennis Weaver
1973–1975

Kathleen Nolan
1975–1979

William Schallert
1979–1981

Edward Asner
1981–1985

Patty Duke
1985–1988

Here in this patrician world the Age of Chivalry took its last
bow. Here was the last ever seen of the Knights and their
Ladies Fair, of Master and of Slave. Look for it only in books,
for it is no more than a dream remembered, a Civilization
gone with the wind . . .

Ben Hecht's uncredited prologue to *Gone with the Wind*, screenplay
by Sidney Howard

Chapter Four

UPHEAVAL

Despite its labor troubles, the motion picture industry was booming at
the close of World War II. In 1946, 1947, and 1948 an average of 90
million customers a week attended American movies, tying the all-time
record year of 1930 and up a third from the tally in the leanest days
of the depression. Because ticket prices had risen, these extra customers provided box-office receipts of over $1.5 billion a year, which
was two and a half times the take of a decade earlier. America's victory
in the war had ensured open markets for the country's products, so to
Hollywood's domestic gross were added further millions from foreign
theaters.[1]

The industrial system that produced this prosperity seemed at the
time to be a model of rational organization. Of the seven major Hollywood studios—Metro-Goldwyn-Mayer, 20th Century-Fox, RKO, Paramount, Warner Brothers, Columbia, and Universal—all but the last
two were just one component in a vertically integrated corporate
scheme. The typical corporation, headquartered in New York, also
owned chains of "first-run" theaters which exhibited the movies made
by the studios, distribution networks which made sure that each theater
received the films on time and in the proper order, and advertising
departments whose function was to keep the theaters full of patrons.
Each organization thus controlled its whole production process, from
the first idea for a film to the final time it was shown; this made planning easier and allowed executives to adjust the activities of one section
of their empire to the needs of the others. Columbia and Universal,
and a few other exceptions to the dominant pattern such as Disney,

which only produced films, and United Artists, which only distributed them, coexisted with the integrated giants, but their rarity only emphasized the pattern of control that prevailed.[2]

The smaller "independents" managed to survive in this system by tailoring their activities to the desires of the majors. Independent exhibitors received a hit film if the majors saw fit to rent it to them, after the first-run theaters were finished with it and at the price of also showing other movies made by the majors whether or not they wanted to. The handful of independent producers could get their films distributed to the majors' theaters, but only if they made the kinds of films the majors wanted, and frequently only by allowing a major to participate in the film's financial backing. In other words, executives of the five integrated corporations largely decided the content of American films, when and where they were seen, and for how long.[3]

As the corporations dominated the industry as a whole, the studios controlled the possibility of work inside Hollywood. This was especially true in regard to actors. The majors kept stables of performers under their power by means of the standard seven-year contract; by unspoken agreement, they would not generally bid for a star's services when the contract expired. Since independent producers also had to bow to the wishes of the studios or find most theaters closed to their films, they also respected the majors' "ownership" of a star. Thus under the absolute power of the studio, actors had almost no influence over the roles they played. They accepted those that were assigned them, rebelled in usually self-defeating ways, or left the industry. Moreover, studio bosses not only traded their services among themselves (as MGM lent Clark Gable to Columbia for *It Happened One Night*, for example), but frequently meddled in their private lives as well. Studio chiefs told the stars whom to date or avoid, whom to marry, what political opinions to hold, what parties to attend, and often what to wear in public. In scores of movie-star autobiographies, actors and actresses have raged against this system, giving many examples of the effronteries and humiliations it imposed upon them.[4]

But there was also a benign side to this relationship between master and slave. First and foremost, contract actors in general, and the stars in particular, were very well paid. But beyond that, the studios viewed "their" performers as valuable properties to be protected and developed. Studio personnel nurtured new contract players, teaching them how to walk, speak, use makeup (and frequently, how to act), becoming their friends, and giving them a warm and, if they behaved themselves, supportive environment. As Lyle Talbot remembers, "If you had any problems, even something as simple as a traffic violation, you could go to the studio and it was taken care of. . . . There was great cameraderie. It was possible to go in and talk to Mr. Zanuck or Mr. Warner. . . . You had security and you got your salary every week."[5]

At the end of the war, therefore, studio heads and their corporate overlords had good reason to feel pleased with their industry, and optimistic about its future. They controlled their world, and it made them millionaires. Little did they know that within five years the system that had seemed so robust would be smashed beyond repair.

The Game Is Over

There was one major problem with the way New York had organized the Hollywood industrial process. It was illegal. The Sherman Anti-Trust Act passed by Congress in 1887 had outlawed business concentrations that acted "in restraint of trade"; that is, suppressed competition. Since the purpose of the major companies' melding of production, distribution, and exhibition into a single system was to allow them to exercise control over the market, they were violating the law.

In 1938, the Justice Department had filed suit against the seven majors and United Artists, charging violation of the Sherman Act. In May 1948 the Supreme Court upheld a lower court's finding that the motion picture industry had engaged in monopolistic practices, and must therefore be broken up into its component pieces. Specifically, this meant that the major companies would have to be divided in two, with film production and distribution on the one hand and exhibition in theaters on the other occurring separately under different companies.[6]

This Paramount decree, as it was called, began a restructuring of the industry. With the majors no longer able to monopolize access to the first-run theaters, the way was cleared for more independent producers to enter the industry. Further, partly because the majors were no longer required to manufacture a certain number of films every month to keep their theater chains satisfied, they cut back on their film production. This left them with excess studio space and distribution facilities, which they were then eager to rent to the independents. The result was an increasing profusion of producers. The forty independent producers in 1945 had multiplied to 165 by 1957 and 1,500 by 1966. As a consequence the proportion of all films made by the majors declined steadily, from 80 percent in 1949 to 35 percent in 1958. Although the majors remained important because of their continued control of distribution, they no longer dominated the screens.[7]

All this had profound effects on actors. With the industry becoming a complex of competing free-lancers instead of an ordered set of feudal baronies, performers discovered their world becoming much more individualistic. This meant that their potential earnings and risks were both greater. Under the new conditions, the majors had far less need for a reliable stable of performers, so they tended to not renew contracts as they expired and to avoid signing new ones. There were thus 742 Hollywood performers under contract in 1947, but only 229 nine years later.[8]

Cast loose from the benign despotisms of the studios, actors became more responsible for their own careers. For the ordinary player, this only increased the insecurities, as the studios were now neither finding and training nor promoting them. No doubt this amplified the traumatic impact of the blacklist, which was becoming established at the same time. On the other hand, for the stars the change created potential bonanzas, for it allowed them to participate in financial deals. There had always been some actor/producers in Hollywood, but the studio system had kept them to a minimum. The splintering of the industry that followed the Paramount decree changed all that. In 1950, James Stewart made an arrangement with MGM for a percentage of the gross receipts from the western *Winchester 73*. The film was a hit, Stewart got rich, and stars were soon attempting to sign percentage deals for every picture.[9]

What was good for the stars, however, was not so good for their union. The rule was that people with financial stakes in films could not be officers in the Screen Actors Guild. When most performers were mere contract players, this did not mean much. As the percentage of stars who were also producers steadily climbed through the fifties, sixties, and seventies, however, the guild's supply of potential leadership was steadily squeezed. By the 1970s, part of the political process before union election time was always a frantic search for "name" performers who had no production interests and who were therefore eligible for guild government.

Despite the great impact of the Paramount decision, however, it was not the largest blow that struck the movie industry during this period. If its market had remained strong, Hollywood could probably have adjusted to its new organization and gone on about its profitable business. Instead, just as it was most in need of strong ticket sales to help it regain its structural balance, it was nearly wiped out by competition from a new form of amusement. And since there is no labor without jobs, the possible demise of the film industry meant potential extinction for the Screen Actors Guild.

The Thing

Although the basic technology of television had been around for a couple of decades, problems of detail delayed its introduction on a commercial basis until after the war. When it was introduced, however, it grew with lightning speed. The ability to watch entertainment without apparent cost and without leaving their living room drew consumers by the hordes. There were only 14,000 receiving sets in the country in 1947, but that grew to 4 million by 1950, and 32 million by 1954, at which point 56 percent of American households owned at least one. In the same period, the number of commercial stations exploded from twelve to over 350. A mere decade after its introduction, television dominated American entertainment.[10]

Motion-picture executives were not unmindful of the potential of the new medium. Beginning in the 1930s, industry leaders had attempted to establish a plan to participate in its future growth, and in the late forties tried mightily to acquire ownership of stations. They were, however, up against a politically stacked deck. Except for the occasional snooping of a congressional committee or the attacks of the Justice Department, the film industry was unregulated by government. Because television was broadcast over the public airwaves, however, and because there was a limited amount of space on the broadcasting spectrum, it fell under the regulatory authority of the Federal Communications Commission (FCC). For the same reason, the radio networks, which also wanted to expand into television, had long been regulated; they therefore enjoyed a history of intimacy with the FCC. When added to the fact that the film industry was in a bad odor in Washington because of the Paramount case, this meant that the moviemakers, as mistrusted outsiders, were competing with familiar insiders for the FCC's favor. The outcome was unsurprising: the networks were allowed to dominate the market for new television stations, and the film-makers were frozen out. They tried to turn to subscription (pay) TV as an alternative, but neither the technology nor the public was co-operative and all the ventures failed. By 1950 it was clear that the film industry was on the verge of being left behind by history.[11]

This failure of the movies to gain control of television had two great consequences for actors, one immediate, the other long-term. It was at once evident that television-watching was cutting into the market for films, as box-office attendance declined with every spurt in TV's expansion. From its 90-million peak during the immediate postwar years, weekly attendance had dropped by a full third in 1950, and by almost half three years later. Because of higher ticket prices, earnings did not fall so drastically, but they still tumbled 26 percent in that short span of years. With the market collapsing around them, producers naturally made fewer films, which meant less work for actors. Hollywood released about 7 percent fewer films in 1954 than it had in 1947; the total number of parts for actors contracted by at least as much. For the Screen Actors Guild, a union already faced with chronic unemployment among its members, the future in the early 1950s had to appear bleak.[12]

Duel in the Sun

The long-term consequence of the domination of television by radio was jurisdictional warfare among the entertainment unions. Until the end of the war, there was no friction between the Screen Actors Guild and the American Federation of Radio Artists (AFRA), which, like the radio networks, was headquartered in New York. Many performers belonged to both, of course, but there was no question as to the jurisdiction of each. Both organizations were members of the Associated Actors and Artistes of America and thereby the AFL. When the radio networks expanded into the new technology, however, the union representing their creative talent naturally wanted to move with them.

But television, unlike radio, was projected on a screen. And although early programs were almost entirely live (live being cheaper to produce), there was nothing to prevent broadcasters from showing film. There thus arose the question of which union should represent performers if and when they chanced to be hired for a filmed television program. In 1948, the year that television went national, this problem began to create unpleasantness between SAG and AFRA.

Anticipating the growth of the then-infant technology, in 1934 Actors Equity, Chorus Equity, the American Guild of Variety Artists, and the American Guild of Musical Artists had formed the Television Authority for the purpose of coordinating the performers' unions' response to television. When potential began to turn into reality a decade later, these unions joined with AFRA in asking that TVA, as it was called, be granted full jurisdiction over all acting for the tube. Since they were a majority within the four A's, the five unions might have been expected to get their way without much difficulty. As it happened, however, the whole idea of TVA was anathema to the Screen Actors Guild. Although it would theoretically subsume all other unions into a larger whole, in the view of the guild's leaders TVA was really just a larger AFRA in disguise, and as such a means by which New York could pirate their jurisdiction.[13]

Like AFRA, TVA was to be a federation of largely autonomous locals, whereas the guild was a California corporation. This would automatically mean that the power in the new union would probably not settle in Hollywood. Additionally, the concentration of radio, the stage, and nightclubs in New York would likely focus that power in the eastern city. When they saw that the executive secretary of AFRA, George Heller, was also to occupy that position in TVA, the guild's leaders' suspicions that they were the target of New York imperialism must have been confirmed. The satellite Screen Extras Guild, also headquartered in Los Angeles, shared SAG's position.[14]

If, as appeared possible in the late forties, television killed the movies altogether, then the only way the guild would survive would be by representing actors making films for the new medium. To give up that jurisdiction to AFRA in the guise of TVA would be to commit slow suicide, for as television suffocated the motion-picture industry AFRA would inherit the right to represent screen actors.[15]

Although this fight over jurisdiction was authentic enough, it also provided an arena for the primeval Left-versus-Right ideological struggle. "I am not suggesting that TVA was a Communist plot, but . . ." wrote Ronald Reagan in his autobiography, after which he proceeded to imply that that is exactly what it was. "The party line will always back anything that simplifies and centralizes. It's easier to subvert one organization where policy decisions are far removed from the rank and file than it is to take over a dozen groups." Despite its red-baiting tone, there is something acute in Reagan's analysis. As we shall see, one of the characteristics of union progressives is an affection for the simplifying and centralizing reform. The conservative unionist cherishes the tiny authority of each little platoon of workers; the progressive dreams of the one big organization that can bring the concentrated power of all laborers to bear on the problems of a few. Although TVA was not a Communist plot (and although AF[T]RA, historically, has been at least as conservative as SAG), leftists did endorse the idea of one actors' union then, as they endorse it today.[16]

The public argument of the time, however, was conducted not on the grounds of philosophy or of who would have the power but on the merits of the case. "While we recognize that SAG and SEG have jurisdiction over motion pictures made for theatre exhibition, we must realize that television is a new concept of entertainment, with new employers and a new method of payment through sponsors," announced Heller during a visit to Los Angeles in November 1949. "Our five AAAA branches have 30,000 members and we have an obligation to them. We cannot and will not delegate the authority to control television motion pictures to a board of directors whose members reside and work mainly in Hollywood."[17]

President Ronald Reagan summed up SAG's reply to this argument in his autobiography: "The plain truth was and is that television is not a new art medium at all; it is simply a new type of theater." The guild was perfectly willing to allow AFRA to represent actors doing live television, but it refused even to discuss ceding its jurisdiction over film work, regardless of the theater in which that work was shown. When co-founder Ken Thomson, then on SAG's executive staff, was asked why he was so resistant to efforts to mediate the dispute, he replied, "A guy comes into your house and says, 'Half of this house is mine; let's mediate about it.' Does that make any sense?"[18]

The two sides wrangled for two years, while television blossomed and films swooned. Then, in April 1950, the AAAA gave up on discussions and simply awarded jurisdiction over all television acting, live, film, or anything else, to TVA. The Screen Actors Guild immediately petitioned the National Labor Relations Board for elections to determine which union actors preferred to represent them.[19]

In the course of the next two years the NLRB held thirteen certification elections. SAG won twelve. In retrospect, this is not surprising. In the balloting, actors who had been working in movies and consequently had been represented by the guild were in essence asked if they wanted to continue with their well-known and successful union, headquartered in the town where they were employed, or whether they wanted to transfer their allegiance to a new, untested organization staffed by people without experience in helping screen actors and headquartered three thousand miles away. When the overwhelming desire of screen actors to stick with SAG became obvious, the AAAA withdrew its attempt to put together one big television union and disbanded TVA. Left with jurisdiction over live TV, AFRA in September 1952 added the word "Television" to its name and became AFTRA.[20]

Besides clarifying who represented whom, SAG's experience with the NLRB had an important internal consequence. During one of the hearings preparatory to the elections, executive secretary John Dales had been examined by a young board attorney named Chester Migden. Dales had been greatly impressed by the intelligence and toughness the attorney had displayed. In late 1951, when the guild's board decided that the increased problems television was causing mandated a larger staff, Dales suggested that they try to hire Migden away from the government. The invitation went out, and Migden, who had in his turn been impressed by Dales, accepted it. From his initial position as agency administrator in charge of enforcing the regulation of agents, Migden rapidly advanced to the job of Dales's assistant. For over twenty years the two would represent the guild in negotiations with producers, and when Dales resigned in 1973 his successor was obvious.[21]

Although both Dales and Migden were present for the beginning of the jurisdictional squabble caused by television, it would outlast both of them. As the technology of TV evolved over the years it created growing confusion about how to distinguish between SAG's jurisdiction and AFTRA's. Additionally, for the next three decades actors resented having to carry two union cards for doing nearly identical work. Periodically, the notion of eliminating the tangle of jurisdiction by merging all screen actors into one union would gain favor. SAG and AFTRA would consult about it and hire a professional researcher to do a study, there would be a good deal of argument back and forth, and after a while the impulse would peter out. By 1980, however, as I shall discuss in chapter 6, the frustration over multiple memberships would boil over into a political movement that would transform both unions. In the meantime, however, there were many more television-caused problems to wrestle with.[22]

Gentleman's Agreement

Being the dominant actors' union in Hollywood was not going to be much to brag about if that city became a ghost town. With insignificant exceptions, television's entertainment programming around 1950 was live and broadcast from the networks' studios in New York. With TV continuing to siphon off customers from the motion pictures, acting jobs migrated to the Northeast and to AF(T)RA. As Hollywood lapsed into a depression, the Screen Actors Guild saw its membership fall to 7,300, a decline of 19 percent, from 1947 to 1951. During about the same period the total annual salary of film actors dropped from $38 million to $32 million. Unless something happened to bring filmed television production to Hollywood, the guild would soon be staring extinction in the face. But what could a mere union do?[23]

The Music Corporation of America (MCA), a talent agency, had an answer to that question. MCA had been founded in 1924 by Jules Stein, a saxophone- and violin-playing ophthalmologist in Chicago. Starting small, booking bands into local nightclubs, Stein had branched out into other entertainment fields, eventually turning MCA into the largest talent agency in Hollywood. In the early 1950s he included Ronald and Nancy Davis Reagan among his long list of actor clients.[24]

Stein, however, also had ambitions to become a television producer. He planned to go against the industry trend by filming television series in Hollywood. One of the potential obstacles he foresaw to this venture was the Screen Actors Guild.

In order to protect its members from unscrupulous practices, the guild had begun to regulate talent agents in 1939. One of the regulations had been a provision forbidding agencies to produce motion pictures. The reasons for this prohibition are clear. If agents employ actors who are also their clients in one of their films, they are functioning both as management and as a representative of labor. Their responsibility as agents is to get as much money for their clients as possible, but their incentive as producers is to hold salaries to a minimum. SAG's rules eliminated the possibility of this conflict of interest. Because its leaders knew that there would likely be exceptional circumstances, however, they left open the possibility that a waiver of the rule might be granted if a specific agent applied for it and presented a convincing case. During the forties the guild had permitted a few of these waivers. Charles K. Feldman of Famous Artists Corporation, for example, had been given a waiver which allowed him to produce three films a year. In 1949 the guild had renewed and updated the agents' regulations, keeping the ban on production.[25]

Because there was so little filmed television in Hollywood, there was no similar ban on agents producing for the new medium. But MCA's executives were naturally concerned that there might be one adopted in the future. It would hardly do for MCA to sink millions into its new subsidiary, Revue Productions, only to have the Screen Actors Guild pass a regulation preventing it from doing business. So in early 1952 MCA asked the guild to grant it a "blanket waiver," giving it permission to produce television shows in general, without having to come back and ask for a specific waiver for each one.[26]

Despite their desperate desire to see filmed television on the West Coast, the officers and board members of the Screen Actors Guild were wary of MCA's request. Before 1939 the relationship between agents and their clients had been full of abuses, and actors had no desire to bring back that situation. Yet they were willing to talk about the MCA waiver, and so negotiations ran through the spring. Although he was SAG president, Ronald Reagan had very little to do with these talks, he later testified, because he married in March 1952 and went on a honeymoon. John Dales handled most of the discussions. The fact that former SAG counsel Laurence Beilenson was now MCA's lawyer no doubt added to the cordial nature of the meetings.[27]

The waiver question was not the only negotiation in which MCA and SAG were disagreeing. In 1951 the guild had begun to talk with all the producers who were making or who wanted to make filmed television about the issue of residual payments to actors for programs that were shown more than once ("reruns"). The producers maintained that once the actors were paid, the film belonged to them and they could do with it what they pleased, without being obligated to make additional payments. The guild insisted that just as authors were paid every time one of their plays was produced, actors should be compensated each time one of their performances was broadcast. The two sides refused to budge, and a strike loomed.[28]

In June, Beilenson suggested a compromise. MCA would break with the other producers and agree to give actors television residuals, and

SAG would grant the blanket waiver. Without even waiting for an official assent from the guild, MCA let it be known that it was giving in
on the rerun position. Faced with this desertion, the other producers
capitulated also. SAG's negotiators signed a contract with the Association of Television Producers providing for residual payments early in
July.[29]

This evidence of good faith seems to have won over the guild's leaders. Before signing the waiver, however, they insisted on a set of protective stipulations being attached to it. In a letter they sent to MCA
over Reagan's signature, they required MCA/Revue to agree to abide
by certain conditions, the two most important being that if it employed
any of its own clients in its own productions, it could not charge the
usual 10 percent commission, and that Revue would have to pay actors
the maximum that they had ever been paid for similar work in television. MCA agreed. After warm discussion at the board meeting of
14 July 1952, Walter Pidgeon moved that the waiver be granted, Leon
Ames seconded, and it passed. Although the minutes of the meeting
record the vote as unanimous, this concealed persistent doubt among
some board members. Chick Chandler, for one, is remembered as having never truly assented to the deal.[30]

Waiver in hand, MCA went on to become the dominant force in
filmed television production.

The next year, Revue Productions hired Ronald Reagan, no longer
president of SAG, to host its anthology drama program "GE Theater,"
at a starting salary of $125,000 per year. Reagan stayed with the show
for nine years, attaining considerable financial security.[31]

Ever since, there have been suspicions that his employment was part
of a corrupt bargain in which the Screen Actors Guild president would
help push through the blanket waiver that would enable MCA to become an entertainment octopus, receiving as a payoff the lucrative position in "GE Theater." Reagan himself later testified that his position
as a client of MCA while he was presiding over a discussion of the
waiver made him "uneasy" lest there be a "misunderstanding" about
his role. Others were more than uneasy. The Justice Department in
Washington began various investigations which culminated in a suit
against MCA in the next decade. Reporters have written articles and
books over the years implying with greater or lesser subtlety that Reagan took a bribe. In 1972, Henry Denker published *The Kingmaker*,
a *roman à clef* novel in which a thinly disguised Jules Stein character is

aided by an even more thinly disguised Ronald Reagan character in return for a job in television. Given Reagan's subsequent history, it is safe to say that these innuendos will never stop.[32]

Those involved in the waiver have, of course, repeatedly denied that there was anything underhanded about it. In a way, however, to even wonder if corruption entered into the agreement is to misunderstand both the Screen Actors Guild and the historical situation in which it was maneuvering. In the first place, as president, Reagan did not even have a vote on the board. Given the fact that the guild's staff negotiated the waiver, and the board approved it, the conspiracy would have had to be a good deal larger than simply between Reagan and MCA. In the second place, neither the Justice Department, nor historians, nor journalists have ever been able to come up with any solid evidence that there was chicanery between Reagan, MCA, and SAG. Thus, to assert, as Dan Moldea does in his book *Dark Victory*, that Reagan "engineered" the waiver, or to argue, as does Anne Edwards in *Early Reagan*, that it was "undoubtedly won with the help of Reagan's position within the SAG," is to substitute fanciful speculation for informed discussion.[33]

More important, however, to believe that MCA had to bribe one or many people in the Screen Actors Guild to get its waiver is to disregard the historical context. In 1952 it was entirely realistic to anticipate that in another decade television would have killed the movies, just as the movies had killed vaudeville. Without movies, the guild's members would have had to rely on filmed TV, which in that year comprised only 25 percent of everything shown on the tube, the rest being live. With so much screen acting live and in New York, AFTRA would indeed have absorbed the majority of nonstage actors, and the Screen Actors Guild would be vestigial at best. "We were just scared that we were going to lose television," is the way that John Dales summarized the situation years later. When Reagan was asked to testify as to his motives, he said, "Our attitude was where we could see no harm to one of our members, to our membership, that we should do everything we could to encourage production, because the great problem we have had has always been unemployment. . . . If somebody comes to discuss and tell us they want to make pictures, we are inclined to go along with them." He was speaking for himself, but it was the attitude of his union. In other words, if Ronald Reagan had never been born, the guild would still have granted the waiver to MCA. Given this circumstance, the question of corruption is irrelevant.[34]

Showdown

Partly because of the television series produced by MCA, and partly because of technical and economic changes, Hollywood did not become a ghost town. As the 1950s advanced, it became clear to the networks that filmed television was superior to live. For one thing, film could be shown at the same time in each time zone. For another, it could record a performance on one day and be broadcast on another. Moreover, film could be saved and reshown, thus generating revenue many times, whereas once a live performance was over it and its earnings were gone forever. As a result, by the second half of the decade most entertainment programs were filmed, which meant that they were made in Hollywood. All of the major movie studios were making series. By the early 1960s, three-quarters of Hollywood's work force was employed in turning out products for television.[35]

The flow of production back to Los Angeles had salutary effects on the Screen Actors Guild. From its low of 7,300 members in 1951, it bounced back to 9,832 four years later, and continued to grow through the next decades. Despite the permanent problem of high unemployment, many of SAG's rank-and-file members were prosperous, and as an organization it could look forward to a secure future.[36]

There was, however, one serious worry facing the guild's members. Because film could be shown on television, the major producers' enormous backlog of movies was a potential source of instant competition for present-day actors. When the older performers had made those films there had been no television, so they were paid once, without any possibility of residuals. Now their previous work was arising to haunt them, for every ten-year-old movie that was shown on TV in 1957 meant that whatever would have been broadcast if that film had never existed had instead not been made. Actors discovered that they were competing with their former selves for jobs, and losing.

The problem did not catch the guild by surprise. In 1948, anticipating exactly what happened later, SAG had included in its list of contract demands to the motion-picture producers a request that residuals be paid to actors for all films made from that point forward, if they ever appeared on television. "Up until that time the only thing you could see on television were a few low-budget westerns and wrestling matches. We didn't care about the wrestling but we thought that the few low-budget westerns were the handwriting on the wall," explained

Reagan in an article in the guild's magazine, *Screen Actor*, twelve years later. The producers, however, had no intention of granting the right of residuals. They argued that they paid actors for their performances, and that they, the producers, then owned the films and could do with them as they pleased. Besides, they maintained that they had no intention of selling their backlog of films to television—would they be so obtuse as to provide their major competition with product? There the negotiations stuck.[37]

The only way the guild could have attained the residuals in 1948 would have been to strike. But at the beginning of the television-induced Hollywood depression, a work stoppage was the last thing anybody wanted. In addition, SAG's leaders would have been asking their members to go out, not over any actual injustice, but over a potential threat. As Jack Dales put it later, "How do you get a strike vote on something that's not happening and there's no threat of it happening?" So the guild and the producers agreed on a stop-gap clause in the new contract in which SAG in effect laid moral claim to residuals without demanding any specific payment, and the producers in effect denied the moral claim, but both sides agreed that if movies ever started showing up on television in the future, they would negotiate about residuals again. Agreeing to talk about agreeing at some future time, the two sides avoided a strike.[38]

Through the 1950s, when the basic contract would come up for renewal, the guild's negotiators would again raise the issue of movie residuals, and the producers' negotiators would again decline to discuss it. Meanwhile, the unthinkable was happening. The year after the interim agreement, Columbia Broadcasting System (CBS) began buying motion pictures from Monogram Studios. In 1953, Republic Studios sold $4 million worth of pictures to the new medium. Two years later television purchased 740 films from RKO, and the next year 725 from MGM. In 1957 Warner Brothers sold its entire library of pre-1948 movies. By 1959 there were few talkies that could not be encountered on the tube. SAG's fears had come true.[39]

RKO and the smaller studios had included residual payments to actors in the agreement with which they sold the packages. But the heads of the other major studios refused to pay residuals. Privately, they warned the guild's leadership that it was a matter of their economic survival, and that they would never give in on this issue. As contract-negotiation time rolled around in late 1959, therefore, the guild's staff and board members resolved that it was time for a showdown. They had laid moral claim to all residuals since 1948; now they would not only demand residuals in the future, but insist that the studios pay retroactively for all the movies in the last eleven years. Deciding that they needed a strong and experienced leader to see them through the coming trial, they prevailed upon Ronald Reagan to resume the presidency.[40]

If residuals had been the only major sticking point between the two sides, it would probably have been enough to start a strike. But they were also at loggerheads over the issue of beginning health and pension and welfare plans. In nearly all major industries, every company included some variety of health insurance in its list of benefits to its employees. In addition, most unions had worked out with the corporations in their industry a plan whereby a worker who retired received a pension based on the number of years he or she had been employed in a given company. The company would contribute a small amount to a fund on each payday, which would have grown to a sustaining level by the time the employee retired. AFTRA had won such a network-supported pension and welfare plan, and an industry-supported medical plan, in 1954.[41]

The Screen Actors Guild, however, had no such employee benefit plans. Actors worked neither steadily at their craft nor consistently for one employer, which meant that contributions for both health and pension would have to come from the producers as a group, go into a central pool, and be distributed to sick or retired performers according to some formula which took account of the peculiar rhythms of their careers. Although SAG had in 1959 paid the Martin Segel firm for advice on the possibilities of such welfare programs for actors, the conclusion being that they were feasible, the motion-picture producers rejected the specific plan that the guild's negotiators put forward.[42]

The guild also made the usual demands for higher minimum wages for day players and so forth, but everyone knew they were peripheral. In the early months of 1960, stubbornness on the two major issues froze the two sides into paralysis. Spyros Skouras, head of 20th Century-Fox and the major producers' representative in the negotiations, cried real tears when he explained to Dales, Migden, and the actors on the negotiating committee that payment of residuals would bankrupt the studios. The guild's leaders therefore launched a publicity campaign in the union's magazine and the local media to stiffen the actors' resolve. This was successful. After voting by 83 percent to authorize a strike, the members obeyed their leaders and walked out of the studios on 7 March.[43]

Although the strike was entirely successful in closing the major studios, halting production of eight feature films in the process, it was not easy to sustain. Because of the popular perception that all actors are rich and pampered, in any labor dispute the public is apt to regard them as behaving like spoiled children. In 1960 the media played up this aspect of the struggle, describing the "two handsomely dressed doormen" who "parked the workers' limousines and sports cars" as they arrived at a membership meeting, and seeking out such celebrities as John Wayne, Jeff Chandler, and David Niven to comment on the issues. The producers, quite aware of SAG's image as a country-club union, took out ads in the trade papers and circulated flyers to their employees hammering at the theme that the actors wanted "to be paid twice for doing one job" by demanding television residuals for their motion-picture performances. Although the guild's leaders asked reporters to remember that 69 percent of its members earned less than $4,000 a year, and took out their own advertisements to neutralize those of the producers, they could never seem to counter the impression that as a labor organization they were merely slumming.[44]

There was also trouble from other unions. When the studios shut down, the bosses were forced to lay off at least five thousand employees, and the leaders of the unions to which these belonged were none too pleased about it. Richard Walsh of the IATSE, apparently not grateful for SAG's help during his own union's struggle with the CSU fifteen years earlier, repeatedly and publicly criticized the strike. Although the guild's leaders pleaded with him to be loyal to brother unionists, he stood his ground, nearly coming to blows with an enraged Ronald Reagan at one meeting.[45]

The most serious trouble, however, came from inside the guild. One of the ways in which a performers' union differs from a more typical labor grouping is in its leaders' inability to suppress dissent. Since a significant proportion of actors are rich, famous, and well-versed in the uses of publicity, they can always get their complaints heard if they wish to. Some wished to. Before the strike started, over two hundred of SAG's members held a meeting at the Players' Ring Gallery Theater to protest. Hedda Hopper, who had not acted since 1942, made a speech in which she declared, "I don't think it is moral to accept money twice for a single job." She neglected to point out that she accepted money every time her column was reprinted. Naturally, this gathering of dissidents drew almost as much attention as the strike itself.[46]

As the weeks wore on and neither side budged in the negotiations, the initial determination of some of the membership began to waver. A few of the stars, many of whom themselves had production agreements and were therefore experiencing a conflict of interest, started to grumble in public that the strike had been a mistake. The guild began to receive dozens of phone calls every day from performers demanding to know when they would be able to resume looking for work. Delegations of angry actors walked into John Dales's office, accusing the leadership of asking for the impossible and insisting that there be some movement in the talks. The negotiators could feel support melting away under them. As Gilbert Perkins, on the board of directors since 1954 and a member of the 1960 negotiating team, states flatly, "We were losing the strike."[47]

And so they compromised. The guild dropped its demand for residuals on films made from 1948 to 1960, and the producers agreed both to pay residuals beginning in 1960, and to set up pension and health plans, to go into effect immediately. (Officially, the pension and welfare seed money was a lump-sum compensation of $2.25 million for the abandoned residuals, although it was not based upon a calculation of what those films would have earned for actors.) Five weeks and a day after they quit the studios, the membership ratified this contract by a vote of 6,399 to 259, and the strike was over.[48]

To the neutral observer, this looks like at least a partial victory for the guild negotiators. Although they renounced claims to the pre-1960s residuals, they won the principle of payment for reuse of their performances, which would of course grow in importance with the passage of time. Moreover, by achieving immediate pension and health plans they were at once able to come to the aid of sick and/or old actors (most of them nonstars) who had put years into the industry but had never made enough money to make themselves financially secure. To have achieved both these goals in one year would seem to be cause for satisfaction, if not celebration.

Yet, ever since 1960, there has been an undercurrent of bitterness directed against the leadership, especially from stars of pre-1960 movies. Seeing their old films on television over and over, knowing that those films are making money for somebody, but not for them, is a continuous spur to their resentment. "The pictures were sold down the river for a certain amount of money," stated Bob Hope years later. "I made something like sixty pictures, and my pictures are running on TV all over the world. Who's getting the money for that? The studios? Why aren't we getting some money?" Mickey Rooney, imagining the income he might have received from his series of "Andy Hardy" films, told a press conference, "SAG screwed us and I am mad about it." Their bitterness is echoed by many other stars.[49]

There is more to the attack than personal disappointment, however. To progressives, the 1960 settlement symbolizes what they consider to be Ronald Reagan's sweetheart unionism. They believe that a more militant, aggressive leadership in 1960 would have won both the 1948-to-1960 residuals and the health and pension plans. To leftists today, some of whom were children during the 1960 strike, it is an article of faith that Reagan crumbled in the clutch, and that the guild's leadership must be ever-vigilant to ensure that such a thing does not happen again. As the actual memory of 1960 fades into myth with the passing of time, it becomes a shibboleth of failure, to be used to spur the consciences of the troops to greater fervor.[50]

Needless to say, those who were involved in the negotiations scoff at this notion. They point out, of course, that Reagan was only one of the people in the room, and that the main burden of the negotiations fell on the staff. More to the point, however, they ridicule the idea that a greater show of resolve would have forced the producers to cave in. Chet Migden, then SAG's number two negotiator, speaks for many of the others when he insists that producers would never have capitulated on the 1948-to-1960 issue. "I don't believe they would have ever given retroactive rights; I think the strike would still be on."[51]

Having come to symbolize larger concerns, this argument over the 1960 contract will probably never entirely fade away.

There is a further way in which the events of 1960 are relevant to the arguments of later decades. In an issue of *Screen Actor* published soon after the end of the strike, Dwight Weist wrote an article decrying the compromise, and raising an issue that would be just as lively twenty years later. "If we strike and still can't get what we want, where then is our negotiating power?" he asked. "Let's merge with AFTRA and establish a union so powerful we can get fair demands for our performers—*without having to strike*." Here was the succinct statement of the progressives' dream—to have a union so big and powerful that it only

had to threaten to strike to make management tremble. Although few
in SAG rallied to Weist's banner at the time, the idea of merging with
the other actors' unions percolated for the next two decades, to boil
over in exactly the same sort of disappointment with a strike in 1980.[52]

Circumstantial Evidence

By the beginning of the 1960s, television had more than substituted
for the movies as the premier American commercial entertainment.
The nearly 46 million households with at least one receiver placed 87
percent of the population within reach of one of the 515 stations span-
ning the continent. Since these sets were turned on an average of five
hours a day, they created a demand for product that quite dwarfed
Hollywood's capabilities even in its golden era. In the late 1930s the
motion picture industry had produced about 450 films a year. Since
the average running time of each was about an hour and a half, movies
offered in the neighborhood of 700 hours of entertainment to the public each year. But television offered over 3,400 hours in prime-time
alone. Any important television-producing company could consequently expect to shoot more film in a year than all the major motion-
picture studios combined. Therefore, although movies were still being
made, in terms of industrial output they had become a minor part of
the business of screen entertainment.[53]

The shift in employment was, of course, reflected in the types of
work actors could expect to find in Los Angeles. By mid-decade only
a little more than a quarter of the jobs available were for theatrical
films. The rest were in television, with the majority of those being in
commercials. While motion-picture acting continued to guarantee the
highest prestige and usually the most artistic satisfaction to screen actors, as wage-earners they had to aim their ambitions at a different
target.[54]

Armed with the Screen Actors Guild's blanket production waiver,
the Music Corporation of America had quickly grown into the behe-
moth of this industry. As both a company representing talent and a
producer turning out television, it had a great advantage over everyone
else in town: it could make deals with itself. While TV in general prospered, therefore, MCA quickly grew not only rich but also powerful.
A decade after the granting of the waiver, it produced about 60 percent
of filmed television.[55]

When they were considering the waiver in 1952 (and its extension two years later), SAG's leaders had not anticipated this. Their concern was that MCA might use the waiver to exploit actors; it did not occur to them that the company might instead use it to dominate Hollywood. The conditions they had insisted on writing into the waiver were all intended to protect actors from attempts to lower their salaries, not to protect MCA's potential competitors from what amounted to its monopoly power over a large part of the available talent. As the new decade dawned with the company the most important entity in the city, they were a bit embarrassed by the monster they had helped to create. As a consequence, in September 1961 they told MCA that the waiver was off. It had one year to decide whether it wanted to represent talent or produce television, for after twelve months it would no longer be permitted to do both.[56]

But it was too late to resolve the situation quietly. The United States Justice Department had been suspicious of MCA for years. Two months after SAG put MCA on notice, the Justice Department began federal grand jury hearings in Los Angeles into the company's possible violation of the antitrust laws. On 5 February 1962 Ronald Reagan had to testify before a federal grand jury under the examination of United States Attorney John Fricano. Although he put all his questions politely and never directly accused Reagan of anything, the direction of Fricano's examination makes it clear that he believed that Reagan had been party to a conspiracy in which officers of the guild would help MCA, and MCA would in turn help them.[57]

For his part, Reagan consistently maintained that the entire reason for the waiver was that the guild desired to assist anyone who would increase the number of jobs available to actors. Although his own replies to Fricano's queries betrayed no annoyance, he was perfectly aware that he was on the grill; in his autobiography he wrote that he "spent a long, unhappy afternoon being interrogated by a federal lawyer who'd seen too many Perry Masons." A week later the government subpoenaed the income-tax returns for the years 1952–1955 of Reagan and his wife, plus those of John Dales, Chet Migden, and four other members of the 1952 SAG board, looking for some evidence of payoffs. It found nothing incriminating.[58]

Nevertheless, in July the Justice Department filed an antitrust suit against MCA, naming SAG and the Writers Guild of America as unindicted coconspirators. The inclusion of the Screen Actors Guild was based on the allegation, which everyone associated with the guild strongly denied, that it had rejected requests for similar waivers from other talent agencies.[59]

MCA avoided going to court by negotiating a consent decree with the Justice Department in which it promised to divest itself of its talent agency while keeping its production facilities—in substance what the Screen Actors Guild had already required it to do. By September, the arrangements were made and MCA continued on as the dominant producer in Hollywood, minus legal problems. Because of this dominant position, and because of the subsequent career of Ronald Reagan, interest in the agency, and in the fabled blanket waiver, continues.[60]

The Awful Truth

The arrival of television transformed Hollywood, and caused wrenching adjustments at every level, from its top management down to its labor unions. It would be a mistake, however, to see the crisis associated with the introduction of the new amusement device as an unusual period of turmoil set against a more normal background of placid progress. The truth is that it is upheaval, not business as usual, which is the constant in the history of the entertainment industry.

Consider the situation in 1985: videocassette recorders and cable television were everywhere on the ascendant, and the old broadcasting networks seemed to be drifting in panic. Twenty years earlier, neither VCRs nor cable had existed as anything more than a technological potential; network television reigned supreme. Twenty years before that, in 1945, television was but the dream of a few entrepreneurs, as talking motion pictures dominated American amusement. Twenty years prior to that, there were no talking pictures, and the silents held seemingly unchallengable sway. Twenty years earlier, in 1905, there was no motion-picture industry, movies themselves were merely a vulgar novelty, and what mattered occurred on the stage. The business of mass entertainment has undergone five technical/economic revolutions in this century. There is no reason to expect that the pace will slacken. Any worker starting young in this industry can expect to see it wrenchingly transformed at least twice.

This certainty of onrushing change creates enormous problems for the business concerns attempting to ride technological inventiveness and public tastes to profits. But it is even harder on the labor unions.

Part of their purpose is to buffer their members from economic uncertainty and create a climate in which people can plan for the future with a reasonable assurance that they will have one. But the hard truth which emerges from an examination of the reaction of the Screen Actors Guild to the arrival of television is that there is no safety for a labor organization in anything except quick wits and nerve. At the very moment that unions are fashioning a haven for their members, history is changing the rules of the game they have to play. Although the Screen Actors Guild managed to survive the transition to television because its leaders were bold and decisive, there is no guarantee that it will always have such leadership. Whoever its leaders are, they had better keep awake.

Democracy is a—a—a system of self-determination. It's the—the right to make the wrong choice.

Glenn Ford to Okinawans, *The Teahouse of the August Moon*, screenplay by John Patrick

Chapter Five

DEMOCRACY

Two concerns dominated the public posture of the Screen Actors Guild in the decade after the 1960 strike. The first was the increasing tendency of motion-picture producers to shoot theatrical films elsewhere than in southern California, and especially in foreign countries. Although Hollywood continued to be the place where deals were struck and much technical work done, producers liked to take advantage of lower foreign costs to shoot overseas. As a result, about half the "American" movies made during the decade were filmed outside the United States. These pictures typically featured American stars in leading roles but local actors in supporting parts. Every film made outside the country was thus a number of lost employment opportunities for Hollywood performers. Repeatedly during the decade, guild leaders harangued the industry about its exporting of jobs, lobbied Congress to pass tax legislation offering incentives to filmmakers to stay in America, and made contract concessions to encourage domestic production. These efforts had no visible effect.[1]

Since theatrical films were no longer the major source of work for actors, however, "runaway production," as it was called, was not their most important worry. That was the problem of television reruns. Television's enormous appetite for product—3,432 hours a year in prime-time alone—had initially seemed to promise a bonanza of employment. But the networks soon discovered that audiences were happy to watch endless repetitions of their favorite series. Economics therefore dictated that an episode, once shot and paid for, be reshown as many times as possible. The increased number of reruns each year, of course,

92

caused the proportion of new episodes to contract. As the total of original episodes produced annually in any given series declined from thirty-nine to twenty-six or even fewer during the decade, the opportunities for new jobs for actors contracted at the same time. Although the guild had negotiated residuals for reshown TV episodes in the 1950s, these agreements did not enable the actor to recover 100 percent of his or her original salary; residual checks became smaller with each screening. And residuals did not solve the problem of the actor who had not performed in the original series and wanted a job now.[2]

In the late 1960s and early 1970s, the guild pursued a major lobbying campaign to persuade federal policymakers to restrict reruns. This effort reached its peak when SAG president John Gavin visited the White House in 1972 and talked with some of President Richard Nixon's staff. Shortly thereafter, Nixon publicly endorsed SAG's position. In 1972, however, Nixon had no great influence with the Democratic Congress, and anyway the guild's position was solidly opposed by the networks. The antirerun campaign went nowhere, and Gavin's successors adopted other strategies to deal with the problem.[3]

While the guild's activists were thus wasting their energy in fruitless attempts to alter industry practices, its membership was nearly doubling from 14,768 in 1963 to 27,904 in 1973. The advent of television had indeed created thousands of new job opportunities, but those had, as usual, attracted far more star-struck hopefuls than could ever be expected to make a living from acting. In addition, advertising agencies had fallen into the habit of using "real people" in their TV commercials. Once they had appeared on screen, these nonprofessionals were eligible for a SAG card, which many of them acquired for its prestige value. No one in the guild knew how many members were thus nonactors, but there was widespread agreement that they swelled the membership lists without adding to the talent pool. As a result of these two factors the official unemployment rate among the guild's members hovered around 85 percent through the 1960s, with more than two-thirds of them earning less than $2,400 a year. It seemed that the more things changed for the film industry, the more they stayed the same for the Screen Actors Guild.[4]

This was also true for the type of people who ran the guild. As with almost every other labor union in the country, a relatively small group sat on the SAG board, served as officers, and set policy. Moreover, as with almost every other union, the people in this ruling group were all more or less conservative in their philosophy.[5]

There was one great difference between the dominant group in the guild and those in other unions, however. In most other unions, officers were paid. They naturally came to rely upon their salaries and perquisites and to view the union as a means to their own enrichment. The "business unionism" philosophy they espoused, which emphasized amicable relations with management and lack of participation by the rank and file, was at least partly a ruse to legitimate their own oligarchical rule. In the Screen Actors Guild, however, there were no paid officers (although there was a small paid staff). The volunteers who sat on the board and devoted hours to committees received no tangible reward. They were motivated by the spirit of service. Indeed, so far were they from attempting to oppress their fellow performers that they frequently passed policies that ran contrary to their own interests. For example, although most of them were quite successful in the profession, they had instituted a formula for eligibility for the pension and welfare system that discriminated strongly in favor of the less successful actor.[6]

If SAG was run by an oligarchy, therefore, it was an *oligarchy of ideology*: its leaders were not interested in hogging the spoils for themselves but in ensuring that a certain outlook and temperament dominated union policy. When, in the political contests of the 1970s, progressive challengers accused the conservatives of belonging to a "self-perpetuating group," the conservatives were hurt and bewildered, for they knew that they had allowed many new actors into the circle of power. The charge was true enough, however, for the governing group had taken pains to ensure that only actors with the right philosophy and character attained influence. By shutting out those whom they deemed irresponsible or obnoxious, they had, perhaps without realizing it, restricted guild government to a narrow segment of the ideological spectrum.

The means they used to perpetuate conservative rule were informal and imperfect, but on the whole quite effective. Because the casts of almost every movie and television show are different, working actors come to know a large number of their colleagues. Additionally, on any set there are long waits between shots during which the performers usually sit around and talk. Consequently, the members of the board as a group were familiar with the outlooks of thousands of actors. With this knowledge they were able to engage in a continuous process of filtration of likely candidates for guild government.[7]

Although the guild's constitution stipulated that the members of all committees would be appointed by the board of directors, in actual practice the membership of every committee was under the control of the president. The custom in the 1960s and early 1970s was for the chief executive to appoint a Nominating Committee (responsible for choosing the invariably successful "official slate" in the yearly elections) consisting of twelve members, nine from the board and three from the rank and file who had been suggested by the president's confidantes on the board. During the process of deliberating on potential candidates, the nine "inside" members would observe the three outsiders. Those whom they found acceptable were appointed to the board when vacancies occurred (as they did frequently, because actors leaving town to work on location often resigned). Furthermore, the official slate itself, of course, consisted of people whose philosophies were known to be conservative. Finally, there was a Board Replacement Committee which used the same network of personal recommendations to fill vacancies between elections. Each board and set of officers therefore exercised strong influence over the stream of volunteers into the boardroom. This did not ensure a unanimity of outlook, but it did guarantee that the great majority of those who were allowed to participate in SAG government shared a basic philosophy.

Like any other system, this one did not always work. In 1969, a well-known character actor named Robert Easton asked the members of the Nominating Committee for their endorsement for his board candidacy. At that time, there was a settled opinion among the guild's leadership that actors should not be allowed to serve on both the AFTRA and the SAG board of directors. Since Easton was a member of the AFTRA board, the Nominating Committee turned down his request. Easton then ran as an independent and became the first such candidate in twenty-two years to be successful. As it turned out, this exception did not disturb the reigning pattern, for Easton proved to be not only a relatively conservative unionist but an able board member. Within four years he had advanced to first vice-president of the guild. Nevertheless, despite such occasional breakdowns the system of screening functioned tolerably well, and assured a consistent tone and direction to the union's government.[8]

The conservatives who ran the guild in this manner resented sug-

Robert Easton

gestions that their procedure was somehow undemocratic. They pointed out that SAG had more member mobility and a larger turnover of board members than other unions, and that, as the Easton example proved, it was possible to successfully challenge official candidates in elections by running via petition. And indeed, compared to many other unions, with their presidential dictatorships, fixed elections, and violence, the Screen Actors Guild was a model of clean and fair government.[9]

Still, from an analytic point of view the critics were right. Among those who have studied democracy in labor unions, there is a consensus that *participation by the rank and file* and *closely contested elections* are the defining characteristics of the truly democratic union. Although it preserved the possibility of both of these, in actual fact the guild until 1971 had neither of them. Indeed, the best indicator of authentic democracy, in a nation or in a labor union, is the defeat of incumbent officers, and in its almost four decades of existence no guild officer had even come close to being unseated in an election. But the times they were a' changin'.[10]

The Intruders

Because the great problem facing actors was unemployment, it was only natural that some of them should want to constrict the labor supply in order to increase job opportunities for those remaining in the talent pool. Controlling the number of people who are available to work so that they will be continuously employed and so that they will receive relatively high wages is, after all, one of the chief functions of labor unions. The fact that SAG was called a "guild" and not a "union," however, was perfectly indicative of the fact that it did not govern the number of workers available to management, but simply negotiated wages, hours, and working conditions for those whom management chose to hire. Nevertheless, it had always contained some actors who wanted to make it into a "union" that would tightly govern the labor market. Performers who shared this opinion were not in power, but in the early 1970s some of them began to make things difficult for those who were.[11]

In 1970 an actor named Charles Briggs began to pepper the guild's staff, officers, board of directors, and Guild Government Review Committee (GGRC) with schemes to enable SAG to restrict the number of performers competing for the available work. For example, Briggs suggested that the guild's initiation fee be raised from two hundred to one thousand dollars, which would have eliminated both those who were not really dedicated to becoming actors and those who were too poor to raise the money. He also demanded that SAG establish a "screening committee" to more tightly enforce the "preference of employment" clause in the guild's contract, which supposedly penalizes producers who employ amateurs in film roles. The new committee would have prevented people from working who did not have the proper training. Since nobody knows what constitutes proper training for an actor, this would have given a small bureaucracy the power to cut off the supply of new competitors, thereby improving the prospects for those who were already members. The conservative establishment found these and other similar proposals repugnant, and rejected them unanimously.[12]

But Briggs was tenacious. He gathered around himself a group of like-minded actors and launched an organized assault on guild government, attending committee meetings, questioning guild procedures, and barraging the officers and staff with proposed reforms. Neither Briggs nor his group were polite; their attitude toward management was confrontational, and toward the conservative actors, contemptuous. Guild government was soon a battleground of personal insult and ideological quarrel.[13]

The Briggs group was small, and by itself would never have been able to capture the government of the Screen Actors Guild. Just as any of history's revolutions has its roots in a large number of separate discontents, however, the insurgency that toppled the conservatives in SAG drew from many disparate sources. Briggs and his coterie were the nucleus around which the accumulated resentments of actors congealed.

One major source of unfocused opposition was frustration at unsatisfied claims. It is very common for actors to believe that management is somehow ignoring a contract provision or cheating them of salary through accounting manipulations. Almost every actor I interviewed had some story of being defrauded of thousands of dollars by a swindling producer or studio. Most of them never bring these complaints to the attention of their union. Those that do, however, are frequently disappointed. Because of the guild's small staff, the executive secretary has had to make choices about which claims to pursue. Traditionally, he solves this problem by trying to help only the "scale" player, that is, the unknown actor working for SAG minimum salary. Contract players, those whose relative eminence enables them to work for above-scale pay, are deemed able to protect themselves. When they call the guild and request help in a personal contract dispute, they are told to hire a lawyer. This naturally engenders resentment in the complainer, who now believes that he or she has been betrayed twice.[14]

There is thus a permanent reservoir of dissatisfaction with guild government, waiting to be mobilized by a dissident group. In the early 1970s, in addition, there was a special sort of this kind of resentment. Many working actors believed that SAG board members alone, among those who worked above scale, could get their claims pursued by the staff. Whether or not this belief was true, it reinforced the arguments of dissidents that a closed, privileged group was running the guild, and that the time had come for a housecleaning.[15]

The next push toward rebellion came with the motion picture and television contract of 1971. Sitting on the board at this time was a veteran character actor named Bert Freed. Although he was hardworking

Bert Freed

and intelligent, Freed was one of the conservatives' partial mistakes. Coming out of a left-wing background himself, he was somewhat in sympathy with the malcontents outside the boardroom, and felt that the opinions of ordinary actors were insufficiently consulted by the group in power. He was, further, the leader of a small faction on the board who wanted to push for 100 percent residuals in the contract (guaranteeing, in other words, that every time an episode was rerun its cast would be paid as much as they had originally received for their roles). Among dissidents, he had the reputation of being, in Howard Caine's words, "the lone, beat-up liberal" on the board.[16]

As a member of the Wages and Working Conditions Committee, charged with the task of formulating contract demands in 1971, Freed sent out a mailer to all members asking them what sort of contract changes they would like to see. Out of this informal poll came a proposal to change the way television residuals were paid. Every time an episode of filmed television was reshown, the members of the cast received payments based on a proportion of the SAG scale (that is, a percentage of the minimum wage). Actors who earned above scale, however, felt that their residuals should at least be based on a percentage of their salary, which would of course give them more money. Freed succeeded in getting this included in SAG's package of contract demands for 1971.[17]

As part of the give-and-take that is inevitable during every contract negotiation, however, guild leaders had allowed this demand to be severely watered down, settling for an additional 15 percent of over-scale earnings on top of the minimum residuals. Under ordinary circumstances the membership would neither have known nor have cared much about which demands were won or lost or compromised in a negotiating session. Because of Freed's innovation in soliciting ideas, however, there had been a widespread expectation that the new contract would contain this particular provision, and its near-absence caused an explosion of resentment.[18]

Here was the widespread public dissatisfaction that Briggs and his group had been waiting for. Invitations went out, and at a meeting of some forty actors in Briggs's living room in the late summer of 1971, the Concerned Actors Committee (CAC) was formed. Although its organizing members had been attracted to activism by their desire to close the guild to further enlistees, once other actors became involved the focus changed. CAC became a vehicle for demands to open SAG to greater participation by the rank and file. The original purpose of the dissidents became submerged in CAC's demands for democratizing the guild's election process and committee structure.[19]

The First Time

In the summer of 1971, after six years in office, Charlton Heston decided to step down as president. Heston's decision was based on the personal belief that he had served his union long enough, but it could not have been better timed as far as the members of CAC were concerned. An articulate conservative, Heston not only possessed the prestige of the incumbent, but was and is an actor of great stature. No challenger of any philosophy could have hoped to defeat him in an election campaign. For that matter, it would have been most difficult to find a serious candidate willing to run against him. But with Heston declining to succeed himself, the guild's Nominating Committee put up first vice-president John Gavin as its candidate. Although undoubtedly a star, Gavin was not nearly so prestigious within the acting community as Heston. Moreover, he would not be running as an incumbent. The members of CAC saw a chance to win power. Thus began democracy in the Screen Actors Guild.[20]

Briggs and another CAC founder named Michael Vandever first approached Dennis Weaver, who had a reputation as a progressive, and asked him to run against Gavin. Never having been involved in SAG government, Weaver felt that it would be presumptuous of him to try for the top position, and declined. Later, however, he decided to run for a board seat, and succeeded in persuading the Nominating Committee to choose him as part of its official slate. Briggs and Vandever next turned to Bert Freed, who accepted. Donald Sutherland ran for first vice-president against Ed Platt, Frank Maxwell for second against Robert Lansing, Barry Sullivan for third against Robert Easton, John Randolph for fourth (in New York) against Joyce Gordon, Beah Richards for recording secretary against Kathleen Freeman, and Don Knight for treasurer against Gilbert Perkins. In addition, CAC fielded a full slate of thirteen candidates for the board of directors.[21]

This was not a gaggle of individuals running separately for office but a true slate with a common platform, shared mailers, coordinated public appearances, centralized financing, and designated spokesmen. The insurgents spent $35,000 as a group, mostly for ads in the trade papers. As the biggest star among them, Canadian Donald Sutherland was given much of the burden of campaigning, appearing on local television and constantly talking to reporters. For his part, Freed managed to goad Gavin into a public debate, which produced no particular enlightenment but did make it appear that the two candidates were more or less equal in stature.[22]

The independent platform nicely blended progressive philosophy with promises calculated to appeal to the members' self-interest. "The main issue is work," Sutherland told the *Hollywood Reporter* in a discussion of the platform. "We propose to borrow $50 million from Congress (the way Lockheed did) to make 50 films, with production funds governed by a union board. The films would be on American historical subjects, and all would be completed in time for the 1976 Bicentennial Celebration." The platform went on to detail additional plans for increasing employment. Nor did the progressives neglect the union's responsibility to protect its members, promising to employ enough shop stewards to "insure contract enforcement so that every actor gets his full overtime payments." The independents also hit the theme of rank-and-file government hard, with Sutherland claiming that SAG "hasn't been a participatory, democratic union, and that's what we want it to be," while proposing quarterly, rather than yearly, membership meetings plus special precontract meetings to get ordinary actors involved in the negotiations.[23]

At first this full-scale assault took Gavin and the conservatives aback, accustomed as they were to quiet, decorous campaigns without real opposition. In the first few weeks of the race, Gavin tried to pretend that he was above politics, telling reporters, "We did not consider a political campaign. Politics should not be germane to what we are discussing here." The conservatives had not even prepared a platform of their own, hoping that the prestige of office would carry them to victory. But with the trade papers full of election news, and Freed and Sutherland generating obvious support, Gavin was forced to abandon his pose of Olympic impartiality. Once he did, he showed that he, too, knew a thing or two about campaigning.[24]

The conservatives' strategy was to ridicule the obvious demagoguery of some of the progressive planks, while offering a few equally fatuous promises themselves. Reasoning that his more serious opponent was the star Sutherland, rather than the lesser-known Freed, Gavin concentrated most of his fire on the Canadian. In "An Open Letter to Donald Sutherland," written in conjunction with his friend Robert Easton, and published as an ad in the trade papers, he took on the independents' platform plank by plank.[25]

"Lockheed had customers already committed to buying its product, the L-1011. Do you? . . . Do you honestly feel the American public will buy $50 million worth of tickets to see 50 films on historical subjects? And if they don't, how will the Guild repay this loan? . . . You also state the $50 million in production funds would be governed by a union board. Doesn't that put the Guild into the role of producer?" In like manner Gavin attacked every one of the opposition's proposals.[26]

The conservatives issued their own platform on 6 October. On the one hand, they too offered a string of unlikely projects for increasing employment, such as (to quote *Daily Variety*'s summary) "current, other plans for new, modern studio complexes to outcompete foreign production," and a "residual policing system using electronic monitoring to insure residual payments." On the other hand, they did come up with a few realistic proposals for being a better union, such as the establishment of workshops for actors and working with the AFL-CIO to fight the drain of jobs overseas in all industries. They did not, however, suggest any new plans for opening up guild government to greater rank-and-file participation.[27]

The campaign's most memorable incident illustrated the extent to which unhealed wounds from the blacklisting era continued to underlie actors' politics. Although he entirely supported his friend John Gavin's candidacy, Charlton Heston had originally intended to keep clear of any involvement in the campaign. The independents' attacks, however, were obviously not aimed solely at the presidential candidate of the moment but at the way the guild had traditionally been run; although they did not mention Heston by name they clearly included his administration in the indictment. Taking personal offense, Heston one day walked into a progressive press conference and began rebutting their charges and attacking their own platform proposals ("Heston, SAG Indies In Hot Clash," read the next day's headline in *Daily Variety*).[28]

During the course of this impromptu debate, Heston had occasion to suggest that the members of the independent slate owed their allegiance to a "shadowy constituency." By this he meant that they were creatures of CAC, which was true. The candidates themselves, however, took the statement to mean that Heston was accusing them of being Communists. Since some of them were veteran leftists and a few had indeed been party members decades earlier, they had reason to be sensitive to red-baiting, and they reacted with outrage. For a brief period charges of McCarthyism filled the air, and the Screen Actors Guild seemed transported back two decades in time. Although it embarrassed him then, this episode evidently taught Heston an important lesson. In the future, he would be careful never to assert or even imply that a political opponent was loyal to any hidden agenda or organization.[29]

When the ballots were counted in the first week of November, the conservative slate had swept the field. Gavin beat Freed almost exactly two-to-one, 6,407 votes to 3,237, with the other conservatives winning by similar margins.[30]

On the one hand, this was a victory decisive enough to give the conservatives reason to feel justified. On the other hand, it was not altogether discouraging for the insurgents. They had, after all, established the legitimacy of challenging the Nominating Committee's choices, thrown together a political slate in a few weeks, taken on an entrenched establishment, run a relative unknown against a star, and still managed to mobilize a credible amount of support. Moreover, they had a toehold on the board, for Freed had retained his seat while running for president, and their potential ally Dennis Weaver had also been elected. All in all, it was enough to motivate them to try again.

Revolution

Gavin and the conservatives were neither stupid, inflexible, nor power-mad. They realized that winds of change were blowing through the Screen Actors Guild and that wise leaders would have to bend to them. In the next two years they initiated a range of reforms and concessions that they hoped would deflate the ongoing rebellion. Fulfilling a campaign pledge, they created a Workshop Committee to coordinate free classes to aid actors in mastering their craft. They adopted a different method of choosing members of the Nominating Committee that would allow more input from ordinary actors. Responding to progressive criticism that the guild was indifferent to the problem of women and minorities, they created committees whose purpose was to study and publicize the problem of discrimination. Taking seriously the charges that lack of participation was shameful in a supposedly democratic organization, Gavin created the Apathy Committee (its name soon changed to the less ambiguous Anti-Apathy Committee) to study ways to increase rank-and-file involvement, and appointed Freed and Weaver to sit on it. He also appointed those two, and later, other dissidents, to the Membership Relations Committee, charged with upgrading the services the guild performed for its members.[31]

All this was sincere, but it did not quell the insurgency. For one thing, the opposition had moved beyond being merely an expression of discontent and had become an institution devoted to seizing power; a few concessions were not going to slow its momentum. For another, many of the gestures were halfhearted. For example, although Gavin did appoint progressives to the committees named above, he kept them off those that had real power: Wages and Working Conditions (which formulated contract demands), Government Review (which recommended changes in the constitution or bylaws), and Nominating. For another, he and his allies continuously rejected proposed changes that were dear to the insurgents' hearts, especially plans to further reform the nominating process and schemes to give more power to the annual membership meeting.[32]

This was on the surface. But there was also another, more subtle conflict of style between the two groups. The establishment conservatives were as a group more formal and less personal. They addressed one another as "Mr. So and So" (or the feminine equivalent) in the boardroom. With a few exceptions (including Gavin, who favored sweaters) men wore coats and ties during meetings. On the other hand, the insurgents as a group were more representative of the style that emerged from the 1960s. They tended to be less conventional in speech, dress, and personal comportment. To the argument over substance was thus added a cultural friction that increased the annoyance the members of each group felt for the members of the other.[33]

Moreover, the insurgents contained within their ranks a number of people who were either full of neurotic hostility, unschooled in common politeness, or both. They refused to keep any discussion to the substantive point, but insisted on heaping personal abuse upon the conservatives, sometimes to their faces and sometimes behind their backs. These attacks, which went on inside and outside the boardroom, ranged from mere rudeness to outright slander. They enraged the conservatives, who were thus even less disposed to treat dissident proposals seriously.[34]

Further, some dissidents began leaking board business to the trade press, naturally offering their own interpretations of the proceedings at the same time. The conservatives suddenly found themselves in a distorted fishbowl, with highly colored accounts of yesterday's board meeting appearing as today's headlines. They took steps to try to protect their decisions from public scrutiny, but these were in vain. From 1972, the internal business of the Screen Actors Guild became the common conversation of anyone who read the trade papers (which meant, in effect, almost everyone in Hollywood).[35]

All this would have tried the patience of a saint, and tested the skill of the wisest politician. But John Gavin was neither saintly nor skillful. Instead of rising above the partisan ugliness, he contributed to it. An able man himself, he could not hide his disdain for those he considered less able, which included all the progressives. An intelligent man, he flaunted his contempt for those he thought stupid. An honest man, he let show the doubt he felt about the integrity of others. In the chair at board meetings, he allowed himself to be overcome by partisanship, ignoring the raised hands of those whose views he did not want to hear. He persistently mispronounced the names of some board members,

and although he (no doubt truthfully) claimed that he did so acciden-
tally, progressives noticed that it was always actors on their own side of
the political fence who provoked his lapses of memory. His behavior
alienated a number of fair-minded board members who at first considered themselves centrists, the most important of whom was Dennis
Weaver. Not too many months into his term, Gavin had changed the
progressive cause from a crusade based on issues into a vendetta
against himself.[36]

The concessions made by the conservatives thus failed to blunt the
progressive attack. All during Gavin's presidency the guild's Government Review Committee was busy dealing with proposed reforms by
Briggs, Vandever, and others. The progressives attended the 1972
membership meeting en masse, and pushed through two resolutions
expanding rank-and-file influence over nominations and policy making. The boardroom and trade papers were full of personal attacks on
the character and judgment of Gavin and his allies on the board.[37]

In the 1972 elections, the dissidents again ran a slate for the board,
although they refrained from the challenging the officers. Only one
of these independent candidates, Kent McCord, was successful. Once
again, while the conservatives took the results as a vote of confidence
from the membership, the insurgents had reason to feel optimistic. In
the first place, even this single victory proved that progressive independent candidates could win; psychologically, the dike had been
breached. In the second place, McCord's victory was instructive about
the sorts of progressive candidates who might be expected to win:
stars. As one of two leading actors in a top-ten television series ("Adam-
12"), McCord's name and face were familiar to most of the guild's voters. Progressive leaders began a private effort to recruit well-known
actors to run on their slate in 1973.[38]

As the election approached, the progressives benefited from a conservative defection. Kathleen Nolan had been on the board since 1964,
had been a fund-raiser for Gavin in 1971, and had become the first
female (third) vice-president in guild history in 1972. An extraordinarily energetic person, she had been involved in an amazing variety
of union activities during her tenure. Board minutes for the years preceding 1973 are full of commendations to Nolan for her work in organizing panel discussions on the craft of acting, chairing meetings
with federal government officials on the rerun problem, preparing an
information pamphlet to be distributed to new members, and the like.

She had also single-handedly founded the Women's Conference Committee in 1972, and had toured the country giving speeches on women's problems to Screen Actors Guild branches. Ambitious and assertive, she felt that she deserved to move up in the union hierarchy.[39]

Nolan had also undergone a philosophical evolution which was pulling her away from the Gavin camp. In her first years on the board, she had been conventional and cautious, willing to go along with the (male) guild leadership. When she was in New York to do a play in 1969, however, she had joined a women's consciousness-raising group. Returning to Los Angeles in 1971 and again serving on the board, she discovered that her attitudes had changed. "I became much more aware that, sitting on the board, the man to my left and the man to my right were saying essentially the same things that I was saying, and many times I felt that I was saying it better," she remembered in 1986. Along with her new feminist perspective came a greater sympathy for progressive arguments, especially those on the subject of rank-and-file participation. "I was beginning to feel that there was a great part of the membership that was disenfranchised. . . . I saw the fear that the establishment had of change." Repelled by the self-righteous, abusive style of some of the dissidents, she had remained loyal to the conservatives in the 1971 and 1972 contests, but she was a potential progressive convert, waiting for the right circumstances.[40]

The right circumstances arrived with the deliberations of the official Nominating Committee in September 1973. The third vice-presidency filled by Nolan had just been given to New York. There were therefore three possible slots that she might fill if she wished to advance in the governmental structure. One of these, the presidency, was out of reach because Gavin was running for reelection, and anyway she did not yet feel ready to try for the top spot. The first vice-presidential candidacy was unlikely because Gavin's friend and confidant Ed Nelson wanted it. Nolan would consequently have settled for the second vice-presidency.[41]

But the conservatives controlling the Nominating Committee miscalculated. Instead of Nolan they chose a black actor named Robert Doqui, the moderate and highly respected chair of the Minorities Committee, as their candidate for second vice-president. Since the third vice-presidency was now the province of New York, this left only the fourth, a technical demotion, for Nolan. When Leon Ames, chair of the committee, called Nolan, who was in Sacramento doing a play, and told her of the Nominating Committee's decision, the disappointment and betrayal she felt finally cracked her allegiance to the conservatives. Exploding with anger on the phone, she refused to accept any nomination. Subsequent calls from several of her conservative friends on the board failed to calm her or change her mind. Finally the committee gave up and chose Kathleen Freeman to run for fourth vice-president.[42]

When Nolan returned to Los Angeles the insurgents lost no time asking her to run as their candidate for president. Not ready for such a move, she declined, but joined them in a concerted plan to win the upcoming election.[43]

Meanwhile, the committee had declined to renominate second vice-president Joe Flynn and board member Robert Hogan because of their progressive leanings, and Bert Freed for obvious reasons. These three planned an organizational meeting with the insurgents at Arthur Hill's house, also inviting Dennis Weaver.[44]

At the meeting, the assembled dissidents tried to persuade Weaver to run on their slate for the presidency. He was reluctant. A man who detests partisanship and political labels, he did not want to be the leader of any faction. Moreover, since his popular television series "McCloud" was frequently shot on location, he knew that he would often have to be away from the guild. Yet, his observation of the struggles within the board had convinced him that something had to be done, and he was certain that Gavin was the wrong person to do it. "When I got on the board, I saw total divisiveness there," Weaver explained thirteen years later. "I saw a group of people who had no voice in what was going on. . . . Their energy and their talent and their feelings were not utilized on any type of committees that had any substance. . . . A great body of people in the guild were trying to say something, and they felt as though no one was listening to them." Torn between his feeling of responsibility to his fellow actors and his distaste for factionalism, Weaver compromised. He agreed to run against Gavin, but as an individual rather than as part of any slate. The progressives jumped to agree to this, for they knew perfectly well that in the heat of a campaign technical distinctions about individuals and slates would soon be erased; Weaver would be viewed as their leader. As part of this nonslate they then "nominated" Nolan for first vice-president, Joe Flynn for second, Elizabeth Allen for recording secretary, and a number of others, including Freed and Hogan, for board seats.[45]

The campaign was essentially a rerun of 1971, with Weaver expressing discontent with the 1971 contract and promising more rank-and-file involvement in SAG government, and Gavin accusing the dissidents of interjecting "politics" into the guild and attempting to refute charges that he was undemocratic and uninterested in the welfare of minorities.[46]

When the ballots were counted in November, however, the results were entirely different. Weaver won over 70 percent of the votes, and Nolan, Flynn, and Allen crushed their own opponents. The independent slate captured only four of the fourteen vulnerable seats on the board (with Hogan and Freed winning), but with the conservative leadership decapitated, the insurgents, although still technically in the minority, enjoyed a complete strategic dominance.[47]

One of the questions that emerges from this watershed election is whether the vote was indeed a choice between philosophies made by an informed Screen Actors Guild electorate or whether it was merely a case of the bigger stars drawing more support. In a national election it is possible to address such questions with reference to the many public-opinion surveys that become available both during and after the campaign. There are no such polls conducted for SAG elections, of course, so the answer will have to be much less precise.

The argument that Weaver beat Gavin because he was a bigger name is quite plausible. Partly because of his fondly remembered and Emmy-winning portrayal of the character Chester in "Gunsmoke" in the 1950s, and partly because of his current hot television series, Weaver was undoubtedly a brighter star than Gavin. Moreover, Joe Flynn's victory over Robert Doqui for second vice-president was probably because Flynn was a much more familiar name. Here the argument falters, however. Ed Nelson, defeated by Kathleen Nolan for first vice-president, was at least as well known, and Robert Easton, defeated by Elizabeth Allen for recording secretary, was more eminent. Therefore, although Weaver's triumph alone might be ascribed to star-voting, the victory of the insurgents as a group can be explained only with reference to a deliberate choice by SAG voters. The "Revolution of 73," as it is often called among progressive activists, was not an accident, but an exercise in democracy.

To emphasize that the change was indeed a revolution, Weaver delivered a militant inaugural address to the annual membership meeting on 18 November, promising that SAG would insist upon achieving the principle of 100 percent pay for reruns in the contract negotiations to be held in 1974. "If the networks feel that it is necessary to pollute the airwaves with re-run after re-run, at least let us have an equal share of the pie," summarizes his cry, which drew standing ovations from the assembled multitude.[48]

He was as good as his word. Although the contract ratified in July did not establish the entire 100 percent return immediately, it did achieve the principle of complete residuals. In subsequent years compensation would rise to the 100 percent level. Further, after 1974 actors would receive residuals based on their actual salary, rather than on scale. By removing the causes for the discontent of 1971, the 1974 contract helped to establish the legitimacy and popularity of the new regime.[49]

If Weaver was militant toward management, however, he was conciliatory in dealing with factions within the guild. Many insurgent movements, attaining power, deal vindictively with their defeated opponents. But Weaver proved that his proclaimed dislike of partisanship was genuine by adopting a tolerant and open-minded attitude toward everyone, including dedicated conservatives. Unlike his predecessors as president, who while presiding at board meetings would sometimes cut off a speaker in order to hurry along the discussion, Weaver allowed everyone to have their full say. He was, moreover, conspicuously respectful of and polite to everyone. Despite the ideological division that continued in the guild, civility returned to the boardroom, and personal attacks subsided.[50]

Although Weaver's benign toleration was good for the emotional atmosphere, it was bad for efficiency. With more people talking longer, the length of board meetings naturally grew. Under Heston, Gavin, and Easton (who as first vice-president presided during Gavin's frequent absences), meetings had begun at eight in the evening and normally were over by eleven. But the democratic give-and-take of the Weaver regime often lasted far past midnight. When Weaver left the presidency, the tradition he inaugurated continued, and seemingly endless board meetings became the norm. A number of capable actors resigned from guild government because they could not bear to sit through the filibustering of the progressive era.[51]

Weaver's practice of allowing everyone a say extended to his approach to filling positions on committees. He appointed not only board members of all factions to the important committees but also rank-and-file members who expressed an interest in serving the guild. "Anybody who bellyached got put on a committee," is the way he later explained his strategy. SAG's committee system thus expanded from a relatively streamlined institution under the control of the president to a large, noisy, and willful tangle of individuals pursuing their personal agendas.[52]

In retrospect, two changes in Screen Actors Guild Government seem to symbolize the beginning of the new era ushered in by Weaver. The first in publicity (although second in chronology) was quite consciously a repudiation of the conservative past. In 1974, the board repealed the bylaw requiring all candidates in guild elections to swear that they were not members of the Communist party. Soon afterward, several previously blacklisted actors ran for and were elected to the board. (These were, of course, not necessarily former Communists. Many progressives had simply objected to such an oath, finding it personally insulting, and had consequently avoided board service as a matter of principle.)[53]

The second change seemed less important at the time, but probably had more of an effect on the tone of SAG government. In January 1973 John Dales had resigned as national executive secretary and been replaced by his longtime assistant, Chester Migden. Although this changing of the guard had been planned for a long time and had nothing to do with the Weaver victory later in the year, the personalities of the two executive secretaries nevertheless conveniently embodied the eras they presided over. Dales was quiet, modest, and courtly, which was appropriate for the restrained style of the conservative decades. Migden, in contrast, was aggressive, outspoken, and brash, which fit in with the more agitated style of progressive government.[54]

In summary, although Weaver himself had a calming influence on guild government, he presided over and helped to set in motion changes which sowed the seeds of later tumults.

The altered style and policies of SAG government after the revolution of 1973 cannot, however, mask what was not changed. The original impetus for rebellion in the early 1970s, the desire to make SAG a real "union" that controlled the labor market for actors and thus improved employment opportunities for those on the inside, received no encouragement from the newly victorious insurgents (although with time and national inflation the guild's initiation and transfer fees were raised). None of Charlie Briggs's early proposals to make entrance into the guild more difficult were ever passed into policy, and although Briggs himself served on the board for a short time, he never achieved personal power. The movement he founded turned in a direction he did not intend and left him behind.

Woman on the Run

Originally, SAG presidential terms had been for a single year. In 1972, however, this had been extended to two years, beginning in 1973. Whereas all previous presidents had had to stand for reelection every twelve months, Dennis Weaver's term did not expire until 1975. As the year began, everyone anticipated a quiet campaign, because Weaver had won such wide approval that he was expected to draw no serious opposition in the fall. But Weaver, believing that he had done his bit, decided not to succeed himself.

Weaver had been so consistently nonpartisan, and his policies so popular, that the ideological divisions on the board had become muted. Contrary to what might be expected, therefore, no organized conservative push to reclaim the presidency materialized. Nevertheless, the tradition of independent candidacy begun in 1971 and continued over the next two elections had now become institutionalized; the Nominating Committee's recommendations had lost their mystique. The choice of the committee, progressive Robert Hogan, drew four opponents running by petition. Conservatives Whit Bissell and Claude Akins ran as individuals, not as members of an ideological slate. First vice-president Kathleen Nolan and Robert Kerr also tossed their hats on the stage.[55]

With none of the candidates choosing to make ideological appeals or even spend much time discussing issues, the campaign turned on personal appeal and the organizational ability of each. And here Kathleen Nolan emerged as a phenomenon. For energy, imagination, and political savvy, none of her male opponents could touch her. At "election headquarters" at her home in Brentwood she had friends phoning actors every day for months, soliciting votes and money.[56]

As first vice-president, she had traveled to the guild's smaller branches, and realized that they were no longer so small. "I felt very strongly the winds of change . . . that it was not a Hollywood industry anymore," she recalled later. "There were already in 1975 probably twenty-five states that had Motion Picture Development Commissions. Later I learned that as of 1975 no president had gone to the membership meeting in Detroit for seventeen years." Seeing, like any entrepreneur, a chance to appeal to a new market, she was the only candidate to target special appeals to the dozen non-Hollywood branches. At a cost of $10,000, she made up and mailed out two types of campaign brochures, a general version to every SAG member, and specific versions to the members in each branch, discussing their problems in familiar detail. Moreover, her general brochure contained, not just the usual list of endorsements from prominent actors, but expressions of support from state and national political figures—Governor Jerry Brown, Mayor Tom Bradley, Senator John Tunney, member of the House Alphonzo Bell (who represented western suburban Los Angeles, where many actors lived), and four other members of the United States Congress.[57]

When the votes were counted on 3 November, Nolan was perhaps the only person in the guild who was not surprised to learn that she had won 54 percent of the total. The distribution of support fully justifies her strategy. Whereas once the vote from the hinterlands would have been infinitesimal, in this election members from all the branches combined cast close to half of all the 10,862 ballots. And whereas Nolan was the largest vote-getter of the five candidates in Hollywood, she still fell far short of a majority at 44 percent. Meanwhile, she was winning two out of every three ballots cast in the branches. Hogan came in second overall with 22 percent.[58]

Shortly thereafter, the new president received a telegram from the chief executive of British Equity, who informed her that in his opinion "the best man won."[59]

If Nolan was an energetic campaigner, she was a positive dynamo as president. Full of ideas, radiating determination and ignoring opposition, she embarked on a personal crusade to reshape the Screen Actors Guild into an activist, politically liberal labor union.

In the few years preceding 1975, the Hollywood branch of the guild had created institutions, such as the Minorities Committee and the Women's Conference Committee, that sought to connect it with larger social changes in American society. Upon taking office Nolan decided that these committees should be national, and not just a creature of the Los Angeles membership. At the general membership meeting immediately after her election, she worked out a plan for representation on these committees, with nine delegates from Los Angeles, six from New York, and three from the other branches. In the ensuing years she attempted to divide the chairs and cochairs of these committees equably among the branches so as to give actors in other sections of the country a larger sense of participation. Additionally, under her prodding the board of directors created additional national committees, such as Telecommunications (to analyze the present and try to anticipate the future of the film and television industries) and Legislation (to track and monitor proposed laws in Congress and the states). The guild was soon abuzz with meetings.[60]

Believing that it was the duty of artists to be activists, and that as the president of a labor union she had the responsibility to try to influence public policy, Nolan began making regular forays to Washington to give her views on all manner of issues relating to her profession and the industry. Other SAG presidents had lobbied occasionally, but Nolan broke all records for cross-country travel. In one year she made forty-seven trips to the East Coast. And lobbying was just the start of her journeys. In one short span in the spring of 1977 she went to Ojai, California, to attend a conference on the Project on Human Sexuality (which was devoted to finding a way to better portray personal relationships on television); to Miami to attend a rally for the Equal Rights Amendment; back to Washington for a conference on the effect television has on children; and then to Tampa to address the Florida Film and Television Association. In a similar vein, her personal persistence prior to both parties' presidential nominating conventions in 1976 had resulted in each of them including an "Arts Plank" in their platforms.[61]

On a more personal level, also, Nolan made an indelible stamp on the guild. She was acutely aware that, as a woman, she was a pioneer in a man's world, and she constantly tried to recruit actresses to serve on committees and run for the board. At her personal invitation numbers of women became involved in SAG for the first time. Some of these then recruited their friends into participation, and soon there was an informal "Women's Bloc" on the board. Norma Connolly, Janet MacLachlan, and Sumi Haru, in particular, formed a friendly coalition to push for greater sensitivity to the problems of women, especially minority women. Later, Nolan made the acquaintance of Walter Annenberg, who was overseeing an investigation into the representation of women, minorities, and the aged in television. When the research was completed, Nolan set up a press conference hosted by herself and the other three actresses, at which Annenberg and his associates discussed their findings. From this cooperative venture Annenberg got a good deal of publicity, and the guild got access to his data.[62]

At first, SAG's board of directors was inclined to endorse, or at least to acquiesce in, this whirlwind of activity. But not very far into her first term, Nolan's style began to cause widespread annoyance.

There was, first, her habit of forgetting to ask permission, or even to inform anyone else in the guild, before flying off on some project. Nolan would arrive home and announce that she had testified before some committee of Congress, or been a speaker at a conference, or attended a convention, and her fellow officers and board members would have to find out what she had said (in their name) as best they could. Nor did this forgetfulness happen only with activities outside the guild. One day the officers arrived for a meeting at SAG headquarters on Hollywood Boulevard to discover that the president's office had been redecorated, at a charge of $2,300 to the guild. No doubt they would have approved this if Nolan had asked them, but she had simply done it on her own authority. Some of them began to complain that this was the sort of imperious presidential behavior that had offended them in John Gavin, and to wonder if one revolution had been enough. By the start of her second year in office, this group formed a large anti-Nolan bloc on the board that fought a series of guerilla actions with her over such internal issues as the president's power to appoint members to the various committees.[63]

Then there was her behavior in the chair. One of the duties of the president is to preside at board meetings. Supposedly, the chief executive not only has no vote but does not participate in the discussion; it is his or her responsibility to be a neutral arbiter. But Nolan seemed unable or unwilling to follow these informal rules. She would jump into the discussion, arguing passionately for one side, and rambling on for so long that others were ready to explode in frustration. When her will was thwarted on some issue, she occasionally burst into tears. Now and then, she used profanity from the chair, which offended some of the members. Her behavior at meetings, then, did nothing to soften the disapproval caused by her willfulness outside the boardroom.[64]

Throughout the rising curve of these complaints, there was an undertone which everyone was uncomfortable in talking about publicly, but which was rarely absent. Part of it was that Nolan at times seemed more interested in pursuing the issue of women's rights than in any of the other problems facing the guild. But even more of it was the feeling many of the men had that her behavior was somehow unfeminine. Her outspoken aggressiveness and ferocious determination were simply not ladylike, and were therefore improper. To feel this way embarrassed some of the men, political liberals that they were, but there it was. There consequently arose in the boardroom a conflict between the male and female activists, with the men automatically opposing Nolan and the women automatically defending her, that twisted arguments about her presidency away from the substance of her policies.[65]

As the 1977 elections approached, the opposition coalesced around the issue of misappropriation of funds. Not only was Nolan far more active in the outside world than her predecessors, but she was the first SAG president who was not either a star or a very well-known character actor and therefore personally wealthy. When previous presidents had occasionally made trips on behalf of the guild, they had sometimes financed these themselves, looking upon the expense as one more contribution to their union. Whereas Nolan was spending much more on travel, hotels, dining, and the like, however, she was at the same time less able to pay for them herself. The bills she presented to the guild's accounting department for reimbursement were, consequently, entirely unprecedented. When combined with her refusal to ask permission before embarking on many of her trips, and the other resentments simmering in the background, this began to make some officers and board members suspicious that she had actually been diverting guild money for her personal use.[66]

The issue might have faded had Nolan simply succeeded herself without opposition. But by 1977 the guild had come a long way from being an organization in which the president dominated internal events. In September, the Nominating Committee reported the shocking news that it was repudiating its own sitting president, choosing instead Bert Freed, the point man for the insurgency of 1971, as its official candidate for the top job in the guild.[67]

It would of course have been entirely out of character for Nolan to accept the committee's judgment and retire in disgrace. She ran for reelection by petition. Although three other male actors also ran as independents, the real contest, in terms of publicity and endorsements, was between Nolan and Freed.

In this battle between two progressives, ideology was again absent from the campaign. Freed chose instead to attack Nolan as an opportunist seeking to use the guild to further her own career, and as a person not above a little pilfering of the till. For her part, Nolan helped to confuse the situation by labeling Freed's tactics as "McCarthyism," which was, in the context of actors' politics, a sort of reverse smear. With prominent members of the guild taking sides without regard to political principles or former personal loyalty, the campaign quickly degenerated into an exchange of insults and slanders.[68]

As the candidate with the track record, Nolan was far more vulnerable to this sort of campaigning than was Freed. Some of the innuendos circulating around Hollywood about her handling of guild finances not only wounded her personally, but stained her public image. Although a guild committee, after a thorough review of all the records, completely exonerated her of financial malfeasance, the charges haunted her for years afterward. When President Carter later nominated her for the board of the Corporation for Public Broadcasting, for example, one of the assignments of the FBI agents investigating her background was to discover if she really was a thief.[69]

But a track record can be an advantage also, and Nolan knew how to use hers. Her campaign pamphlets emphasized her impressive range of activities in politics and the labor movement, and again carried endorsements from nationally known figures. One of these, for instance, simply reprinted in journal notation form her activities during one month, January 1976:

> Los Angeles—8th—Breakfast with industry leaders and Senator Tunney re Tax Incentive/flight to San Francisco—inauguration of mayor . . . 9th—meeting re film-making in San Francisco . . . 10th—San Francisco AFL-CIO staff meeting, etc.[70]

Once again, her campaign expertise and strength in the outlying branches pulled Nolan through. Her margin of victory was slightly smaller than in 1975, however. Allen Garfield, a candidate who did not even bother to campaign, received surprisingly strong support, perhaps as a protest against the ugly tone of the contest between Nolan and Freed.[71]

The Impatient Years

Her name cleared, her grip on power strengthened, and her travel allowance increased, Kathleen Nolan in her second term was as she

had been in her first, only more so. Her second two years were a whirlwind of testimony, speeches, and news conferences, which earned her
frequent appearances on the nightly news.

Yet through the two years, Nolan was drifting to the Left in her personal philosophy. In her first term she had been concerned with gaining an entry into conventional politics and big labor. Having attained
those, she discovered that they were not the allies she had hoped for
in the struggle to bring about social change. Her fundamental concern
was the status and well-being of the artist, and as she learned more
about how things work in America she came to believe that artists
would always be vulnerable under the present system of power and
property. She therefore began to advocate fundamental reorderings
in the economy, and especially in the telecommunications industry.
Most prominently, she wanted to redistribute control over what Americans saw on television, to overthrow the "tyranny of the minority—
the networks," in determining what was broadcast. An economic restructuring, she believed, would both improve and widen the content
of television shows and enable artists to move into their rightful place
in society—radical views from a labor leader.[72]

To move the union in such a direction would, of course, require time
and patience. But one step on the road to a more politically conscious
Screen Actors Guild would be a more politically conscious communications organ. The editorship of the guild's house publication, *Screen
Actor,* had customarily been given to a Hollywood publicist. When the
job opened up in February 1979, however, Nolan saw an opportunity
to give it a more left-wing, union-activist flavor. Two years earlier, in
Washington as part of the AFL lobbying effort to defeat the Labor Law
Reform Act, Nolan had met and been impressed by Kim Fellner, a
progressive young assistant editor of the house paper of the Service
Employees Union. Now, in Washington once again at a meeting of the
Social Security and Unemployment Committee of the AFL, Nolan
contacted Fellner and persuaded her to apply for the vacant SAG
editorship.[73]

Back in Hollywood with Fellner, Nolan knew that the appointment
was by no means assured, for there were actors on the Executive Committee (consisting of all the guild's officers) who would vote against
anyone she supported. To counter the anti-Nolan prejudice, however,
she remained quietly in the background during Fellner's interview
with the committee, while one of her allies, first vice-president Victor

Jory, took the lead in introducing the applicant and speaking on her behalf. This bit of legerdemain, plus Fellner's own award-winning record, won her the job. As we shall see in the next chapter, it was an appointment that had all the impact Nolan hoped for.[74]

As her second term drew to a close, Nolan decided to refocus her attention on her acting career, and declined to run again. Not wanting her feminine presidency to be a fluke, however, and trying to ensure that a strong activist would succeed her, she tried to persuade a number of prominent actresses to run. She found none willing to put up with what she had endured. She then turned her attention to men she thought qualified. Burt Lancaster was willing to run, but learned that he was ineligible by reason of his ownership of a production company. As a result, Nolan exercised no influence over the presidential contest of 1979.[75]

But several of her strongest backers in guild government approached William Schallert, an articulate progressive who had served on the board from 1974 to 1977 and had been prominent in defending Nolan from Freed's charges, and persuaded him to make the race. Partly because he had the Nominating Committee's endorsement, and partly because his face and name were familiar to most actors (for, among other accomplishments, important roles in the TV series "The Many Loves of Dobie Gillis," "The Patty Duke Show," and "Nancy Drew"), he easily defeated challenger Ron Soble, who also had much experience in guild government but who was not as prominent a performer.[76]

That Uncertain Feeling

For most of the twentieth century, sociologists and historians have been studying democracy in labor unions. They have come up with a number of generalizations about when insurgencies are likely to arise in union politics, and when they are likely to be successful. Because a progressive movement arose and seized power in the Screen Actors Guild in the 1970s, it is logical to wonder if the regularities that the scholars have noticed apply to it, or whether it is such a peculiar union that it cannot be compared to others.

The guild differs from typical labor unions in three important ways. First, it is not a hiring hall; that is, it does not control the supply of labor to management. Second, a significant number of its members are celebrities, which means that they are rich, and have easy access to publicity. Third, SAG activists receive no tangible rewards for winning office. Do these differences make a difference?

The primary question is, Under what conditions do insurgencies occur? Summarizing various studies, and discarding those rules that are too vaguely stated to permit testing, there seem to be five generalizations that might constitute a plausible theory of union insurgency. Organized opposition is more likely to arise against the ruling group of a union if (*a*) the work milieu encourages movement and conversation among the workers, out of the observation of management;[77] (*b*) there is a sudden reduction in wages, for whatever reason;[78] (*c*) there is a major strike, especially if it ends badly for the union;[79] (*d*) new technical devices, changes in legislation, or jurisdictional rivalry threaten the workers' jobs;[80] and (*e*) a leader steps down, especially if there is more than one heir apparent to the leadership.[81]

The first of these generalizations plainly applies to actors. Their extremely fluid work situation and large amount of spare time are ideal for fostering fellowship and the circulation of ideas away from the notice of management. Furthermore, the presence of so many celebrities in the guild, with such superb access to the media (not to mention skill at using them), means that any dissidents who want to can easily bring their complaints, and their appeals for support, to the attention of the entire membership. Put broadly, if all union insurgents could run Dennis Weaver against the incumbent president, American unions would be awash in democracy.

The problem with this explanation, however, is that it always applies. The actors' milieu was no more conducive to insurrection in 1971 than it was in any of the preceding years. By this rule, the history of the guild should have been one long example of hard-fought election campaigns. It may be that the terror of the blacklist suppressed dissent within SAG in earlier years, but this is only conjecture. We must look elsewhere for a good indication of why the progressive challenge arose at the moment that it did.

The next three of these generalizations directly address the question of timing. Together, they suggest that challenges to traditional leadership tend to occur when the jobs of the workers are in danger, and they perceive that the leadership has not defended them competently. In a general sense, these apply to the SAG of 1971. Consider the following table of the gross earnings of all of the guild's members

for all product for which contributions were made by management
to the pension and welfare plan, in millions of dollars (figures are
rounded):[82]

	1965	'66	'67	'68	'69	'70	'71	'72	'73	'74	'75
Earnings	98	105	109	113	121	114	114	124	137	153	165
% change		+7	+4	+4	+7	−6	0	+8	+11	+11	+8

The country entered a recession in 1970, and actors' earnings contracted, not rebounding until two years later. The insurgency thus began precisely when performers as a group were feeling an economic
pinch. Whatever the specific grievances of the dissidents recounted in
the earlier part of this chapter, this overall earnings decline must be
considered an essential part of the explanatory background for the
attempt to make a revolution in 1971.

Moreover, the final generalization applies, for Charlton Heston's de-
parture from the presidency clearly triggered Bert Freed's challenge.
Thus, the timing of the insurgency, coming in the middle of an economic crisis and occurring as a long-term leader was retiring, fits in
smoothly with social-science notions about the origins of rebellion in
the labor movement. Although by the time the movement triumphed
in 1973 the gross earnings of actors had improved dramatically, the
progressive crusade had by that time acquired its own momentum.
From this perspective, the Screen Actors Guild does not appear to be
such an exceptional union after all.

The second question commonly asked by scholars is: Under what
conditions are insurgencies, once launched, likely to be successful? We
can say that there are two kinds of tentative answer to this question.
The first takes union structure into account and suggests that insurgencies succeed when the union (a) is geographically decentralized,
that is, when it consists of a number of locals of roughly equal size and
power;[83] (b) has many levels of full-time officers (to provide potential
bureaucratic rivals to the president);[84] (c) is large;[85] (d) has power divided more or less within the union between two executive officers;[86]
(e) has frequent elections;[87] and (f) has a leadership unable to dominate the means of communication to the membership.[88]

The first four of these generalizations are of no help in understanding the SAG insurgency. The guild was small and geographically centralized, and had few officers but only one president. The second to
the last, however, is important, and the last is crucial.

If the guild had had elections spaced several years apart, the insurgency might easily have evaporated between contests. Instead, the quickly spaced elections allowed the people in the movement to learn from their mistakes and adjust their strategy, while maintaining their fervor.

Most important, although the conservative establishment controlled the official guild publications, the opposition could circumvent those at any time through the trade press. Indeed, the *Hollywood Reporter* and *Daily Variety* took obvious delight in magnifying and sensationalizing all conflicts within the guild. Any actor with an accusation or a gripe could count on reaching his or her colleagues by contacting these papers, and independent candidates were given at least as much space as the Nominating Committee's picks in their election coverage. This access to publicity neutralized most of the advantage of incumbency, and ensured that dissidents would be able to mobilize their potential support. Without it, SAG's politics would have been much more typical of labor politics elsewhere.

The second kind of answer to the question of what conditions make for successful insurgencies looks to the strategies of the insurgents themselves. They are more likely to prevail if (*a*) they nominate a challenger who enjoys a status approximately equal to that of the establishment candidate;[89] (*b*) in their operation as an organization they are themselves relatively democratic;[90] and (*c*) they stress political ideology in their campaign statements, as opposed to merely trying to appeal to the momentary complaints or personal problems of the members.[91]

Here lies the real key to understanding the success of SAG's progressives. After something of a false start in 1971, they nominated a candidate in 1973 who enjoyed at least as high a status within the acting community as did the conservative incumbent. In their own caucuses they operated according to majority rule, and allowed, indeed encouraged, free speech. Although including a variety of appeals in their campaign material, they did not neglect to emphasize principled notions of rank-and-file participation and worker solidarity.

I must conclude that it was good leadership that turned the guild progressives from a noisy faction into a governing group. The revolution was not inevitable; it was made by shrewdness, boldness, and a genuine concern for the common good.

Leadership, however, is not inherited; it must be created anew by each generation. Nor is it the monopoly of one side. Just because the progressives had the better leaders in the 1970s does not mean that they enjoyed the same advantage in the 1980s. Revolutions beget counterrevolutions, and competent leaders can arise anywhere. As it entered a new decade, the Screen Actors Guild was about to illustrate these maxims in dramatic fashion.

I'm not *living* with you. We occupy the same cage, that's all.

Elizabeth Taylor to Paul Newman, *Cat on a Hot Tin Roof,* screenplay
by Richard Brooks and James Poe, based on the play by Tennessee
Williams

Chapter Six

POLARIZATION

Hollywood was changing again. In the late 1970s, cable television began to challenge the dominance of the three broadcast networks over
American entertainment. As television had grown with breathtaking
speed in the forties, undermining the movie studios, so cable started
to spurt upward in popularity, draining revenue from the three networks. At the same time the arrival of the video recorder, which ena-
bled ordinary citizens to watch relatively new films in their own homes,
was threatening to render the movie theater obsolete. By 1980 the entertainment industry was on the brink of crisis. The Screen Actors
Guild faced the prospect of protecting its own membership against
the storms that obviously lay ahead.[1]

Meanwhile, the guild was still struggling with old problems. As producers continued to look outside the Los Angeles area for cheaper or
more attractive locations, jobs radiated away from Hollywood. By the
1980s less than half of the guild's membership resided in its founding
branch. Perhaps because they were now shot outside its jurisdiction, or
perhaps because they merely redistributed the available work, these
new films had no effect on SAG's official unemployment rate, which
held steady at 85 percent. The growing importance of the junior
branches also strained the guild's centralized governmental structure,
as it became more difficult to coordinate decision making across a continent. The New York branch especially, which had always been restive
under the domination of California, became increasingly assertive as
its size approached that of its West Coast sister.[2]

Nor were things going well between the Guild and AFTRA. Originally, in the early 1950s, the two unions had divided jurisdiction over television acting so that SAG had authority over programs made on film, and AFTRA over programs shot live. With the decline of live programming and the introduction of videotape in the succeeding years, however, this arrangement required modification. Officially, by the 1970s SAG still had jurisdiction over film and AFTRA over tape. But producers often ignored these distinctions. Those who shot in the old-time motion-picture studios signed with the guild, while those who made their films in a studio associated with a television station went with AFTRA. It was not uncommon for a television series ("It's A Living," for example) to switch studios for financial reasons, thus abruptly changing unions. Since the contracts for each were quite different, this caused confusion and resentment among the cast. Actors had always chafed under the necessity of holding two union cards (or three, counting Equity) for doing the same work, but by 1980 the absurdity of the situation was becoming intolerable.[3]

If the Screen Actors Guild was troubled, the Screen Extras Guild was facing serious adversity. The actors' union's power derived from the fact that it controlled an irreplaceable resource, for amateur performers could not act in films and look anything but amateurish. But extras, as mere living props, could always be replaced. The extras' union therefore had almost no market power. After the two unions had split in the 1940s, SAG had customarily lent its personnel and clout to SEG during each contract negotiation, and as long as the industry was dominated by a few large studios, this system worked smoothly. As a result, union extras were by 1980 very well paid, earning almost ninety dollars a day for easy, unskilled labor. But with the decline of the studio system and the multiplication of independent producers, SAG's inability to police them all left SEG vulnerable to the forces of competition. The result was foreseeable. In the 1970s, casting agencies for non-union extras sprang up, supplying bodies to independent producers for about a third of the cost of SEG extras. As it lost an ever-larger proportion of the market, SEG's very existence became threatened. Leaders in both unions began to consider reuniting what had been rent asunder a generation before.[4]

With the approach of negotiations with motion-picture and television producers in 1980, therefore, the Screen Actors Guild faced a lineup of old and new challenges. In previous times of trial it had almost always met its problems with fairly strong internal cohesion. It was about to enter an era, however, in which its unity would collapse. This would be the worst problem of all.

Nightmare

In preparing for the 1980 negotiations the guild was attempting to anticipate the changes that were about to descend on the industry. When the producers informed the actors that they wanted to discuss the topic of made-for-cable movies, guild negotiators were entirely agreeable, although there were as yet no significant revenues to discuss. Many of SAG's leaders, including national executive secretary Chester Migden, had lived through the frustration of the 1950s, in which producers had refused to grant residuals to actors for movies shown on television, and the disappointment of the 1960 settlement, in which the guild had been forced to compromise on revenues from films made between 1948 and 1960. Now, with cable poised for an economic takeoff, they were determined to win a contract ensuring that actors would share in income from the new medium from the very beginning. Residuals from films made to be shown in theaters or on network television were already covered by existing contracts; the crucial demand in this negotiation would be for revenues from those films made originally to be shown on cable.[5]

There were signs of trouble from the outset. SAG was the first of the Hollywood "creative unions" (the others being the writers' and directors' unions) to attempt to negotiate an accord on cable residuals. Since there was no industry performance record, nobody knew if the guild's demand for 12 percent of the "distributor's gross" (Hollywood jargon for what would normally be called gross, as opposed to "producer's gross," which is distributor's gross minus distribution costs), after the producer had recouped the cost of the cast, was too high, or too low, or perhaps wrongly stated. In addition, the guild had begun in 1974 to negotiate prime-time television contracts jointly with AFTRA. As the two unions attempted to coordinate their plans in early 1980, the actors' leaders discovered that the TV union had already negotiated a 2 percent cable residual with the networks. The AFTRA board had not ratified this agreement, but its status as a precedent promised to undercut the guild's position. As the talks got under way in the late spring of 1980, the SAG negotiators were therefore unsure of their own position and not on the best of terms with their supposed allies.[6]

Adding to the difficulty of the situation was the fact that the producers were disposed to be unusually uncooperative. They had no more idea than the unions about the future shape of the cable industry, and so were reluctant to commit themselves to a payment formula that might prove to be overly generous. In addition, the financial structure of the studios had evolved to a point at which they lost money at first on prime-time television shows, only showing a profit as the programs went into syndication. This meant that a work stoppage in prime-time would actually be financially to their benefit in the short run. Finally, the producers had been divided and feuding during the contract negotiations of 1977, which had allowed the unions to win very favorable contracts. Firmly united this time around, they were determined to right the balance. They thus had no incentive to be conciliatory, and several reasons to dare a strike.[7]

At first the discussions went smoothly, with the two sides agreeing on many important points. On the subject of residuals for cable, however, there was little progress for several weeks. The two unions asked for and received a strike vote from their members, and broke off negotiations on several occasions, only to postpone a deadline and come back to the table each time. In the wee hours of 21 July, however, while the Negotiating Committee was caucusing in a room separate from the producers' representatives, executive secretary Chet Migden pointed out to them that they had technically been without a contract for some hours and that it would soon be time to report for work in New York. Strongly urging a tough stance on the weary negotiators, he persuaded them not to go back to the table. The strike was on. Many of the actors on the committee felt that they had been intimidated into a walkout, but they temporarily kept their complaints to themselves.[8]

Outside the negotiating room the strike was a great success. Strike captain Kent McCord organized teams of actors to come into headquarters on Hollywood Boulevard to mail out literature to the members explaining and justifying their demands, answer the extra telephones that had been installed, and coordinate picketing. The picketing itself went beautifully: 1,500 marchers at Warner Brothers on 24 July, 3,500 at 20th Century-Fox on 5 August, 5,000 at Disney on 21 August, and so on. Teams consisting of both celebrities and board members were dispatched to press conferences and talk shows, the first to draw the cameras and the second to plead the unions' case, so that for the first time an actors' strike was treated by the media as a labor dispute instead of a freak show. One of the celebrity volunteers, Ed Asner, was invited to appear on the late-night public affairs program "Nightline," where his sober performance advanced both the unions' credibility and his own. Kim Fellner, SAG's public information director, was so articulate in explaining the actors' point of view to the media that she herself inadvertently became a minor celebrity. On 16 September over two dozen performers volunteered their time to "An Evening Of Stars" at the Hollywood Bowl, which raised more than $300,000 for SAG's strike fund. As workers' theater, it was a dream.[9]

But inside the negotiating room it was a nightmare. Almost as soon as the two sides resumed talking on 21 August, the actors' consensus on what they wanted began to dissolve. Before the strike, they had dropped their percentage demand for residuals from 12 to 6 percent. Under this plan the producers would still have been allowed to recoup the cost of the cast before beginning to calculate their gross and the residuals they owed the actors. President William Schallert, calculating the revenue to performers under various assumptions on the blackboard, concluded that for the typical program this would mean that a producer would be allowed to take in $1 million before having to begin to pay residuals. Thinking that this amount was far too high, he decided that his own union's major demand was fatally flawed. He convinced several of the actors that the Negotiating Committee should change its proposals. The balance of the negotiators, however, preferred to stick with the original plan. The committee, in essence, began to try to negotiate with itself before it sent Chet Migden out to try to negotiate with the producers.[10]

That was the beginning. As the days went by, the original demands became completely shredded as other proposals arrived from the producers and from within the committee itself. Each suggestion received the enthusiastic support of some actors, but none could command a majority of the committee. Worse, as tempers wore out under the continued frustration, the arguing degenerated into personal attacks and irrelevant emotional outbursts, so that it often seemed as if the actors had gathered together to insult one another instead of to negotiate a contract. "It was almost as though there was a predetermined decision *not* to negotiate, but to create total and abject failure," Migden characterized it five years later.

Moreover, the executive secretary himself was beginning to lose his grip, not only on the negotiations, but on his job. His predecessor, John Dales, had maneuvered his way among the touchy temperaments around him behind a persona of mildness and humility. But as soon as Migden had taken over the position in 1973, his dominating personality had begun to offend some of the activist actors with whom he constantly dealt. As long as things had gone relatively well for the guild, Migden's unquestioned competence had protected him from resentment. But with the negotiations collapsing around them, many of the actors remembered the way he had pushed them into the strike, and turned on him.

Not all of the opposition was personal. Part of it derived from the different roles of an executive secretary. During normal times, he was a counselor to whom the actors could go for advice. In a negotiation, however, many felt that he became someone advocating his own agenda, which not only gave them an additional set of suggestions to consider, but deprived them of their main advisor. "I wanted to go to him and say, 'Tell us what you think of Chet's proposals, Chet,' " is the way Yale Summers expresses it.

But whether personal or principled, the opposition poisoned the atmosphere between the committee and its chief negotiator. "It's very easy to be emotionally swayed by a group of actors sitting around at three or four o'clock in the morning, saying 'Chet's selling us out,' " remembers Janet MacLachlan. The actors actually held caucuses away from the negotiating room to try to decide whether they trusted Migden. Although nothing concrete happened as a result of these meetings, they reinforced the sense of hopelessness and dread that began to permeate the committee room as the summer waned.

A strong president might have instilled some coherence into these proceedings, or at least suppressed the squabbling. But William Schallert could not seem to bring himself to impose his ego on the group. A gentle, intelligent, avuncular man, he had been elected to the board in 1974 and soon discovered that he had a penchant for detail work on the contract. Before the 1977 negotiations, as chair of the Wages and Working Conditions Committee, he had made a name for himself as a whiz with numbers and concepts. Narrowly defeated for first vice-president that year, he had helped to streamline policy making even while out of office, convincing the guild's Government Review Committee to make a recommendation to the board, subsequently en-

Janet MacLachlan

dorsed, that *Robert's Rules of Order* be adopted as the official manual of procedure for all meetings. Inspiring affection by his personality and respect by his professional success, he had been easily elected to the presidency in 1979. In the first year of his incumbency he had been responsible for a variety of progressive advances, including overseeing the founding of a committee to consider the problems of disabled performers, establishing a "branch liaison office" which members in the branches could contact when they were dissatisfied with the service they had received from the staff, and participating in the creation of an industrywide drug and alcohol abuse program. Ever the concerned liberal, he had been a rational and civil presence in all the guild's activities.

But here and now was a problem with the irrational and the uncivil. The actors on the committee felt that Schallert hated personal conflict and could not deal with it. Faced with emotional ugliness, he withdrew, leaving a leadership vacuum that was filled with rancor. "I was a classic instance of the Peter Principle," he remarks with considerable self-insight. "I was a damn good mechanic. With the contract, and research,

I was one of the most valuable tools the guild had. But instead, they made me shop foreman." And so the actors, with one leader discredited and the other miscast, spiraled down into futility.

Meanwhile, although the studios responsible for making motion-picture and prime-time television programs were quiet, the networks (proceeding under the AFTRA contract) were happily cranking out daytime soap operas and game shows. The irony of this situation was forcibly brought home to the negotiators every evening. Two members of the committee, Norma Connolly and Frank Maxwell, were employed in the cast of the soap "General Hospital," and as such had to report for work every day, returning to the negotiating room at night. This constant reminder of the imperfection of their strike reinforced the actors' feeling that something was amiss with their contracts, and that something had to be done so that the situation would not recur.

As the hopeless negotiations continued, the stress of spending endless unpleasant hours accomplishing nothing began to tell on the performers. Several developed insomnia. One actress broke out in hives from the neck down. Another astonished herself by bursting into rages at inappropriate moments during the day. A usually healthy actor mysteriously developed an ulcer (which disappeared just as mysteriously the week the strike ended). After having fought with all their hearts for one particular proposal and seeing it defeated by a majority of the committee, two actors, each known for his macho screen presence, excused themselves from the negotiating room, walked to separate parts of the building, and wept bitter tears of humiliation and rage. By the third week of September the Guild and AFTRA negotiators as a group were so beaten down physically, emotionally, and intellectually that they were looking for any excuse to end the ordeal.

And so they accepted the proposal that was on the table 25 September. It was not a bad contract. Besides the usual increases in daily and weekly minimums, it contained advances in wages and working conditions for children and a variety of provisions for enhancing the comfort and convenience of actors shooting on location. More important, it established the principle that performers would receive a proportion of the revenue from films produced especially for cable. But it also permitted producers to receive revenue from those films for a "window" of ten days each year on each cable system before they had to begin paying residuals. Most actors viewed this free-play window as

Rhodes Reason

effectively guaranteeing that they would in practice receive no residuals at all. They therefore regarded the settlement, quite simply, as a defeat.[11]

The psychological damage caused by this botched strike was immense. As news of the free-play provisions in the tentative contract filtered out to the membership, it caused dismay and a growing anger. Many of the people on the Negotiating Committee, exhausted and disappointed, felt that they had somehow betrayed their trust. "I was so upset after the strike," reports Rhodes Reason, "that if the membership had formed a lynch mob and said 'We're going to hang all the negotiators,' I would have been very happy to give my life for that purpose." Some of those on the Negotiating Committee took immediate "temporary" leaves of absence from the board of directors, never to return. Others flew off on vacation, leaving to someone else the job of explaining the contract to the rank and file. Those who stayed blamed Schallert, or Migden, or each other for not making them stay and hold out for a more palatable agreement. From the end of the strike, things began to go very wrong for the Screen Actors Guild.

The Group

In the final weeks of the strike, a dozen or so actors who had worked the phone banks, walked the picket lines, and helped organize "An Evening Of Stars" began meeting together to discuss strategy, trade rumors, and shore up one another's morale. As word began to circulate about the tentative contract, they rented the Writers Guild Theater on Friday, 26 September, getting out the word to many friends to come, and asking Schallert and Migden to show up to answer their questions. These two declined on the ground that the contract had not yet been presented to the board of directors. Several members of the Negotiating Committee attended in an unofficial capacity, however, fielding increasingly hostile questions from the audience. Since this meeting only vented frustration without supplying much information, the same group rented the Hollywood Palladium for the following Friday, 3 October. They petitioned board members to attend.[12]

By the time the day arrived, the details of the contract had been pretty well circulated by word of mouth, and the meeting had been sponsored by the guild as a semiofficial event. In the morning, the performers had learned that the boards of SAG and AFTRA had voted to order the rank and file back to work, although the contract had not yet been ratified. Given the mounting resentment of the way the negotiators had conducted themselves, this struck the malcontents as further evidence of the leadership's disregard for their wishes. That night hundreds of furious actors faced Schallert, Migden, and several members of the Negotiating Committee on the stage. Questions about the settlement turned into speeches against it, and there were numerous implied charges of treachery and cowardice hurled at the guild's leadership. One member of the negotiating team, a stunt man, became so offended at the remarks from the audience that he offered to step outside and fight anyone who thought he had not bargained in good faith. No one took him up on this challenge, but neither did anyone back down from the accusations.[13]

As he drove home that night, veteran character actor Howard Caine began to think of the Los Angeles AFTRA local's monthly meeting, which would be held to vote on ratification of the contract the next Monday. A decade before, Caine had been a member of the Concerned Actors Committee which had wrought the progressive revolution in

Howard Caine

SAG. "It seemed to me that if we could cash in on all this anger by putting together something like the old CAC—a caucus, meeting monthly, passing the hat . . . and develop an effective war chest, (we could) get the dinosaurs off both boards. We could change the face of each of the two unions, and even, hopefully, bring about a merger." As a start, they could get some people elected to the board "who were not so willing to go back to work for less than what artists deserve."[14]

Spending the weekend making phone calls, Caine organized a guerrilla raid on the AFTRA meeting. Taking the leadership by surprise, dozens of insurgents packed the event and succeeded in getting a vote of 226 to 217 to reject the tentative contract. That Thursday, 9 October, twenty-two temporarily victorious rebels met at Bruce Weitz's home to discuss a larger strategy.[15]

There and in a series of larger meetings at various actors' homes over the next several weeks, an organization took shape. In addition to rank-and-file performers, the group's size was swelled by several members of the Screen Actors Guild board of directors, who felt that it was inappropriate for them to join officially, but who nevertheless pledged their support. Some of those at the meetings were, like Caine, militant progressives who thought the moderate progressives in power in the guild too cautious, and the conservatives ruling AFTRA an abomination. Some wanted to move toward the one big performers' union that would be able to overawe the entire industry with just the threat of a strike. Some were primarily interested in trying to defeat the contract. But all agreed on two points: first, all actors' contracts should run coterminously, so that if they struck, production everywhere would be paralyzed, and second, the three actors' unions must be merged. Because the last point was the most important and specific, they named their society the Caucus of Artists for Merger, or CAM.[16]

"The present system encourages divisiveness within the performing community," read the "Declaration of Interdependence" that CAM adopted at a meeting 15 November, "pitting for example prime time against day time, film against tape, radio against television, and actors, stuntpersons, singers, dancers, announcers and journalists against each other. . . . The rank and file memberships of AFTRA, SAG and Equity *for over thirty years* have expressed overwhelming desire to merge, only to be blocked by a majority of their Boards and staffs. . . . Be it resolved that we . . . take all the legal and political steps required by the electoral process to direct the Boards of Directors, Councilors and Executives in all of our unions to bring about the merger demanded by the rank and file."[17]

Meanwhile, a former president of the Screen Actors Guild had been elected president of the United States.

Because the national memberships of both unions had by this time ratified the new contract, the people in CAM turned their attention to the next item on their long-run agenda—capturing power in SAG and AFTRA. Infiltrating, organizing, and agitating, they were spectacularly successful in their first test, their entire slate sweeping to victory in the Los Angeles AFTRA local's balloting in February 1981. In the next few years they would transform AFTRA's national organization by winning contests in its locals across the country. After the triumph of February, however, the next immediate problem was the Screen Actors Guild national election, to be held in November. Although progressives were already more or less in the majority in the guild leadership, CAM's members wanted to elect officers who were committed to merger in particular. They also wanted a president who would be responsive to their advice and who had enough prestige among other actors to carry them along in the movement.[18]

The guild was a somewhat different political problem than was AF-TRA. Because power in the television union was structurally dispersed, candidates who had attained mostly local fame could be successful. SAG's centralized organization, however, meant that every member in the country was eligible to vote for the major officers. This gave a great advantage to candidates with national reputations, that is, to the stars. But the typical actor, upon becoming a force at the box office, naturally wished to retain as much of his or her earnings as possible, and was therefore forced by the tax code to get into production. By law and custom, however, performers with production interests were forbidden to serve in union government. For over thirty years, therefore, a major problem at the guild's election time had been finding candidates who possessed a name big enough to draw votes, but who had never cashed in on that name by becoming producers.

As they cast their eyes over the profession, CAM's leaders could see only one actor who was a big star, had never bothered with production, might be available to run for the presidency, and was on their side. As luck would have it, that actor was sitting at the table with them, having been involved in CAM from the beginning. His name was Edward Asner.

The Hero

From a variety of viewpoints, Ed Asner looked like the perfect candidate for the presidency of the Screen Actors Guild. He was a bona fide celebrity, having won national affection on television in a supporting role in the "Mary Tyler Moore Show" and presently starring as the title character in the top-ten-rated "Lou Grant." His skill at his craft was underscored by the five Emmy awards he had won for playing the crusty journalist. He was revered by his fellow performers as a generous, sincere, warm-spirited colleague, the sort of actor who would never upstage them and was always ready to listen to their problems. He had a long-standing interest in the labor movement and in guild government itself, having participated in CAC a decade earlier. After being perhaps the most visible spokesperson for the recent strike, he had then emerged as a vocal opponent of ratification of the contract. Unlike many performers, who prefer to hide behind characters on stage and dislike appearing before audiences as themselves, he was a dynamic and eloquent public speaker. He was committed to merger.[19]

In view of what happened over the next four years, however, it is important to understand that Asner did not want to run for the SAG presidency. He was acutely aware that he had no experience in guild government, never having served on the board of directors or even on a committee. As not only an extremely busy actor but also a political and social activist, he felt that he had no time left over to give to running a union. Moreover, he understood that his far-Left views on national and international politics would not sit well with many of the guild's conservative members.[20]

But the delegations of friends who began to approach him in the spring of 1981 were prepared to meet his objections. His role as president was to be the symbol and statesman of the merger movement, they told him. He did not have to worry about performing the tedious day-to-day chores of government; they would see to those. They would be available to offer experienced advice on any topic that might come up. As to his political activism—if former conservative presidents such as Ronald Reagan and Charlton Heston had not had to give up their political lives to become president of the guild, why should he? His friends appealed to his disgust with the recent contract, to his loyalty to the labor movement, to his devotion to his profession, and to his affection for them. Finally they prevailed. Reflecting on his decision to run, Asner told a reporter for the *Los Angeles Herald-Examiner* even before the election, "I must have been in a suicidal mood."[21]

With many board members already sympathetic, CAM was able to pack the Nominating Committee with its allies in July. Dumping the incumbent Schallert, this committee picked Asner and a slate of promerger actors as the guild's official recommendations. Stung, Schallert ran as an independent, the second sitting guild president (after Kathleen Nolan) to be forced to do so. He made a surprisingly strong showing, but he was running against a celluloid hero. When the mailed ballots were opened in November, many of them had no marks by Asner's name. Instead, the voters had written in "Lou Grant." They counted anyway. Asner received 54 percent of the total, Schallert 40 percent, and a little-known conservative candidate, Morgan Paull, 6 percent.[22]

As 1982 approached, therefore, the promerger forces had every reason to anticipate a quick and easy victory. They were in control of the guild and rapidly gaining the upper hand in AFTRA. They had a popular leader. They faced no systematic opposition. In August, even before their slate's victory, the guild's membership had voted by over 94 percent to approve phase 1 of the merger, the combination of the two unions' negotiating committees. Talks were under way to prepare for phase 2, the joining of SAG's governmental structure with AFTRA's, and phase 3, integration of their pension and welfare funds. Unless somebody made some terrible error, they would soon be able to throw away one of their union cards.[23]

Return from the Ashes

Since the revolution of 1973 there had been no organized conservative presence in the guild. John Gavin had left acting to pursue other careers. Robert Easton had withdrawn from participation in guild affairs (although he continued to be active in AFTRA, serving three times as vice-president of the Los Angeles local). Charlton Heston had been elected to the board in 1974, where, as he wrote in his journal, he had "become a surly curmudgeon, bitching about policies they go ahead and vote through anyway." He had resigned in May 1975, to be replaced by Yale Summers. A few holdovers from the pre-Weaver era, such as Ed Nelson, Don Dubbins, Anthony Caruso, and Marie Windsor, remained on the board, but they had no identity as a group, no cohesion in their voting, no issue to rally around, and no recognized leadership.[24]

Not yet. In August 1981 the members of the national union of air traffic controllers (PATCO) had walked off their jobs in a labor dispute. Strikes of federal employees are illegal. President Ronald Reagan promptly fired them all. When the Asner administration came into office in November, its members viewed the PATCO firing as an opportunity both to proclaim their solidarity with the labor movement and to symbolically repudiate Reagan, whom many regarded as a sweetheart unionist. On 9 November, at its first meeting after the election, the Hollywood board voted fifteen to nine, over much fervent dissent, to contribute $5,000 to a fund for the assistance of the families of the unemployed controllers. Asner, as president, had no vote in this decision, but there is no doubt that he approved of it.[25]

From the standpoint of the conservatives this was bad enough, but worse was soon to follow.

Back in the 1960s, when guild government had been quiet, its leaders had been concerned about the abysmal attendance at the annual membership meetings. To spur interest, they had hit upon a scheme

Anthony Caruso

to present an award to some long-lived superstar who had also achieved distinction in a humanitarian pursuit outside the entertainment industry. The idea had been to keep the name of the recipient a secret until the membership meeting, thereby using suspense to increase interest. Over the years this Lifetime Achievement Award "For Outstanding Achievement in Fostering The Finest Ideals of the Acting Profession" had been presented to such worthies as Bob Hope, Barbara Stanwyck, Gregory Peck, and Katherine Hepburn.[26]

A twelve-person national committee, chaired by Hollywood branch members Anthony Caruso and Marie Windsor, was designated to choose the award recipient for the membership meeting to be held in late November. Caruso and Windsor devised a three-stage method of voting. At first, everyone on the national committee could vote to nominate any three names from an extensive list supplied by Hollywood. On the second ballot, the twelve voted for their favorite among the nine performers receiving the most support in the nominating round. Finally, the top three vote-getters in the second round (or, in this case, four, because there had been a tie) were voted on, the plurality winner receiving the award.[27]

Marie Windsor

There was some difficulty in the tabulation of the vote, because on the second round Caruso and Windsor could not locate one of the New York members of the committee. This was of no serious significance, however, because on each round Ronald Reagan's name led all others by a wide margin. On the final tabulation he was the winner by a clear plurality, although not a majority. The two actors, privately pleased with this choice of a man they regarded as a friend and had themselves supported for the award, informed executive secretary Migden, who notified the White House.[28]

All of this was foolish in the extreme. Reagan deserved the award, of course, but it was disingenuous to try to give it to him while he was an incumbent; the proper thing to do would have been to wait until he had left office. To try to present him the guild's highest award in the first year of his first term was bound to be perceived as a partisan endorsement, and run into a buzz saw of opposition from progressives. Moreover, since the guild had just finished officially insulting Reagan with the PATCO contribution, to turn around and give him an award the same month would look severely addled at least.

But no matter. In Hollywood and Washington plans progressed secretly for Reagan's return to the site of his first political office.

At this point Kim Fellner entered the picture. Since being hired as public information director in early 1979, she had established a strong progressive identity for herself in guild administration. The summer after assuming the position she had edited a special issue of *Screen Actor* devoted to interviews on guild history with surviving actors who had been important in the union's early years. The tone of this issue had been extremely sympathetic to blacklisted radicals; it had been nearly silent on the dominant anti-Communist position. The conservatives were not amused. During the strike she had emerged as one of the key spokespeople who had persuaded the media to take the actors' arguments seriously. A militant unionist, she had reoriented guild publications to emphasize more a "labor" theme and less an "acting" theme than in previous years. More than being just a servant of the board, she had become a player in the game.[29]

It was part of the job of the public information director to order the Lifetime Achievement Award trophy, and so Fellner had to be informed of the name of the recipient. She was amazed at the inappropriateness of it. The winner was supposed to be so secret that not even the members of the board could be told, but here was being done in their name something that would violate their own preferences in a particularly humiliating way. After a good deal of indecision, Fellner resolved that in this case silence was not golden.[30]

"While I know that confidentiality is the rule . . . I feel that I would be remiss in my obligation to this union if I did not ask you to review the [Awards] Committee's selection," she wrote to all Executive Committee members on 12 November. "I am asking your intervention because I believe the Committee's selection of recipient will cause this organization great harm. I feel certain it will alienate us from the rest of the labor movement, subject us to embarrassment and ridicule, and cause severe and unhealthy disruptures within the membership. I believe the proposed award will erode the fine union image we have worked so hard to build and that the damage will be difficult to repair."[31]

She was right. The award subjected the guild to embarrassment and ridicule, and caused severe and unhealthy disruptures within the membership. This was not, however, because it was given to Ronald

Frank Maxwell

Reagan. At a stormy meeting on 24 November, the board voted first to rescind the authority of the Awards Committee to pick the recipient, then to avoid presenting a Lifetime Achievement Award that year, then to invent a new "Ralph Morgan Award" (named after the guild's co-founder and first president) and present it to Chester Migden, who had just announced his retirement. Once again Asner had no vote in the decision, but once again there is no doubt that he supported it. Naturally, the news leaked out immediately. The press had a field day with the fact that the only labor leader ever to be elected president of the United States had just been repudiated by his own union.[32]

Some of the progressives were not displeased at having thus discomforted the president. Frank Maxwell, then and now on the guild board and now also national president of AFTRA, speaks for others when he says, "What has he ever done for the union or anything else, or for humanity, for that matter?" Not only had Reagan collaborated in "all that horrendous blacklisting stuff," but he had "sold the Screen Actors Guild down the river" in the 1960 contract. "I mean, [he] gave away our lives. . . . I felt that the public should know that his own people didn't think very much of him as a union person."[33]

This attitude, added to the revocation of the award itself, made the conservatives apoplectic.

But this was still not all. The basic intentions of the Asner administration offended conservatives. They were not particularly hostile to merger. As a group, conservatives were willing to wait for a plan to be produced before making up their minds on that particular issue. But the additional baggage of progressivism was anathema to them.

In the first place, they regarded as pernicious the progressive enthusiasm for closer ties with the national labor movement. "Unions giving each other moral and financial support is a very archaic principle that has been widely repudiated," asserts Charlton Heston. He argues that big labor exploits guild leaders for their publicity-drawing power without ever giving much in return. "In the public eye, far and away the best known labor figures in the history of the union movement have been presidents of the Screen Actors Guild."[34]

The different philosophical positions on the labor movement are distilled in a battle over nomenclature. Progressives invariably refer to SAG as a "union." By this they seem to want to express the idea that actors are workers, and that their interests are best served by an organization that emphasizes their class solidarity with other workers. Conservatives, on the other hand, always speak of a "guild." By this they seem to want to express the idea that actors are artists who must rely on mutual aid to protect their interests but who have little in common with workers in other professions. The insistence on using one or the other term can become quite heated. In fact, listening to whether actors refer to SAG as a "guild" or as a "union" is the single easiest shortcut toward grasping their ideology.

In the second place, conservatives were dismayed at the progressive penchant for taking liberal stands on national and international social issues. In its first months, for example, the "Asner board" voted to boycott the Nestlé company for distributing allegedly inferior baby formula to Third-World countries, and to support multilateral nuclear disarmament. Moreover, Asner and many of the progressives wanted the guild to begin endorsing political candidates. Although the national board eventually voted down this proposal, its very consideration served to reinforce the conservative fear that SAG was careening to the Left.[35]

The official conservative position on this issue is that the guild should, if at all possible, relegate its activities to negotiating wages, hours, and working conditions with management, but that if pressed, it can lobby legislatures on proposed laws that deal directly with the careers of actors. Conservative propaganda either states or implies that the guild never dabbled in wider "politics" until the rise to power of the progressives. As I hope I have shown in the preceding chapters, this is a gross mistatement of the organization's history. In the forties and fifties, during the anti-Communist era, it was deeply involved in the politics of Hollywood and the nation.

The conservatives are correct in maintaining that the depth and breadth of political involvement have increased under progressive administrations, but this is hardly the same thing as asserting that the party in power has despoiled a virginal guild with politics. The fact is that the conservatives, when in power, engaged at various times in conservative politics, and that once the progressives got into office, they wanted to engage in liberal politics. Merely crying "liberalism!" was not likely to stop the swing of the pendulum, however, so instead the conservatives fantasized a pristine past so that they could accuse the progressives of "politics!" They are sincere in this error, but that does not excuse it.

There was a final, largely unspoken anxiety underlying the conservative renaissance. Many saw the invisible hand of the hard Left behind the rise of CAM and Ed Asner. Marie Windsor explains her concerns:

> Though I wasn't in the fight against Communism, when Reagan was doing his thing, and John Wayne, I have always been scared to death of Communists, and I know a lot of people that then and now feel that they're working their way into our country and taking over. So that bug has always been in the back of my head, so I suppose I'm oversensitive, and when anybody [is] far too liberal or seems to lean in those directions, like Jane Fonda, I believe they're worth fighting. And I felt that this element was creeping into our guild. There were too many in that group [CAM] that I felt were thinking along those lines."[36]

This attitude is not shared by all the conservatives, and it is specifically disavowed by some of their leaders. But it is unquestionably held by many in the movement. Progressives, upon encountering it, are apt to become hysterical. Partisans of the two ideologies consequently harbor a bedrock hostility for and distrust of one another that disrupts their attempts at genuine discussion. Thus do American politics of the 1940s poison Screen Actors Guild politics of the 1980s.

By the early months of 1982 the conservatives had acquired grievances, leaders, a sense of identity, and an ideology. To become a force in guild politics they lacked only an organization, and as a spur to that, an issue. They found it.

The Greatest Thing That Almost Happened

There was a minor problem that had to be disposed of before the SAG/ AFTRA merger could move into high gear. Where AFTRA had jurisdiction over television, it also had jurisdiction over extras. SAG itself included extras in New York and several other eastern cities. Since the 1940s, however, a separate union, the Screen Extras Guild, had represented nonspeaking players in the movies and in areas of television where SAG had jurisdiction on the West Coast.

The separation between actors and extras in Hollywood caused difficulties for the guild elsewhere. Nonunion extras were paid roughly thirty dollars a day, while those under the protection of one of the performers' unions could expect to earn almost three times that much. The producers naturally preferred to pay the lower rates, and so hired nonunion extras whenever they could get away with it. More important, just the possibility that they would do so gave them leverage against the unions during contract negotiations. "How long can you say to a group of employers in New York, 'We want you to pay ninety dollars,' when your own members are working for twenty-five dollars in another part of the guild's jurisdiction?" asks Chester Migden. "Sooner or later the employers say 'Screw you. What kind of double standard is this?' You are undermining your own contract." In order to protect a merged actors' union from this kind of erosion, SAG leaders decided even before the Asner administration began that they first had to fuse with SEG.[37]

There were a variety of other good reasons for SAG's 50,000 members to absorb 2,500 West Coast extras. Whereas nonunion extras were essentially amateurs who could be counted on to pester actors for autographs and cause similar small disruptions on the set, union extras were professionals who would leave the other performers alone. Whereas a separate SEG was annoyingly exclusive, preventing actors from performing extra work in their periods of unemployment, a combination would allow actors who could not land speaking parts to at least earn a living in show business instead of having to park cars or wait tables. Whereas television producers who moved from an AFTRA studio to a SAG studio were able to put pressure on the first union for contract concessions for extras, under the threat of switching to SAG and dumping the union extras, this would be impossible under merger.[38]

The unpublicized assumption lying in back of all these reasons was that once SEG was eliminated the Screen Actors Guild would not admit any more extras. As their numbers declined through attrition, more and more nonspeaking parts would be filled by actors, until eventually there would be no more extras, just actors doing extra work.[39]

By the end of January 1982 the accumulated force of these reasons seemed irresistible. There was little public opposition to a merger with SEG. Confident of receiving the 60 percent membership referendum vote that was necessary to authorize a merger, the guild's leaders were already planning the next step.[40]

Then president Asner made his first great mistake. At a Washington press conference on 15 February, he joined with several other well-known actors in presenting to a representative of the El Salvador guerrillas a check for $25,000, to be used for medical aid. The money was not the actors' own, but had been raised through a mail campaign. The celebrities' function was to help publicize the gift by virtue of their ability to attract television cameras. In this they were successful, for the presentation made that night's evening news.[41]

The reaction was immediate. Here was the president of a labor union, the star of one of the most popular television series in the land, publicly giving aid and comfort to Communist revolutionaries. "Here we go again," wrote Ricard P. Winston in a letter to the Los Angeles *Herald Examiner*. "The left-leaning, weak-kneed nellies such as Ed Asner are telling their lies, giving aid and comfort to the Communists." Another letter writer opined that "sending American dollars to aid the guerillas, however humane the motive, borders on treason." Shortly thereafter, the chief executive of a corporation that owns several television stations read an editorial just before "Lou Grant" came on, denouncing Asner and warning that "if El Salvador falls to the Communists, next comes Guatemala and then Mexico. We have a 1,300-mile open border with Mexico. The Rio Grande river is not an ocean; in fact, half the year it's a dry riverbed anyone can walk or drive a tank across." The president of Vidal Sassoon, Inc. wrote a letter to CBS board chairman William Paley containing a strongly implied threat to pull out all his company's advertising. A group calling itself the Congress of Conservative Contributors held a press conference in New York to announce a call for a boycott of the "Lou Grant" program. In May CBS canceled the series, ostensibly because of slipping ratings.[42]

And overnight, opposition to the SEG merger was a roaring inferno.

The nonactor is likely to be surprised by the universal antagonism actors hold toward extras. The jobs of the two types of performers appear to be similar; why should not they be in the same union?

To actors, however, not only are the jobs of the two completely different, but any confusion of them is both an insult and a threat. Actors are artists. Each one is unique and irreplaceable, or so they think. In contrast, anybody can be an extra. To ask actors to admit extras into their union is to tell them that they are not special people, not different from the herd, but merely cogs in an industrial machine. It is an assault on their self-concept and their status in society.

Until the flap over El Salvador, this attitude among actors was subterranean, almost unconscious. It was somehow a violation of etiquette to express it publicly. But when the national bellow of rage hit Ed Asner over his Central American opinions, it knocked the politeness out of his union's discussions. The unconscious became conscious. Where there had been a resigned silence, there was now a determined and vocal opposition.

The conservatives had their issue. Former president Charlton Heston had been occasionally criticizing the board of directors ever since the aborted Life Achievement Award. Now he launched a full-scale assault on Asner and the SEG merger, making dozens of speeches and giving a statement to local newspapers almost every day. Soon the national media were full of references to the "Star Wars" in the Screen Actors Guild between Heston and Asner.[43]

To his credit, Heston was very careful never to introduce red-baiting into this conflict. Moreover, despite the personal aspects of the situation, he always attempted to keep the argument focused on the dispute over principle. "I don't think extra work should be organized," he says now. "It's casual, unskilled labor, work that can be very easily done by students, by retired people, by disabled people." He was soon joined in the attack by the conservatives on the board, and others, such as Robert Conrad, in the wider acting community. "They want to call us the Performers Guild," Conrad remarked of one plan for merged unions. "Seals perform. I still think I can act." "No one expects that Legal Secretaries should be admitted to the Bar Association simply because they do work that is 'similar' to a lawyer's," wrote Marie Windsor. "The merger with the Extras Guild forever collapses the membership standards of your union in the name of big unionism for no benefit to actors," is the way Morgan Paull expressed it.[44]

Despite their focus on principle as opposed to personality, however, Heston and his associates entangled several different strands of argument until they had thoroughly obfuscated the real issue. They managed to fuse the issue of merger with the extras with the issue of SAG's widening political involvement, and then to make it seem as if Asner's personal social agenda in Central America was becoming the guild's. So successful were they at this intellectual sleight of hand that there are still many actors who believe that Asner was constantly delivering harangues about El Salvador in the boardroom. In truth, he never mentioned it. It didn't matter; a month after the president's fatal press conference, a vote for the SEG merger had become, through a process of symbolic transmutation, a vote for the Communist rebels in El Salvador. Thus, when a group of actors demonstrated outside SAG headquarters on Hollywood Boulevard against the SEG merger, most of their picket signs referred, not to the subject at hand, but to seeming irrelevancies: "Keep SAG Out of Politics," "Reagan In, Asner Out."[45]

Meanwhile, the progressives flailed about in befuddlement. By continually attacking Asner for not stating at the beginning of the press conference that he was speaking as an individual and not as a representative of a union, Heston managed to convince Asner that this was the issue. Asner and his allies spent endless energy attempting to point out to the world that he had indeed made clear later that he was speaking for himself alone, as if that mattered. He could not seem to understand that a president of any organization automatically becomes the symbolic spokesperson for that organization. Disavowals to the contrary, when the president of a union speaks in public, he or she speaks for the union. If Asner had wanted to represent only himself, unencumbered by organizational baggage, he should not have run for president. This blindness was no doubt the result of his inexperience in leadership, but that is an explanation, not an excuse.[46]

More important, the confusion about speaking for oneself alone is symptomatic of a more fundamental progressive misunderstanding. Throughout the controversy, Asner and some of his friends seemed to believe that if the irrelevancies about his manner of expression, the

Life Achievement Award, and the PATCO contribution would just go away, then no one would mind that he was publicly supporting a Communist revolution. But this issue was the heart of the matter, as it deserved to be. Asner had quite consciously used his status as a celebrity to work up publicity for the $25,000 contribution. Evidently he and his friends believed that the public affection for "Lou Grant" was so great that he could persuade millions of people to alter their views on communism. Having made the attempt, he then seemed shocked that the population, instead of changing its opinion about El Salvador, had changed its opinion about Ed Asner. But that was the risk he ran when he stepped in front of the television cameras. Having traded on his celebrity, he was in no position to argue that the public did not have a right to object to his private opinions. He had stated his views and would be judged by them.

The tremendously confused campaign, with headlines and mass meetings, lasted into May. There is no way to tell how much of the eventual vote was based upon the actual issue of merger, and how much was really a referendum on Asner, or American policy toward Central America, or guild involvement in politics, or the memory of Ronald Reagan, or any other nongermane factor. All that is known is that the SEG merger was endorsed by 56.7 percent of SAG's voters, and therefore, failing to reach the required 60 percent, defeated.[47]

The merger with AFTRA suddenly came to a screeching halt. Morale in CAM was devastated. In New York, where there had been almost no opposition to the merger, SAG leaders were stunned. Meanwhile, the guild's newly created conservative opposition party was celebrating its first victory.

It Had to Happen

After Morgan Paull had run unsuccessfully for president in 1981, the Board Replacement Committee had appointed him to fill a vacant slot on the Hollywood board of directors. There he had felt thoroughly frustrated, so frequently did he vote in a small minority. He also became angry with Kim Fellner, who, believing that the function of a house publication is to reflect the views of the administration, refused to run anti-SEG merger articles in *Screen Actor*. In March 1982 he decided that he could be more effective by organizing outside the boardroom.[48]

Morgan Paull

Paull was friendly with Windsor, Heston, Don Galloway, Don Dubbins, and several other conservatives from having worked with them. Making phone calls to those he knew, and urging them to make other calls, he arranged a meeting of about fifteen sympathetic actors at Windsor's house on St. Patrick's day. Although the major concern of those who attended was the guild's increasing left-wing political involvement, the SEG merger was also much on their mind. There was in addition a general consensus that Kim Fellner should be fired, both for her publication policies and for her intervention in the Lifetime Achievement Award process.[49]

Those present discussed a name for their organization. They wanted a title that emphasized that they represented working actors, not stars, extras, or the unemployed, and that they desired the guild to pursue only those goals that were directly of interest to actors. They also needed something that would provide an acronym that was easy to say and remember. The name chosen was "Actors Working for an Actor's Guild," or AWAG.

Having observed and been impressed by CAM's impact on performers' unions, they were resolved to copy its tactics for different purposes.

They thought they knew the secret of CAM's success: "scream and holler" to the press, thus reaching all those who were potentially sympathetic, in Marie Windsor's summary. Paull was elected chairman, and he and Heston were designated group press spokesmen. Also imitating CAM, they resolved to run a slate of candidates in the upcoming November elections, and to try to influence the Board Replacement Committee to appoint more conservatives to empty seats. Writing a combination declaration of principles and appeal for support, they placed it as an ad in the next day's trade papers.

Within a week about five hundred actors had written in to endorse the new organization, many sending money. Another thousand joined in the following months. Meanwhile Heston had been talking to his superstar friends in the profession, and collecting pledges of support which AWAG then publicized. Before long it was regularly taking ads in the trades listing hundreds of members, among whom were, besides Heston, six former SAG presidents and such names as Clint Eastwood, Burt Reynolds, Frank Sinatra, Bob Hope, Joel McCrea, Barbara Stanwyck, and James Stewart.[50]

Progressive and centrist members of the board of directors had great difficulty dealing with these attacks. For example, one of the AWAG missives to the trades read in part,

> The Screen Actors Guild is in a time of crisis. The current leadership proposes to shift the Guild from its historic focus on the professional needs of the working actors to a political concern with a wide spectrum of issues and candidates on every level of the national scene. . . . This formidable agenda can only be paid for out of your pocket.[51]

This is plainly political rhetoric, but it also speaks to authentic concerns. In a long discussion of this ad in the boardroom on 26 April, however, the non-AWAG members demonstrated that they could not recognize that here was a political situation requiring a political response. They kept accusing the AWAGers of having told lies and betrayed a trust by going public with their discontent. Paull and Windsor did their best to defend themselves on ideological grounds, but their interlocutors did not realize that they were facing a complete difference of perspective, not an instance of group pathology or evil. Among the progressives, only Bert Freed, with his long experience in ideological quarrel, seemed to understand the dynamics of what was happening. "He thought that what was going on here was an attempt to return this union to what it was before 1971," report the minutes. ". . . These ex-board members and past presidents of SAG are coming out of their retirement to break down and destroy what the Guild has achieved over the past decade." Exactly. What was happening was a counterrevolution, made all the more effective by the progressives' inability to see (or admit to seeing) its nature.[52]

The progressives quickly evolved various theories to explain the rise of AWAG. Chief among these was the assertion that the conservative leaders were not really actors, but producers. Some of this was unarguable. Such members as Eastwood, Reynolds, and Conrad produced their own films, and as such were responsible for hiring the talent and keeping the shooting under budget. This made them management, and placed them under a conflict of interest when recommending policy to actors. Further, as executives whose movies could be made more cheaply with nonunion extras, their position on the SEG merger left their motives open to challenge. When Morgan Paull and Don Galloway began their own independent production company two years after AWAG's founding, the progressives assured themselves that this proved their contention that AWAG had all along just been a front for the producers. In public and in private, they dismissed the conservatives as "union busters."[53]

While this explanation perhaps accounts for the participation of a half a dozen of AWAG's prominent members, however, it is unconvincing as a general explanation for the organization's appeal. In the first place, several of the conservative leaders, including most prominently Heston, were not and never had been producers. In the second place, the overwhelming majority of AWAG's 1,500 dues-paying members were not big stars and had no hope of ever becoming management. In supporting the conservatives, they were expressing their personal beliefs, not defending their private interests.

Despite its wide appeal and ability to cause trouble, AWAG spoke for a minority of actors. This became clear in the November election, when after a full-throated campaign featuring ads, mailers, and a variety of other publicity, the official Nominating Committee slate (heavily influenced by CAM) erased the AWAG slate in the polling. In the 1983 election, also, AWAG was unable to mount a credible challenge, failing even to recruit a candidate willing to run against Asner. Pretending to boycott this election for reasons of principle, the conservatives saw the president garner 73 percent of the vote against token opposition. This was never going to allow them to recapture power. If the counterrevolution was going to be successful, the progressives were going to have to make another horrendous mistake.[54]

Return to Fantasy Island

After two smashing electoral victories in a row, the progressives were feeling more confident. Although little that was concrete had been accomplished on the AFTRA merger, talks were continuing. Still, the lack of a fusion with SEG was a continuing impediment to the larger goal. Why not try again?

The New York branch, in particular, urged this course upon Hollywood. The New Yorkers were embarrassed. Not understanding the depth of the opposition to extras on the West Coast, they had assumed that the merger would sail through, and so had not exerted themselves to get out the vote. This time, they promised, we will take it seriously. In addition, the progressives were mesmerized by the 57 percent majority the merger had received the first time. A majority, but not a victory. Didn't majority rule mean anything in this democracy? It was maddening. Finally, president Asner had been greatly annoyed at the way AWAG in general and Heston in particular had turned the SEG election into a plebiscite on his private politics, and he was continually frustrated at the conservatives' seeming ability to block closer ties between SAG and the rest of the labor movement. He allowed the New York leadership to talk him into backing a plan to present the SEG merger to the membership for a second referendum. It was his second great mistake. It was not his alone, however. On 10 December 1983 the national board voted 70–1–1 to again try to sell the merger with extras to actors. Eventually they spent over a quarter of a million dollars to do so.[55]

With Asner keeping very quiet about national politics, but vigorously talking up the merger, the campaign this time around was much more focused on the issue at hand. This was not an advantage. The spectacle of their board of directors going to the expense of submitting a question to the members less than two years after seeing it defeated struck many actors as a sign of contempt for their ability to make a decision. The conservative campaign played up this aspect of the contest. "I resent the fact that, despite the membership's rejection of this proposal in 1982, the National Board is forcing this issue on the membership," wrote Tom Selleck in an antimerger flyer. "Why did the board fail to respond to your previous rejection of this merger?" asked Morgan Paull in another. "Our elected leaders tell us . . . that we didn't know what we were doing when we rejected this merger before. This insults our collective intelligence and subverts the democratic process. Does this mean we must keep voting on this merger until the Board gets THEIR way?" inquired three dozen past or present SAG and AFTRA officers in another.[56]

In March 1984, the largest voter turnout in SAG's history—61 percent—rejected the SEG merger for the second time. Once again, more than half the voters supported merger, although the majority had shrunk to 51.5 percent. Some actors who had endorsed it the first time reversed their vote the second time out of anger over the board's arrogance.[57]

Perhaps it is not a coincidence that the AWAG slate swept the field in the November 1984 elections, capturing a third of the seats on the Hollywood board.[58]

We're not quarreling! We're in complete agreement! We hate each other!

Nanette Fabray to Oscar Levant, *The Band Wagon*, screenplay by Betty Comden and Adolph Green

Chapter Seven

WAR

In some ways, Ed Asner was an excellent president of the Screen Actors Guild. His evident concern for the problems of his fellow actors, coupled with his oratorical powers, made a considerable number of them feel for the first time that their union was really on their side. His speeches at such occasions as the annual membership meetings were great successes, full as they were with passionate avowals of solidarity with actors and unabashed admissions of love for his profession. They were also educational, in the sense that they made the connection between the life of the actor and the need for a labor union so clear that it seemed inevitable. Consider how briefly, but with how much eloquence, he makes the following point:

> As an actor, as a member of one of the most insecure professions in the world, I need the strength of my fellow actors. I know that when all else fails, I will act for free, just to act. And starve for a chance to practice my craft. Only our union prevents us from falling prey to our own desperation.[1]

It was not just in this symbolic sense that Asner was valuable to SAG. The most fundamental activity of a union is negotiating with management, and here the president's fearsome reputation as a militant translated into concrete results. His lieutenants in the guild hierarchy reveal, somewhat bemusedly, that Asner knew little about the details of the contract. They nevertheless believe that he was a potent force in the 1983 negotiations. They were the ones who actually met with management, only calling on him to enter the room (to "give them grim aspect," in Asner's words) when the other side seemed about to

Kathleen Connell

become intransigent on some point. So great was the producers' belief in his ability to rally the troops in the event of a strike, the SAG negotiators believe, that his mere appearance was enough to instill reasonableness in the negotiators. As Dean Santoro puts it, "All we needed to do was bring him in and sit him down at the table. He didn't have to say anything. We did the talking. But that perception was valuable. Ed was our big gun." Kathy Connell concurs: "The whole town was terrified that that crazy Ed Asner was going to strike."[2]

As a result, the 1983 negotiations were remarkably peaceful from the actors' point of view. In this there was more than a little irony. Asner's candidacy had, after all, been a reaction to SAG's perceived defeat at the bargaining table in 1980 and the allegedly confiscatory ten-day free-play window for cable movies. It would have been logical for the guild to make the elimination of this window the centerpiece of its demands when the odious contract expired three years later.

It turned out, however, that when the members of the Telecommunications Committee analyzed how cable networks like Home Box Office, Cinemax, and others were using their product, they discovered that the infamous ten-day window was largely irrelevant. The number

Daryl Anderson

of films made for cable was not large, and those that were produced were used in a manner that made the number of showings in a year, not the number in a short period, important. SAG therefore did not even bother with a demand to change the ten-day rule in 1983. "A lot of what motivated 1980 was the Phantom of 1960, and the feeling that we were in a period of great change and that we were going to be left out again," explains Daryl Anderson. "But three years later it looked like we'd really been chasing our tail around a tree. The market wasn't taking off." And so Asner, who had run for president as part of an effort to deal with cable television, ended up frightening the producers into making concessions regarding safety on the set and the union health plan instead.[3]

Asner was thus a successful, even a great, leader in some aspects of the job of president of the guild. In other aspects he was a calamity. When he had run for office he had been assured by his supporters that he would not have to handle the details of the job because they would see to the day-to-day running of the guild. Once in the presidency he astonished them by how faithfully he lived up to his part of that bargain. He rarely came into headquarters, neglecting the minutiae of the job of the executive—hiring staff, deciding on raises for them, signing papers, and so on. More important, he treated the task of presiding at board meetings as though it were similarly trivial. In four years as a presiding officer at board meetings, he never bothered to learn *Robert's Rules of Order,* relying instead on advice from other officers who happened to be present. He could or would not bring himself to appear impartial in the chair, nodding in agreement when someone expressed his own position, and tipping his chair back with his hands behind his head in obvious boredom when someone spoke whose views were contrary to his own. He made personal remarks at inappropriate moments of discussion, and sometimes exploded in profanity when some assertion triggered his temper. In other words, he treated guild board meetings as though they were a college bull session and he was a sophomore visiting in the dormitory.[4]

When added to the fact that neither the SEG nor the AFTRA merger advanced much during Asner's tenure, this makes his record a decidedly mixed one. Even his friends, those who implored him to run for the job in 1981, feel a strong ambivalence when talking about his presidency. While praising his courage and good intentions, they describe his actual performance as embarrassing. Speaking for those who come down on the side of a favorable evaluation, Dean Santoro insists that "when he erred, he erred on the side of the angels as far as I'm concerned. He made some big gaffes, but those gaffes were made with a good heart, and a clean heart." Another early supporter, Joseph Ruskin, expresses the views of many others, however, when he says sadly that "Ed was loved, and is, as a man of great personal integrity, but I think we all know that he really was a disaster as president."[5]

The Talk of the Town

Asner's incompetence in the chair had palpable consequences. *Robert's Rules of Order* are not a series of regulations designed by pedants to increase the tedium of public gatherings. They are a means by which the minority can be treated fairly in policy making, but the majority can still govern. When they are disregarded, either the majority oppresses the minority, or the minority reduces a meeting to chaos. In the case of the Screen Actors Guild in the early 1980s, both occurred. The AWAG representatives and their sympathizers often felt railroaded, and the CAM representatives and their sympathizers often felt as though the animals had taken over the zoo.

This was only part of the problem, of course. Even if Robert himself had presided at board meetings, there would still have been an increasing divergence between the two sides as the Asner presidency progressed. The leftists wanted to draw the guild ever closer to the national labor movement, pursue a social agenda they found imperative, find more ways to protect actors from management in the contract, and vigorously pursue merger with AFTRA. With the rightists being opposed to or only lukewarmly in favor of all these projects, unending conflict was inevitable.

The fight between the two factions was always accompanied by reams of publicity, for the celebrities on both sides had easy access to the town's press. If the rhetoric had been intense in the early years of the Asner administration, however, it became positively purple after September 1983, when Mark McIntire took over as chairman of AWAG.

Contrary to the later claims of some of the progressives, McIntire was a bona fide working actor, having appeared in a variety of small parts in television programs and commercials. In particular, producers sometimes exploited his strong physical resemblance to President John Kennedy to cast him either as an unidentified political figure or as Kennedy himself. Nevertheless, he was in no sense a celebrity, and, until he joined AWAG, can be fairly characterized as obscure.[6]

A man of strong conservative ideology and unbridled assertiveness, McIntire was affronted by the guild leadership's evident plans for a second SEG merger vote in the late summer of 1983. He called AWAG headquarters and volunteered his time for campaign work. Coincidentally, at this moment Morgan Paull was becoming weary of the details of organizational labor and was looking for someone to take over as AWAG chair. Additionally, Charlton Heston, exasperated with the media's insistence on framing a contest of principle as a "Star Wars" between himself and Asner, wanted a lesser-known actor to take over the duty of being chief press spokesperson for AWAG. When McIntire called, he found himself quickly being interviewed by Marie Windsor, then Paull, then Heston, and in less than a week was chairman. "This is the only time I've ever joined an organization at the top," he muses.[7]

Heston made clear what he expected. The long-run agenda was to return the guild to a state in which it was free from entanglements

Mark McIntire

with big labor and liberal social causes. In pursuit of that ideal there were three specific short-run goals. First, AWAG needed an effective campaign organization to fight the SEG merger. Second, Ed Asner was to be harassed into resigning, or otherwise leaving guild government. Third, McIntire was to persuade the guild to fire "that villanous director of propaganda," Kim Fellner. While Heston was to remain available for advice and moral support, he would withdraw from the front lines of the rhetorical battle, leaving McIntire to deal with the media.[8]

The choice of a new leader had thus been made somewhat haphazardly, but it nevertheless turned out to be inspired. Although he is fundamentally a serious person, there is something about Mark McIntire that suggests the manic glee of a ten-year-old boy who has just been given permission to shoot rubber bands at grown-ups. His task, as he understood it, was to "snip and peck away at Asner's outer edges—his nerves—and to keep at him and keep rebutting him. Every time he opens his mouth, we have a spokesperson who opens *his* mouth, and that mouth says something which is inflammatory, outrageous, and intemperate, but nevertheless effective in presenting an [opposite] point of view. Every time he [Asner] made some pontifical announcement,

I would counter it with a pontifical announcement. And every time that he said we should use the guild's resources for whatever social cause he at that point was advocating, I would come out with a "Binaca blast" at him."[9]

The respectable, dignified Heston had never been able to express publicly the anger he felt at the direction the guild was taking under the progressives. Every one of his hundreds of statements to the media had been almost painfully thoughtful in substance and measured in style. But McIntire had no reputation as a responsible person to live up to and no desire to create one. He proceeded to launch a rhetorical campaign that soon drove the guild leadership into a frenzy.

On 18 September 1983 McIntire held his first press conference as chairman of AWAG, and displayed the weakness as well as the strength of his confrontational style. Claiming that Asner wanted "to do away with SAG as we know it," he argued against the SEG merger, and teed off on the guild's new social consciousness. So far, so good. But, criticizing the efforts of SAG's various minorities', women's, and disabled performers' committees to persuade producers to endorse affirmative-action programs, he stated facetiously that the guild should stop "chanting the cause of three or four Buddhist Eskimos in iron lungs."[10]

This was a poor beginning. Affirmative action was of interest not only to progressives, but to a goodly number of conservative minority, female, and disabled actors, who now loudly proclaimed their dissatisfaction with AWAG's new leader. Ricardo Montalban, former SAG board member, longtime activist for Hispanic rights, and AWAG's most prominent minority member, threatened to resign. McIntire hastily apologized, and his sponsors tried to explain that he had meant that the guild should work to improve the condition of all actors, not just a minority. McIntire survived the gaffe, but he avoided the subject in the future.[11]

This did not restrain his blasts on other issues. Soon he was tormenting the progressives with a steady stream of attacks and requests. One of his communications accused the board of being composed of "neo-socialists." In another, he threatened by implication to sue individual progressives and the board collectively for claiming that AWAG members were "union busters." In yet another, he called upon Asner to apologize to the guild's youthful performers for having used the word "bullshit" in a speech on the SEG merger. Elected to the board on AWAG's ticket in November 1984, at his first meeting he asked the guild staff to prepare a compendium of all organizational policies on every topic for the previous fifteen years (his colleagues voted down this motion). In threatening to sue the guild if it employed any dues on behalf of the international campaign against apartheid in South Africa, he accused the board of attempting "to make SAG the moral den mother of the world." When the guild resolved to present the Lifetime Achievement Award to Paul Newman and Joanne Woodward in October 1985, McIntire told the press that Newman represented "far-left political groups" that "believe in disarming the Western democracies first" and which "support Communists" in Central America.[12]

While aiming at the progressives in general and Asner in particular, McIntire did not neglect to fire a few volleys at Kim Fellner. At the annual mid-year membership meeting in June 1984, he introduced a resolution from the floor to have her fired. It carried by one vote. He understood that motions passed this way were only advisory to the board, and that this one was sure to be defeated there, but he also knew that it would be embarrassing. "It was great fun," he laughs.[13]

As Charles Briggs had tortured the conservative establishment in the early 1970s with a seige of proposals, demands, and insinuations, McIntire similarly plagued the progressive establishment in the 1980s. This is the weakness of the open, democratic union: its leaders are vulnerable to hypercriticism from members who are not interested in working from within, but intend to bring down the regime.

Somewhat to the AWAG leaders' surprise, their strategy worked beautifully. As soon as it became apparent that McIntire was guaranteed to supply a provocative quotation on any subject, the media began to seek him out. Every time president Asner made a public statement, reporters would call McIntire for a rejoinder. Within a month he had become a sort of junior-grade celebrity. The trade papers never printed a story on the Screen Actors Guild without quoting McIntire's views on the subject under discussion. In a city where publicity is often confused with reality, he became an important personage. After the election, when he could goad the progressives from inside the boardroom, and had better access to guild documents, he became even more effective as a disruptive force.

The reaction of the progressives, centrists, and even non-AWAG conservatives to McIntire's campaign of aggravation is easy to describe. They hated him. His media attacks were distressing in themselves, since nobody likes to be continually lampooned in the press. And they were draining of time better spent on guild government, since they kept people busy writing letters of explanation and defense. But most significant was that because many of his statements came dangerously close to red-baiting, they awakened the primal terror of the blacklist that hovered in the background of actors' politics. And because Mc-Intire spoke for AWAG, his attacks were not perceived as issuing from an individual personality but from an organized conspiracy, which, in fact, they were. If the relationship between the Right and the Left in the guild had been hostile before McIntire, after his election to the board it became one of open warfare.

The intensity of the resentment of McIntire's tactics, and the way in which it could unhinge rational argument, is illustrated by a discussion within the SAG board of directors on 19 August 1985. On that particular day president Asner was absent, so first vice-president Joseph Ruskin chaired the meeting. By this time AWAG had become a California corporation and McIntire had stepped down as chair, to be replaced by Morgan Paull. As a member of the Hollywood board, however, he was still very much on the front lines of battle. Two weeks earlier, he had spoken to an actors' support group on the subject of the guild and how it affected them. Expecting a nonpolitical talk containing practical information, his audience had instead been treated to a polemic. One of the actresses in the group had written a letter to the board, complaining of McIntire's tone and asserting that he had strongly implied that the progressive regime contained "card-carrying Communists."[14]

The actors' meeting had been a private affair, and no minutes had been kept. There was therefore no independent record of what McIntire had said, and more important, of the context of any statement. The wise course of action on all sides would have been to let the matter drop. Instead, the reading of the letter nearly precipitated a riot in the boardroom.

Frank Maxwell asked McIntire "who he was referring to when he said that the 'present regime' in the Screen Actors Guild were 'card-carrying Communists.'"

McIntire tried to explain that the actress had misinterpreted his meaning. "The only statement I made at that meeting was that 'even AWAG has card-carrying Communists as its members,' because AWAG is not interested in whether someone is a Communist, or not a Communist. And whether SAG has Communists in it or not, is irrelevant and immaterial." In other words, he had intended to convey the idea that the outside political affiliations of people on the guild board were not important; what mattered was the positions they took on guild issues inside the boardroom. Probably because of the inflammatory phrasing in which it was couched, the actress had construed his statement in the opposite sense in which he meant it.

On the face of it, this construction of the situation is plausible, and consistent with the phrase quoted by the actress in the letter. In the absence of a transcript, it should have sufficed to move the board meeting on to other things.

But the progressives were not buying it. Mark Schubb reported that he had talked to two other actors who had attended the meeting, and that they had substantiated the actress's letter. He further argued that he could not see any motivation for the actress to have lied. The fact that McIntire had accused her of confusion rather than falsehood did not seem to have penetrated.

Bert Freed, quoting McIntire's explanation that even AWAG had Communist members, asked, "When you use [the word] 'even' you mean 'additionally,' which in a sense gramatically says there are card-carrying members . . . in AWAG. . . . I now ask you who of these people that are part of this group or are part of AWAG, are you calling 'card-carrying Communists?' "

Howard Caine remarked that "the lady has expressed if nothing else having heard somebody who has contempt for their fellow members."

The record also contains this exchange between a black actor and a conservative board member:

> TOEY CALDWELL: "This is the second time I personally have been insulted by you [McIntire]. First by you calling me a Buddhist Eskimo in Iron Lungs and now by putting a phrase in of me being a card-carrying Communist. . . . This is the last time that . . . [I]—Toey Caldwell—will put up with it personally, and I will deal with it on my own if it happens again."
>
> ED NELSON: "That's a personal threat, Mr. Chairman!"
>
> CALDWELL: "Take it whatever way you want!"
>
> NELSON: "Control the meeting!"

Meanwhile, Ruskin was indeed trying to maintain decorum. "I would like to point out to you [that] those of us who are old enough to have been living through the 50s and attempting to make our living in the business were terribly, terribly scarred. . . . It may be that we are very much on our nerves' ends when those statements which destroyed

Joseph Ruskin

careers are reported again at this time of our lives. . . . The situation is a dangerous one whenever those words are used about American performers. . . . You have a right to express your opinion and your feelings, but please I am asking for everybody to pull the reins in a little."

On that theme, Paul Stewart asked, "Is there anybody in this room who was blacklisted or did not get work during the McCarthy hearings? [He meant the HUAC hearings.] Would they please raise their hand or indicate that?" Three in attendance raised their hands.

After twelve pages of this sort of discussion, without coming to any conclusions or taking any action, they unanimously voted to resume the evening's agenda. The minutes record that "there was a brief recess before going on to the next order of business."

Neither side seems to have learned much from this exchange. At least half a dozen progressives stated flatly to me in interviews that Mark McIntire had publicly, or in the boardroom, claimed that there were "card-carrying Communists" in the SAG leadership, which is at best a problematic assertion. On the other hand, McIntire does not seem to have been educated by the violence of the reaction to his phrasing, or to have seen the wisdom in Ruskin's plea for restraint on this particular subject. Consider this conversation with me on 24 August 1986:

> MCINTIRE: "As far as I'm concerned, some of them are Bolsheviks. . . . There are people in that board room who would like to overthrow the economic system of this country."
>
> PRINDLE: "Does that mean that they would like to install a dictatorship of the proletariat?"
>
> MCINTIRE: "Yes! Yes!"

The Miracle Worker

After four tumultuous years on the job, Ed Asner decided not to try to succeed himself in November 1985. As the election in which his successor would be chosen approached, it was plain to many people in the guild that they were now supporting a two-party system. The summer was full of frantic organizing, recruitment of as many "name" candidates as possible, and fund raising. Activists on each side predicted that the balloting would be a watershed that would turn the guild permanently in the path of righteousness or forever into the darkness. Not only were the Hollywood trade papers crammed with election news, but national media figures were in town gathering background information for "election night coverage." There was even a political scientist from the University of Texas pestering candidates for interviews.

AWAG mounted a full-tilt effort for its slate of board nominees, throwing "meet-the-candidate" parties and supplying reams of publicity to anyone who asked for it. The organization did not sponsor its own presidential nominee, instead endorsing the hopes of Ed Nelson, a strong conservative who had nevertheless never been affiliated with AWAG. By most measures, Nelson was a formidable candidate. Familiar to other actors because of his costarring roles in the prime-time series "Peyton Place" in the 1960s and the daytime soap "Capitol" in the 1980s, and dozens of stage, television, and film appearances before, after, and in between, he was also a very experienced participant in guild affairs. A former vice-president under John Gavin, he had demonstrated considerable levelheadedness in almost twenty years of participation in the guild.

With over a decade of experience himself in the upper reaches of the union, vice-president Joseph Ruskin planned to try for the top spot. The entry of Nelson into the race, however, set him and his CAM allies to recalculating. Despite their comparable service to the organization, Nelson was far better known as an actor. Assuming that a large proportion of the voters would endorse the most familiar name on the ballot, the progressives anticipated that Ruskin would start with a handicap. Not willing to run the risk, they persuaded him to withdraw in favor of Patty Duke, who had no experience in guild government but who was an Emmy and Oscar-winning star. Ruskin agreed to again take the first vice-presidency. As if to emphasize the continuity of progressive hopes, Asner himself made the phone call to ask Duke to run.[15]

Duke had served as a vice-chair of CAM, and had long been active in such safely noncontroversial causes as world famine relief, aid for the blind, and prevention of child abuse. The Nominating Committee, dominated by progressives and containing several CAM members, chose her as the union's official candidate. Thinking that perhaps "Caucus of Artists for Merger" was an unduly restrictive title, Duke's backers then put together a new organization called "Pro-SAG" which was responsible for electioneering.[16]

Despite the massive marshaling of forces and the passions represented on each side, it was a quiet campaign. Nelson proved to be as gentlemanly on the hustings as he was in the boardroom, and Duke, chastened by the example of Asner, was very careful not to say anything publicly that would distract from the issue of merger. As might be expected, the only real color in the campaign was supplied by Mark McIntire.

The shadow of the AIDS epidemic was stealing across the national landscape. As concern began to turn into panic, rumors started to float around Hollywood that some actresses were going to refuse to perform love scenes with homosexual men, and that producers were planning to eliminate kissing scenes from films. The board, anxious to calm the fears and head off anything that would put still more impediments in the way of actors' employment, passed a resolution requiring producers to notify the cast in advance if "open-mouth kissing" would be required in a scene. This policy was supported by all factions in the guild.[17]

Several of Patty Duke's supporters on the board, however, arranged for her to hold a press conference immediately after the guild's, at which she supported the policy. They naturally did not do the same

for Nelson. This made it appear, they hoped, as though Duke was already somehow officially associated with SAG authority. Clever as a
campaign ploy, this angered McIntire, who called *Daily Variety* and
charged that Duke was "dancing on the graves of the dead in a crass
attempt to salvage her floundering bid for the SAG presidency" and
that "it would be a tragic commentary on all SAG actors if she won the
SAG presidency by climbing over the bodies of AIDS victims."[18]

Incomprehensible as anything but hastily invented campaign rhetoric, this statement was the last straw for the progressives. At the next
board meeting on 4 November, they attempted to officially censure
McIntire "for reckless and irresponsible statements not reflecting the
Board's decisions on policy matters," including the "card-carrying
Communist" remark, the attack on Paul Newman and Joanne Woodward, opinions he had given to the press regarding the guild's stand
against apartheid, and the most recent AIDS pronouncement. Considering that the balloting was only a week away, however, the board
decided to postpone voting on the motion until the next meeting.[19]

A week later Patty Duke received 56 percent of the vote to become
the second female president in guild history. Although official, and
therefore largely progressive, candidates won most races, thereby ensuring continued leftist control of policy, AWAG achieved two significant victories. Christopher Mitchum surprised most people by defeating incumbent Joseph Ruskin for first vice-president, and Marie
Windsor ousted incumbent Norma Connolly for eleventh vice-
president.[20]

Like Asner, Duke wanted above all to help put through the merger
with AFTRA. But unlike Asner, she had the advantage of having seen
her predecessor's plans be deflected by extraneous issues, and had
learned from the spectacle. She understood that the most important
thing to be done to hasten the merger would be to smother the partisan
sniping that was draining everyone's energy.[21]

Immediately she moved to calm the waters. During the campaign
she had kept very quiet about her own personal (very liberal) stands
on national politics, answering inquiries with brief politeness, then
turning the conversation in other directions. She intended to continue
to subordinate her private views to the union's priorities throughout
her presidency. During her first press conference after the victory, she
announced, among other things, that McIntire's "dancing on the
graves" charge was probably "not well thought-out," and that she did

not intend to live her life "holding grudges." McIntire could take a hint. He personally apologized to her for the severity of his statement before the next meeting. As a result, her first words in her capacity as chair were to ask the board to rescind the motion to censure him. No doubt heaving a collective sigh of relief, it did so unanimously. Duke proceeded to bolster the truce by quickly proving herself a fair and scrupulous presiding officer, so that the AWAG members felt that henceforth their opinions would receive full due in guild deliberations.[22]

Duke also moved to reorient the Guild's image as a confrontational union, both to its members and to outsiders. In her maiden speech to the annual membership meeting a few days after the election, she stressed the role of actors as artists rather than as workers. Pleading with those in her audience to bring their disagreements to her or to their representatives on the board instead of to the press, she said, "I sincerely hope to lead you through two very boring, but progressive years."[23]

Kim Fellner had resigned as public information director in September to become executive secretary of the National Writers Union. She was replaced by Mark Locher, whose background, unlike his predecessor's, was in the theater. Locher began to de-emphasize the "union" theme in SAG publications that had so disturbed conservatives, and to make *Screen Actor* a "discussion of the craft of acting." In conversations with Locher immediately after taking office, Duke strongly endorsed this new direction of guild public relations, adding that it should also attempt to mute internal conflict, allowing the organization to conduct any disagreements as privately as possible.[24]

All this had a profoundly soothing effect. Mark McIntire believed that "she continues to advocate her causes, but she does it in a way that is humane, intelligent, witty, compassionate, and balanced. She is a moderating force, not a divisive force. She is antithetical to everything Ed Asner ever was." For a while he even took to wearing a "Patty Duke" campaign button to board meetings. Charlton Heston told me in January 1986 that he thought that the guild was "coming back to its proper agenda," and that if he'd known what an excellent president Duke was going to make, he would have voted for her. In June, Anthony Caruso informed me that AWAG had disbanded, there being no further need for it (he was mistaken; it was merely inactive). On both sides of the ideological gap, in the early summer of 1986 guild activists expressed the belief that the misunderstandings of the past had been overcome, and the hope that the guild could now proceed on its peaceful way.[25]

The Long Hot Summer

They were living in a fool's paradise. The conflicts of the past few years were not the result of personal insult or maladroit public relations on the part of Ed Asner, but were the consequence of fundamentally different beliefs and values about the role of a union. They would not go away, even given a president with the superb interpersonal and political skills of Patty Duke. By reining in the prounion propaganda, carefully phrasing her own public statements, and treating all factions with warm courtesy, Duke had eliminated the incidental squabbles. She could do nothing, however, about the critical disagreements which continued to underlie guild politics.

And the conservatives were growing restive about the continued lack of resolution of those disagreements. Through Duke's first six months, they had repeatedly asked her for a formal meeting, at which AWAG members could present their grievances and hope to receive assurances that the guild under Duke would not pursue a liberal social agenda. The schedules of the various leaders never seemed to mesh, however, and the meeting never came about. By June the conservatives were beginning to feel that they had given her a long enough honeymoon period, and that the time was again approaching when it would be appropriate to play hardball.[26]

The truce began to dissolve in mid-July. At one particularly long board meeting, conservative (but non-AWAG) board member Conrad Palmisano made a motion to relegate all nonactor issues to the bottom of the agenda, which would mean, in effect, that they would never come up for consideration. Progressives and centrists voted it down, several stating that they would be proud to continue dealing with problems from the wider world. This convinced the AWAGers that the truce was one-sided. Some of them decided that the guild as it was presently constituted was not reformable, and might have to be dismantled.[27]

A full resumption of hostilities followed quickly, and once again it was the status of extras that touched off the explosion. In May 1986 the contract between SAG/AFTRA and motion-picture and television producers had been up for negotiation. The unions had sought a variety of pay hikes and noneconomic gains. Their negotiators had been shocked, however, to see management's proposals, which called for steep rollbacks in a number of areas, especially residuals on cable and videocassettes. AWAG's leaders, concerned that a perception of internal division within the guild had encouraged this attack on actors' income, had issued a statement that their organization "strongly supports SAG's current position and proposals in the ongoing contract negotiations." It didn't help. With the two sides locked in position, the unions had received a strike vote from their memberships, and Hollywood had braced for another work stoppage. The negotiations crept forward, but by the end of July a walkout looked inevitable.[28]

Then Charlton Heston discovered, through his industry contacts outside the guild, that that one of the chief contentions was over a guild demand about extras. The normal contract contains a clause in which the union agrees not to strike for the duration of that contract. This no-strike clause itself is, of course, negotiable. Heston's sources reported that the SAG negotiators had placed an additional clause in their demands that would allow the guild to go on strike in sympathy with the Screen Extras Guild. This meant, in effect, that SEG would be able to threaten the producers, during its own negotiations, not only with a strike by its puny self, but with a simultaneous walkout by the actors. The guild representatives had claimed that this SEG clause was "non-negotiable." Management had refused to consider it. This had been one of the chief sticking points in the negotiations.[29]

When they learned that their guild was threatening to strike over the extras, the AWAGers felt betrayed. Although this "new" demand was in reality not much more than for a return to the pre-SEG-vote circumstances, the conservatives thought that it represented an effort to circumvent the membership's stated preferences on representing the extras. That the membership had twice voted by majority to support a coalition with the extras didn't matter. They felt that the ruling progressives had used AWAG's quiescence as a window of opportunity to undo the democratic decision.[30]

It was not quite that simple. As it had in the case of the second SEG merger vote, the New York branch of the guild had prevailed upon a reluctant Hollywood branch to include the extras clause in the negotiations. Hollywood board members say that they had gone along basically to placate New York, had known that management would never agree to such a provision, and had expected it to be bargained away as part of an inevitable compromise.[31]

Whatever the real purpose of the SEG clause, Heston considered it to be palpable evidence of treachery. Besides being an insult to the conservatives, he believed that by not informing the membership of the SEG clause when they sent out the ballots for the strike authorization, the guild leadership had violated the rules of the National Labor Relations Board. Furious, he called a number of former guild presidents and a variety of prestigious friends, such as James Stewart. All pledged to support him in whatever he chose to do. He then informed the media that he would hold a press conference on 31 July, and "sent word" to the board that if the extras issue was not taken off the table he and AWAG would "blow the whistle." Although he never actually threatened to lead an effort to break a strike, he planned to say at the press conference that he "couldn't support [his] union" in the event of a walkout.[32]

The implied threat was enough. No guild leadership was going to try to sustain a walkout against the public opposition of many of its celebrity members. The board postponed its strike vote, and took the SEG clause off the negotiating table. In a few days they had come to terms on a new contract, which avoided the give-backs management had originally sought but also lacked several provisions that guild negotiators had hoped to win.[33]

For the Screen Extras Guild, this final abandonment by the actors was the beginning of disaster. Within six months it had signed a humiliating contract, experienced a rank-and-file rebellion that led to a complete turnover in its leadership, contemplated merger with the Teamsters, conducted a brief strike, and signed another contract almost as bad as the first. Its future as a separate union does not look promising.[34]

For the Screen Actors Guild also, the debacle of the 1986 negotiations was a turning point. To a union leadership, a member threatening to break a strike—in essence taking management's side—is perhaps the ultimate felony. In August many progressives decided that Heston and his friends in AWAG had ceased to be the "loyal opposition" that they sometimes called themselves and had openly come out as union-busters. They set about to find some way to discipline the renegades. Further, they resumed the guild's involvement in liberal social issues. For example, in October they contributed five hundred dollars to the journal of Norman Lear's People for the American Way.[35]

Meanwhile, many of the conservatives had concluded that the guild had indeed ceased to be a useful entity, and that some way had to be discovered to allow them to withdraw from it while continuing their work. Not only was the truce over, but the war had escalated to massive retaliation on both sides.

River of No Return

In late August 1986, Mark McIntire circulated a memorandum to the twelve other AWAG-backed board directors calling their attention to a series of court decisions based on a case initiated by conservative political writer and publisher William Buckley. Finding himself forced to join AFTRA because of his syndicated radio and television program "Firing Line," Buckley had sued to escape the obligation. The courts had decreed that a union may levy charges against workers for their share of the expenses of collective bargaining, but may not force them to join or pay full dues. Not surprisingly, members who chose this truncated form of belonging could not vote in union elections or run for office. In his memo McIntire suggested to his colleagues that "in the coming months of our service to the board of directors it may serve us well to consider the benefits derived from the case of Mr. William F. Buckley." The advantage of becoming "Buckley members" would be that they would not be "compelled to belong to a union in order to continue working." This memo, of course, instantly leaked to the press.[36]

"I had reached the conclusion," McIntire explained a few months later, "that we [AWAG] were not capable of turning the Bolsheviki around. . . . I decided that I wanted to hand out parachutes to those who wished to flee a burning and downing plane, and that the parachutes were protected by the courts. . . . but most people were not even aware that there was a parachute in the plane. Although, as an elected official, it was my responsibility to be one of the last out the door, . . . if I do have to leave my guild, it will be with the greatest degree of regret. It will be because I have reached the point where I have been driven out . . . and that will be a tragedy."[37]

In case the progressives were tempted to miss the point or think that McIntire was alone, Morgan Paull told *Daily Variety* that only matters dealing with collective bargaining should be on the guild board's agenda, and that he "wouldn't hesitate to become a Buckley member if they [the board] continue on this path and ask for a dues increase."

Don Galloway

Closer to home, Don Galloway wrote a letter to the board asking, "Would you please tell me what percentage of my dues is utilized for collective bargaining, as opposed to other SAG expenditures?" The implied threat was lost on no one.[38]

Patty Duke was seeing her carefully nurtured organizational harmony crumble to dust. "I am personally insulted," she told the trade paper, "that Mr. McIntire chose to do this negative thing in public prior to mentioning it to me. I'm not saying he doesn't have the right to publicize the Buckley decision. But if he wants to help me, as he states, to strive for unity in the Guild, then I would think that he would have at least had the courtesy to express his discontent to me. . . . My concern . . . is that it stimulates the very destructive anger that Mr. Paull, Mr. McIntire, and Mr. Heston have reassured me at least eight times since last November that they want to deal with in a constructive manner."[39]

It was too late to reprimand the boys for being naughty. The war had entered a new phase. The prospect in front of the ruling progressives was that of a significant proportion of their membership withdrawing from active participation, and, more important, withholding part of its dues. At its next meeting the Hollywood board voted to launch an investigation into whether McIntire had violated rule 1 of the constitution, which provides that any member may be "reprimanded, disciplined, fined, suspended or expelled" for "conduct unbecoming a member of the Guild." Lawyers on both sides began to churn out paper.[40]

Meanwhile, Charlton Heston was opening a new front. In the 1947 Taft-Hartley Act, Congress had allowed the states to pass laws which forbade the union shop, that is, which made it illegal for unions to require a worker to join their organization as a condition of employment. In the ensuing years, twenty mostly southern states had passed these right-to-work laws, as they were called. California was not a right-to-work state, which meant that the guild's founding branch could prevent any actor from working who was not a member. Passage of such a law in the Golden State, however, would mean that the AWAGers could drop out of SAG while continuing to pursue their careers.[41]

Economic theory is clear in holding that right-to-work laws are devastating to labor unions. Without the power to compel membership, organizations of workers face what is called the "free rider problem." Since unions provide benefits such as contract bargaining that are collective in nature, individual workers have no incentive to join. If all the other workers join and one doesn't, that one will still receive the benefits. If the one joins and the others don't, nothing will happen. Therefore the economically rational worker will choose to remain passive, hoping to hitch a free ride on the exertions of others. Of course, if all workers feel the same way, no one will join and the union will either collapse or never be born. It is therefore necessary to eliminate individual freedom of choice in the matter by making membership compulsory. Needless to say, almost every labor leader endorses this argument, and consequently execrates right-to-work laws.[42]

Nevertheless, although the theory is clear, the facts are not. States with right-to-work statutes consistently have weaker unions and lower wages than states without such statutes, but it is possible that the laws merely reflect anti-union attitudes in the states and do not cause labor's weakness there. The empirical studies conducted by scholars, in which such variables as the "southernness" of a state's population are statistically controlled, have found that there is no identifiable relationship between right-to-work and union weakness or wages. The question is still open, but as of now the conclusion must be that the "free rider problem" theory is wrong.[43]

At any rate, by August 1986 Charlton Heston had decided to help make the world safe for right-to-work. The citizens of Idaho were scheduled to vote in November as to whether they would ratify the state legislature's passage of such a law. Heston journeyed several times to that state to campaign, making a television commercial in which he said that "as a former union president" he urged Idahoans to support the law with their ballots. This was the opening effort in a campaign that would take Heston and a retinue including Rory Calhoun, Don Galloway, John Gavin, Mark McIntire, and Morgan Paull to New Mexico for a right-to-work battle there, and, if their plans are successful, to the coming struggle in California in 1988.[44]

That Heston was publicly engaging in what was, in their view, union-busting was offensive enough to the progressives. That he was doing it while draped in the mantle of a labor leader was intolerable. As CAM chair Paul Weisenfeld wrote in a letter to the *Los Angeles Herald-Examiner* in January 1987, "To the members of SAG, it became clear that this man was attempting to subvert their union from within."[45]

At a board meeting in the middle of September, one progressive proposed that Heston be stripped of his dues-free lifetime membership in the guild. In view of the former president's clout among other actors, and especially in view of his recent lobbying in Washington that had been instrumental in removing several provisions obnoxious to actors from the new tax bill, this suggestion was impolitic, and was shelved. Nevertheless, the board authorized president Patty Duke to travel to Idaho and make commercials urging the defeat of the initiative to repeal the right-to-work law. When it passed anyway, the progressive anger at this symbolic blow to their vision of labor was augmented by fear as the realization dawned that Idaho had just been target practice; California and the Screen Actors Guild would soon be in the bull's eye.[46]

Heston had enraged not only the leadership with his campaign. At the guild's annual membership meeting in December, three to four hundred actors (still, of course, only a tiny percentage of the 60,000 card-holders) voted overwhelmingly to censure him for his "antiunion activities."[47]

This particular affront sparked a letter-writing campaign on behalf of Heston's freedom of expression. James Stewart, Richard Dreyfuss, Tom Selleck, and others wrote to the board (thoughtfully sending copies to the trade papers) defending his right to say anything, anywhere.

John Gavin nicely captured the general tone of the letters, and reminded the progressives of their former status as a frustrated minority, by harking back to his own days in the majority:

> During my two terms as president of the Guild, there was some pressure to censure certain other members for their political activities. There were those, for example, who considered the appearances of Miss Jane Fonda in Hanoi not just unacceptable political activity, but treason. . . . The then leadership of the Guild steered a course away from such attempts at political censure . . . I would hope that today's Guild leaders would also be prudent in this respect."[48]

He need not have worried. The progressives were not about to allow themselves to be cast as the heavies in a media morality play. On 11 January 1987 SAG president Duke sent a letter to Heston, and to the trades, in which she made it clear that "it is, and always has been, not only my opinion, but my example, to respect your right—and that of any other citizen—to speak freely." Shortly thereafter, the Western Regional Board confined itself to passing a toothless resolution in which it expressed its "dismay and disappointment" with Heston's behavior, but ostentatiously refused to take any disciplinary action. There the matter rested.[49]

Meanwhile, former president William Schallert, now the ninth vice-president, had been asked to chair a committee to look into the desirability of taking action against Mark McIntire. The five-member panel also contained Ed Nelson and Beverly Garland, who had been backed by AWAG in their electoral campaigns. This inquiry had produced, back in October, probably the calmest and most thorough examination of the philosophical differences between the two sides. In a lengthy conversation, the committee had discussed with McIntire his actions and the reasons for them. He had made it clear that he had well-considered reasons for his disruptions, and that he would not stop them until he observed "a cessation of political and ideological expenditures with which the dissidents disagree."[50]

Given this defiance, the members of the panel had a difficult political problem. If they recommended a condemnation of McIntire, they risked casting him has a victim, which would only increase his media profile. If, on the other hand, they absolved him of guilt, their conclusion might be seen as either a cowardly retreat or an actual endorsement of his position.

They avoided the trap. The panel's final report in January 1987, written by Schallert, concluded that "although Mr. McIntire's actions were potentially harmful to the Guild, their actual effects were so minimal that the Guild suffered no real damage," and that therefore "Mr. McIntire should NOT be charged with violating the Constitution and By-Laws." In other words, he was portrayed as someone who might have been dangerous if only he had been of any consequence; he was not so much condemned as belittled. Both sides were willing to consider the report a victory.[51]

The rank and file's views on all this became clear at the end of March. Facing a projected deficit of nearly $14 million over the next five years, in February the SAG board asked the members to approve an increase in dues and initiation fees. AWAG attacked the proposal, of course, arguing, in Morgan Paull's words, that "the current board of directors of SAG has recklessly and wantonly squandered our dues money. . . . until the board displays some semblance of fiscal responsibility towards our membership, AWAG cannot support, and indeed, strongly opposes, any proposed dues increase."[52]

Coming on the heels of the Heston/McIntire episode, it is safe to say that this referendum was viewed by the membership as a symbolic vehicle to express their opinions on the two factions. Their 71 percent vote for the proposed increases on 29 March must, therefore, be regarded as a ringing endorsement of the progressives. We can consequently expect the current leadership of the guild to continue to pursue the policies it has followed for the past five or six years, and anticipate that some conservatives will continue to try to dismantle the organization.[53]

Things to Come

While progressives and conservatives were pummeling each other in newspapers and boardrooms, the original cause of the political upheaval in 1981—the merger with AFTRA—was slouching toward realization. In a report to the membership in the fall 1986 edition of *Screen Actor*, Joseph Ruskin and Jordyce Bryntesen, cochairs of the National Merger Committee, revealed that their group had a plan that it was just about ready to submit to the boards of the two unions for approval.[54]

The new performers' union, its name still unchosen, would be organized along traditional lines, as an "association of autonomous locals." Gone would be SAG's centralized structure. "Each local would have fiscal autonomy, setting its own dues and budgets as it sees fit. Every local will have representatives on a National Board of Directors." As in most unions, the national president would be nominated at an annual convention. Unlike the case in most unions, however, in which the rank and file have no direct say in the choice of national leaders, the candidate, once nominated, would be submitted to a mail referendum of the entire membership. Since this would make challenges to the convention's decisions possible, opposition, and therefore democracy, would be assured.

Once the two boards approve the merger plan, which they are almost certain to do, the easy part will be over. It will have to be submitted to a vote of both memberships, and must draw 60 percent support from each to pass. It is certain to spark opposition. Although the official AWAG position is one of neutrality toward a merger, and conservatives will almost invariably answer, "I'd have to see the plan," when first asked whether they support fusion with AFTRA, further questioning reveals fundamental hostility to the whole idea.

Conservatives view merger with suspicion for many of the same reasons that progressives endorse it. The ever-bigger union that grows in power as it widens its representation seems to the conservative mind a structure guaranteed to submerge the individual concerns that the small union nurtures. The national officers that progressives desire because they draw prestige from the size of their organization seem, instead, like remote politicians to conservatives. Perhaps inconsistently, the structure based on locals that the progressives regard as fair to the rest of the country is seen as a strategem for diluting Hollywood's power.

Furthermore, AFTRA contains not just actors, but also news broadcasters. The conservative objection to being in a union with these people is similar to their objection to being in a union with extras: not being actors, they neither deserve to be associated with artists nor are trustworthy allies in a dispute. Although Ruskin and Bryntesen argue that "broadcasters and newspeople are already outnumbered in AFTRA now, and it hasn't caused any problems yet," many conservatives dispute this, saying that AFTRA's contracts are generally inferior to SAG's because the nonactors in AFTRA are reluctant to strike on behalf of actors' demands. (Many actors report, in addition, that the newscasters are hostile to the idea of a larger union in which they would be a still smaller minority.)

Finally, while the committee chairs proclaim that they "anticipate several economic savings through merger," conservatives scoff, predicting an endless string of dues increases if the unions are combined.

When the actual plan is submitted to the rank and file, all of these submerged objections will become manifest. Just as the ruling progressives were surprised at the extent and intensity of opposition to the SEG merger, they are going to be startled by the upsurge of hostility to combination with AFTRA. Whether or not the opposition will be strong enough to muster the required 41 percent vote to stop the merger, I can't say. But I predict that the Screen Actors Guild has not seen its last intense political struggle.

It is possible to imagine a future for the guild in which it simultaneously grows larger and smaller. It may double in size by merger while losing members because of Buckley or right-to-work. If that happened, it might in the end be the same size. It would certainly be more militant, as the leadership would not face the problem of having to deal with a large conservative constituency. But with a significant pool of nonguild members available for employment, producers might then decide that they had nothing to fear from a SAG strike, and decide to destroy it. The Screen Actors Guild may be facing the most dangerous era in its history. Stay tuned.

A man ought to do what he thinks is right.

John Wayne explaining his philosophy, *Hondo*, screenplay by James Edward Grant, based on *The Gift of Cochise* by Louis L'Amour

Chapter Eight

IDEOLOGY

Most politics is a struggle between interests over who gets what, partially or wholly disguised by appeals to principles. The principles are, however, real. If the mass of humanity did not believe in a set of ideas that legitimized one kind of decision instead of its alternative, there would be no point in the interests pretending that theirs was the more just cause. Without ideologies, which are systems of beliefs and values justifying one pattern of decision over another, social life would be simply an arena for cunning and force, and civilization would be very much less pleasant than it is.

The tendency of people to disguise their personal stake in a political decision by wrapping their arguments in ideology, however, makes the study of ideas difficult. When hearing a professed conviction, one is always tempted to look for the private motive behind the public declaration. Indeed, much research into the nature of philosophy boils down to the search for the social or personal interest that underlies, and therefore corrupts, the stated positions of political actors.[1]

Historically, this problem has been as acute in the study of union ideologies as in other political inquiry. Critics have frequently accused conservatism (which they like to call "business unionism") of being merely the justification offered by opportunists in the labor movement for the way they collaborate with management for personal gain. On the other hand, critics of progressivism sometimes accuse it of being a smoke screen behind which the antidemocratic forces of Marxism advance to battle.[2]

181

This tendency is, of course, mistaken. Both ideologies are well grounded in defensible values, and intellectually respectable. Because of their occasional association with unsavory motives, however, they are difficult to view in a pure state.

The Screen Actors Guild is perhaps the best laboratory we have for studying union ideologues who are free from distracting motivations. Performers who volunteer their time to guild government—serving on committees, running for the board of directors or a position as officer—do so knowing that they will receive no monetary compensation for their efforts. They further know, or at least believe, that they will not help themselves as actors by doing so. Almost every person I interviewed remarked on the way his or her career had been damaged by service to the guild, either because producers come to think of union officers as enemies, or because its time demands divert the performer from more lucrative activity.

Nor do activists benefit in a personal way from the contracts they negotiate. In the first place, since the great majority of contract provisions refer to the scale or minimum-wage actor, and most guild activists are established performers, very few things that they win in a negotiation are likely to affect them personally. In the second place, those contract provisions that do impinge on their working lives, such as limitations on working hours, apply to everyone equally and therefore cannot be acquired by one set of actors to the exclusion of another.

What this means is that participants in guild government bring to the union political process a set of ideas that are uncontaminated by a selfish perspective. A SAG activist is about as close to that mythical creature, the disinterested, public-spirited citizen, as exists anywhere. Social scientists seldom encounter elites with motives so clean.

As a consequence, they are ideal subjects for a study of labor ideology. When they give their preferences about how their union ought to be governed, we can be sure that it is a forthright set of beliefs and values, not a hidden agenda, that is organizing their opinions.

They Might Be Giants

For this book I interviewed fifty-six actors. Most of them have been involved in guild government, as evidenced by their candidacy, successful or otherwise, for a position on the board or higher office. A half-dozen or so have never run but have participated in other ways, such as contributing money to and allowing their names to be publicly associated with candidates, causes, or the like. Fifty-two are from the Hollywood branch, three from Dallas, and one from San Francisco. The omission of New York is unfortunate, and may skew the results. Since the center of gravity in the guild continues to be in Hollywood, however, that branch contains the overwhelming majority of important activists.

Among the performers in this sample are eight former or present presidents of the guild, at least a dozen officers, and at least three dozen members of the board. These categories, of course, tend to overlap.

In a survey such as this there is always a question about how well the sample represents the universe of people we are trying to study. There is no problem in this case; the sample pretty well covers the entire universe. With a few exceptions (and with the systematic exception of anyone from the New York branch), every important living Screen Actors Guild activist for the past fifteen years has contributed to the information in this survey. It does not include all people of significance to the guild, for it omits staff members, some of whom have been crucial in setting policy. Nevertheless, it captures the opinions of the actors who have governed themselves and their fellow performers through their union.

I have divided the sample into twenty-five progressives, twenty-five conservatives, and six centrists. In the great majority of cases, the actors did the dividing for me, choosing to run with the backing of one of the political factions or parties that have contested guild elections since 1971. In the remaining cases, I assigned people to one of the categories on the basis of their stated loyalties, their admiration for one set of candidates, or, in a very few cases, on the basis of their position on issues.

The centrists have often run with the backing of one or the other party, but they are so resentful of partisan labeling, and so inconsistent on issues, that I have found them impossible to categorize. Partly because they are a relatively small group, and partly because they are less interesting than the ideologues, I will not spend a great deal of time discussing their views in this chapter. Nevertheless, we should always remember that they exist, lest we fall into the error of believing that every important activist in the guild has chosen to live on only one side of the fence.

Table 8.1 summarizes some of the personal characteristics of these

Table 8.1. Screen Actors Guild Activists Summary Statistics

Characteristic	Number	Percentage
Philosophy		
Union philosophy:		
Progressive	25	44.6
Conservative	25	44.6
Centrist	6	10.7
Self-described political philosophy:		
Liberal	25	44.6
Middle-of-the-road	17	30.4
Conservative	10	17.9
Other or missing	4	7.1
Personal Background		
Age:		
Under 40	7	12.5
40 to 60	27	48.2
Over 60	19	33.9
Missing	3	5.4
Sex:		
Female	14	25
Male	42	75
Religious background:		
Protestant	20	35.7
Catholic	14	25
Jewish	14	25
Other	8	14.3
Father's (or mother's, if father absent) political party identification:		
Democratic	18	32.1
Republican	21	37.5
Other or missing	17	30.4
Father's (or mother's, if father absent) profession:		
Entrepreneur or professional	29	51.8
White-collar	9	16.1
Blue-collar	9	16.1
Art, acting, journalism	8	14.3
Missing	1	1.8
At least one parent a member of a labor union?		
Yes	15	26.8
No	28	50
Other or missing	13	23.2
Education:		
High school or below	8	14.3
At least some college	46	82.1
Other or missing	2	3.8

Table 8.1. Screen Actors Guild Activists Summary Statistics (*continued*)

Characteristic	Number	Percentage
Professional Experience		
Years in SAG:		
Under 15	7	12.5
15 to 30	19	33.9
Over 30	30	53.6
Attended acting school?		
Yes	26	46.4
No	9	16.1
Other or missing	21	37.5
Unemployed as an actor for more than a year?		
Yes	12	21.4
No	44	78.6
City where career began:		
Los Angeles	17	30.4
New York	20	35.7
Other	19	33.9
First job in which medium?		
Film	12	21.4
Television series	10	17.9
Stage	31	55.4
Television commercial	2	3.6
Radio	1	1.8
Balance of career in which medium?		
Film	10	17.9
Television series	20	35.6
Stage	6	10.7
Television commercials	1	1.8
No predominance, other, or missing	19	33.9
Other things (such as pay) being equal, prefers which medium?		
Film	24	42.9
Television series	3	5.4
Stage	19	33.9
Television commercials	1	1.8
No preference, other, or missing	9	16
Professional Success		
Type of actor (self-described):		
Character	31	55.4
Leading	19	33.9
Other or missing	6	10.7
Average yearly income from acting over previous five years (in thousands of dollars):		
50 or below	24	42.8
50 to 150	14	25
150 to 500	5	8.9
Above 500	6	10.7
Missing	7	12.5

Note: Figures do not always add up to 100 percent because of rounding.

activists. They differ in important ways from the rank and file they represent. Most strikingly, they are far more successful in their profession than is the average member of the guild. The typical "professional actor" works seldom or not at all. Although these activists are a relatively elderly group, they have been comparatively free from long-term unemployment (and some of those who report several years of no work really mean that they were blacklisted). Similarly, whereas only about 3 percent of SAG's members earn over $50,000 dollars a year from acting, 45 percent of my informants who are willing to report their income do so.[3]

The figures on professional experience, also, emphasize that these activists are unusually successful. Nowadays the majority of actors' employment comes from television commercials. In this sample, however, the great bulk of the work has been done either in television series or in movies, with little time spent on commercials.[4]

The activists are also demographically unlike the rank and file. There are no figures on the average education of screen actors, but 82 percent of activists attended college, undoubtedly making them more educated than the rank and file. Moreover, although the membership of the guild contains only slightly more men than women, three-quarters of the activists are male. Finally, whereas 7 percent of the guild's members are black and 3 percent are Hispanic, in this sample there is only one black (2 percent) and no Hispanics. There is, however, one Filipino-American.[5]

Since this book deals with the differences within the elite and not with those between the elite and the mass, the discussion here centers on just what it is that progressives and conservatives believe that causes so much conflict in guild councils.

Separate Tables

In their classic study of the Printers, Lipset, Trow, and Coleman summarize the ideological cleavage within labor as being one of militancy versus caution, deriving from the workers' identification of enemies. Even in the nineteenth century, they report, "one group saw as the primary foe sickness, accident, and death. The other saw as its primary foe the employer." This assertion is not inconsistent with my basic argument about guild activists, but it is too simple. Progressives and conservatives do tend to perceive different enemies, but that perception is itself the result of a more fundamental difference in outlook. More-over, the tendency to be militant or conciliatory in dealing with man-agement is related not just to the temperaments of the actors but also to their interpretations of their situation as workers and their attitudes about the union itself.[6]

In any discussion of patterns of beliefs and values, there will inev-itably be some distortion because of the need to ignore individual var-iations in pursuit of the general truth. The following discussion is no exception. The actors in this study are just as quirky and inconsistent as the members of any other group of political activists. No more than a handful on each side will conform completely to the "model" con-servative or progressive that I am going to describe. Further, none of them are robots; most of them reflect upon arguments made by the other side before deciding on their own position on issues. Never-theless, the overall direction of their thoughts and the general struc-ture of their opinions are so clear as to justify an assignment into two groups. The very occurrence of two-party election campaigns in the guild confirms that my analytic assumptions are grounded in reality.

Underlying the conflict between progressives and conservatives, then, is a fundamentally different orientation toward labor unions. Conservatives, while they do not necessarily reject the idea of voluntary group action, are primarily concerned with the individual, not the col-lective. They view the preservation of personal choice as the most im-portant value to be nurtured in society; they therefore oppose any or-ganization which threatens to submerge the one person in the many. Progressives, on the other hand, do not recognize a conflict between the organization and the individual. Instead, they believe that individ-uals are defined, supported, and protected by the group. Their out-look is communitarian. In a basic psychological sense, conservatives are loners and progressives are team players.

Conservatives are therefore somewhat uneasy with the whole idea of belonging to a labor union. While acknowledging the good that unions do, they retain a profound ambivalence about collective action, and so are always alert to the possibility that the organization may get out of hand. This ambivalence was most poignantly and ironically ex-pressed by Leon Ames, co-founder of the guild in 1933, longtime board member, multiple-term vice-president, and president in 1957, in a conversation we had in 1985.

Don Dubbins

LEON AMES: "Basically, I don't believe in unions."

DFP (spluttering somewhat in surprise): "Now, you understand that for me—you founded this union, and yet you say you don't believe in unions."

AMES: "I don't believe in unions at all. And the longer I'm connected with them, the less I believe in them. And the proof of the pudding is—look at the history and what's happening to them nationwide now."

DFP: "You're not saying that if you had it to live over again, you wouldn't found the Screen Actors Guild?"

AMES: "No. No. I learned from being a part of the union. It was necessary when they were formed. Back when we formed the actors, we accomplished what we went out to accomplish. And they [the progressives] are destroying it as fast as they can."

DFP: "Are you suggesting that a union is a good thing if it goes so far, but no farther?"

AMES: "That's right."

Although they obviously are not in a position to speak with the same historical disappointment, other conservatives plainly share Ames's ambivalence about the compulsory cooperation that is the essence of a labor union.

Jessica Walter

DON GALLOWAY: "You lose individualism and the needs of individuals when you form this monolith."[7]

DON DUBBINS: "I'm a union member, but I'm not a unionist. I'm not here to forward the union, I'm here to forward the labor" (people, not organization).[8]

MARK MCINTIRE: "I think you have to weigh two counterbalancing values. One . . . is the right of the union to grow and prosper and increase its membership and to simply collect its monies and spend it any way it wishes. Is that an over-riding right to the right of the individual to object? . . . My position is that the right of the individual—it's analogous to religion in a way. Everyone has the right to choose a religion. . . . Every person has the right to choose whether to be a union member or a non-union member."[9]

The progressives don't see it this way. To them, it is not a question of the individual versus the group. In the long run, they believe, group defense is individual self-preservation. Too much emphasis on personal choice must eventually destroy the strength of the group, which will leave individuals undefended in a hostile world.

JESSICA WALTER: "A labor union is not just about wages and working conditions. It's about protecting its members' civil rights. . . . It's about protecting the dignity of its members; it's about making the members feel

Sumi Haru

secure, united and strong. And especially when you're dealing with artists, it's about speaking out against the prejudices against artists in
other countries that are not as fortunate as we are to be allowed free
expression. . . . The union is Everyman. . . . We're related to all artists
everywhere. . . . I really feel very passionately about the union. It's such
an important part of our lives as artists and as human beings. . . . Without the union we'd be dead."[10]

ED ASNER (in September 1981, on why he was running for the presidency): "First of all, to instill in the minds of all our members that we
are a union, that a union carries certain responsibilities in providing
for its members, and that its members are encumbered by the responsibility of taking care of their union. . . . I would seek to ensure that
the big movie names react and respond as unionists, regarding themselves as part of a brotherhood or sisterhood, however they want to term
it. We must show the strength of unity."[11]

BERT FREED: "The purpose of a union is to represent the people who can't
otherwise be represented—they're splintered individuals. If you go on
that premise, it follows that the greatest strength derives from the
greater numbers acting in a unified manner; that's what 'union'
means."[12]

This difference of attitude toward the idea of the union is closely
connected to a disparate belief in actors as workers or artists. All per-

Table 8.2. Are Actors Laborers in the Sense of
          "Labor Union"?

	Yes	No	
Progressive	13 81.3 81.3 48.1	3 18.8 27.3 11.1	16
Conservative	3 27.3 18.8 11.1	8 72.7 72.7 29.6	11
	16	11	27

Notes: Gamma = .84; $p < .002$.

formers proudly consider themselves artists. But progressives go on to assert that in relation to management they are merely laborers, and as such share a common exploitation with other workers. In my interviews with them, here's how they answered my question, "Are actors laborers, in the sense of 'labor union?' "

PAUL KREPPEL: "When it comes time to be paid, yes, but when I'm learning my lines I'm an artist."

SUMI HARU: "Yes. We're trade unionists. We really should think of ourselves that way. . . . We need to be part of the labor movement. It's worker solidarity."

WILLIAM SCHALLERT: "Yes. The great bulk of the union does fall into the laboring category."

DAN CALDWELL: "An actor does labor, but he labors artistically."

Conservatives rejected this idea absolutely.

MARIE WINDSOR: "No. We're artists."

ANTHONY CARUSO: "No. That's why it's a guild [not a union]."

MORGAN PAULL: "No. Artists aren't workers."

The statistical differences between progressives and conservatives on this issue are very strong and significant (see table 8.2).

They also differ along another basic dimension. As Lipset and his colleagues discovered, conservatives do not believe that management constitutes a threat. To a conservative, reason and good faith among well-meaning people on both sides of the bargaining table will allow them to adjust their differences. Their interests are not opposed; all being in the industry together, it is to everyone's advantage to work together amicably. As a consequence, they are always reluctant to strike, although most will do so if the extremes of intransigence have been reached. Consider the following excerpts from my interviews:

JOHN GAVIN: "I never thought that management was the enemy."

CHARLTON HESTON: "It's to the advantage of all actors to bring in pictures as economically as possible" (because that increases the likelihood of employment in the future).

ROBERT EASTON: "You don't kill the goose that lays the golden eggs."

ED NELSON: "Their [the progressives'] concept is that management is always the enemy. That's a union concept. I don't think management is the enemy at all. . . . We're in this industry together, and if we don't cooperate with each other, we can't find justice."

MORGAN PAULL: "I've never understood what recently we have to strike for. . . . [The progressives have an] 'us against them' attitude. It's almost as if [they had] never worked on a set. Because we work *with* producers. It's not us against them; it's us *with* them."

Progressives are not diametrically opposed on this issue. Despite the conservatives' characterization of them as spoiling for confrontation, their actual attitude tends to be one of ambivalence. While acknowledging that without management there would be no jobs, they are nevertheless suspicious of its motives and goodwill. They are therefore likely to express cautious or contradictory opinions when queried about their attitudes toward the owners.

ED ASNER (when I asked him if he believes that there are irreconcilable differences between management and labor): "Not when management is enlightened. . . . There are wonderful plants where management profit-shares with the workers" (but there are none of these in the entertainment industry).

FRANK MAXWELL: "[In this historical era unions are not being confrontational] although there are times when I think they'd be a lot better off if they were."

Table 8.3 illustrates the differences between the two groups on the question of whether there are irreconcilable differences between management and labor. While the conservatives show a strong tendency to say "no," the progressives are split. The statistical relationships are thus weak and not significant. It is consequently fair to conclude that although the conservatives are by and large the cautious accommodationists that we would expect, the progressives as a group are somewhat

Table 8.3. Are There Irreconcilable Differences between Management and Labor?

	Yes	No	
Progressive	10	11	21
	47.6	52.4	
	76.9	57.9	
	31.3	34.4	
Conservative	3	8	11
	27.3	72.7	
	23.1	42.1	
	9.4	25	
	13	19	32

Notes: Gamma = .42; p = .14.

less than the combative militants of their reputation. Progressives appear pugnacious only when contrasted with the conservatives' friendliness toward the producers.

Thus, in the model conservative character a suspicion of group action is joined to a feeling of separateness from other workers and a basic faith in the good intentions of management. In contrast, the model progressive both accepts collective behavior and identifies at least partially with other workers, while harboring somewhat more suspicion of the bosses. The two philosophies thus spring from opposed views of life and work. What progressives urge as community defense, conservatives are bound to fear as an attack on individuality. What conservatives prescribe as voluntary association, progressives cannot but perceive as a threat to the union itself. What conservatives view as a reasonable readiness to trust the humanity of management, progressives are more apt to view as an eagerness to collaborate. Since the members of each group feel their own deepest values threatened by the opinions of the members of the other, it is no wonder that their disputes are so rancorous and so little marked by an advance toward agreement.

Differing as they do at the level of fundamentals, the two groups must also diverge on issues. Progressives see an advantage in joining in ever-larger combinations. Because workers are in some sense under a threat from management, and the labor movement is the means of defending the workers, the closer they are to it the better. For this reason they are receptive to stronger ties with other unions and with the AFL-CIO.

KATHLEEN NOLAN: "If we are going to survive in this industry, we must be activists. . . . As actors, we realize that we can't perform in a vacuum. Just as we need to collaborate with writers, producers, and directors to perform on film, so we will need coalitions, and political involvement with other actors, other unions and outside professionals in order to assure our future dignity and working conditions."[13]

PATTY DUKE: "I believe there's safety in numbers. . . . I think we're a very strong guild, but I don't think we're strong enough to survive out there all by ourselves."[14]

DEAN SANTORO (describing the atmosphere of the first CAM meetings in 1980): "At that point we were very idealistic. We said, 'We should *all* get together—Equity, the writers, the directors. Then we can have some power.' Which is true. It would be the smart thing for us to do. But we will never be that smart."[15]

Conservatives, on the other hand, fear the potentially oppressive hand of organized labor more than the possible domination of management. As a consequence they always resist plans to associate with other unions; they especially dislike the thought of closer ties to the AFL-CIO.

JOHN GAVIN (on closer AFL ties): "I would prefer the union to be pristine, and to be independent" (because involvement with the labor movement always pulls a union into politics, and political participation is bad because) "this organization ought to be about wages, working conditions, retirement benefits, ancillary benefits, etc."[16]

CHARLTON HESTON: "Unions giving each other moral and financial support is a very archaic principle that has been widely repudiated. . . . I think we should reassess and re-evaluate our relationship with the AFL-CIO. We owe our members more than considering ourselves foot soldiers in big labor's batallions."[17]

MARIE WINDSOR: "The AFL-CIO does little or nothing for us. They ask for money, want us to march for waiters, the steel industry and they use our visible actors who are big labor minded to march and speak for them. They need us and our money more than we need them."[18]

Similarly, the basic values of each group determines their perspectives on the question of outside political involvement. To repeat, this is not a question of participating in lobbying campaigns for or against legislative bills on subjects that directly affect actors; everyone endorses that. But the progressives, as a matter of principle, do not want to stop there. Feeling themselves part of a threatened class, they want to take positions on many subjects in order to forestall attack from many different directions, as their comments in my interviews with them reveal:

JEFF COREY: "I don't think a trade union can exist on a stilt."

KATHLEEN NOLAN: "We've always been involved in issues that are not just wages and working conditions, because all these other issues involve, ultimately, wages and working conditions in my mind. Because ultimately the way people feel about you, and your dignity, determines the way they are going to treat you. And right now we are treated very badly."

ED ASNER (on the value of political action by the labor movement): "Just as every progressive act that has gone through Congress in the last hundred years has either been initiated or abetted by union aid, there would be a greater progressive attitude by the average citizen, a banding together of brothers and sisters, and a greater concern for . . . the homeless and the hungry, a lessening of 'I'm all right, Jack,' and a greater drive toward one for all, all for one. . . . Where I'd like to go is less disparity between rich and poor."

Not surprisingly, this attitude gives conservatives the willies. Although conservative SAG administrations did participate in politics during the anti-Communist years, that participation was an exception to their general aloofness. It is not just that progressives invariably want to support a liberal political agenda, but that they seem to want to rush into all manner of endorsements and commitments. Conservatives, with their constant focus on individual rights, behold in this promiscuous cascade of activity a steady stream of violations of personal choice. Here's what they said to me:

ROBERT EASTON: "[Robert Montgomery, Leon Ames, and others founded the guild] primarily to help their fellow actors. . . . [It was] a thing of service . . . altruism. I wish to God it had stayed at that level. Before the guild became political it quite properly represented a wide cross-section of views."

DON DUBBINS: "[Conservatives call progressives] the 'giveaway group.' They want to spend actors' money on four million different things that have nothing to do with actors. [We want to] concentrate on wages, hours, and working conditions. We don't need to worry about day schools for children, or things like that."

MARK MCINTIRE: "The basic problem under the Asner regime, which he inherited from his predecessor, Bill Schallert, was that there were no priorities. The guild was just wandering like a centipede, sniffing to the right, sniffing to the left . . . and whatever squeaky wheels demanded action, got it."

On the issue of union membership in general declining: "I believe that one of the reasons they have been declining is because they simply rake money in and ship it out to political candidates, causes and issues with which a large section of their working constituency disagrees, and when these objections are made known they say, 'Poof. Poof. Poof. Nothing you can do about it. We're a union shop'. . . . And I believe if a sufficient number of members took advantage of financial core status. . . . If they dissent . . . then it would force the union to do the thing that it does best: negotiate the contract and stop right there."[19]

In a like manner, progressives see a value in attempting to bring pressure to bear within the industry to correct wrongs they perceive being visited on some actors. A threat to one group, in their communitarian world view, is a threat to everyone. The guild consequently has a variety of committees working to persuade producers to adopt affirmative action programs to increase the proportion of female, minority, elderly, and handicapped actors in their casts. So far these efforts have been only slightly successful, but the progressives are nonetheless determined to persist. As William Schallert pointed out to me:

"If they [children] never see a black face on television, if they never see a Chicano, if they never see a disabled person, and if they only see women in certain kinds of roles, they're going to get a very strong imprint from that, at the tender age that they start watching. . . . That's why I think our affirmative action programs have a very strong defensible posture about them, that is, they serve a larger social purpose than simply employment. . . . You want television to reflect what real life is about."

The conservative position is, of course, directly contrary. Mark McIntire told me that in his view, "affirmative action is a form of discrimination. Therefore, it is unconstitutional, and we [AWAG] oppose it. The guild would be better served by dismantling all of those committees and reapportioning all of those staff people, and concentrating on getting more jobs and better working conditions for *all* actors."

The philosophical cleavages between progressives and conservatives are therefore sharply etched and passionately felt. We must then ask, from where do these divisions come? Are workers in general and actors in particular born with different attitudes? Do they derive from family training? Or is there something about the experience of working that tends to form the variations in outlook that give rise to union ideologies?

The Way We Were

As part of their study of the Printers, Lipset and his colleagues attempted to uncover background variables that would explain, through statistical relationships, the tendency of union activists to endorse either progressivism or conservatism. In this they were not notably successful. One of their major problems was that printers are all pretty much alike: they earn roughly the same pay for doing roughly the same job. It is difficult to find variations where almost none exist. Their only two definite findings were that printers from lower-class backgrounds leaned more to the Left than those from higher on the class scale, and that Protestants tended to be more conservative than Jews.[20]

In the ensuing decades scholars have made much progress in learning about union politics, especially in regard to the circumstances that tend to enhance the possibility for democracy within labor unions. They have not paid much attention, however, to the problem of explaining the sources of different union ideology.[21]

Unlike the Printers, the Screen Actors Guild contains members of wildly different backgrounds. Activists come from all sections of the continent and from every social milieu. They have experienced extremes of success in their careers, from many years of obscure struggle to almost instantaneous celebrity (Patty Duke, for example, won an Academy Award at the age of sixteen). Various performers among them have spent their time acting under quite dissimilar conditions. If anything in the personal or professional background of unionists can help to explain their choice of philosophy, we should be able to detect it in these actors.

I started with a general theory of the sources of a worker's orientation toward organized labor. In the first place would be the general variations in personal background which we know are correlated with political belief and voting choice in the larger society. These include a citizen's religious background, social class background (in this case, measured by reference to father's occupation), political party background (father's identification), whether or not either the mother or father were members of a labor union, and the amount of education received by the actor.

Second, it seemed to me that any employee's professional experience must play an important role in forming his or her attitudes toward working, management, and the union. Specifically in regard to actors, the number of years in SAG, and the amount of time unemployed would most likely have an impact on attitudes toward labor organization. So also would whether or not the performer attended acting school. In addition, because actors work under different conditions depending on whether they are on stage, in television series, in the movies, or making commercials, there are three questions which I expected to be related to ideology: In what medium did you get your first job? In what medium have you spent the balance of your career? Other things (such as pay) being equal, in what medium do you prefer to work? (There are other possibilities, such as industrial films, but they are relevant mostly to actors outside Hollywood.) Finally, because the folklore of the industry emphasizes the differences in "political culture" between New York and Los Angeles, I expected to find that actors who began their careers in the different cities would have different unionist orientations.

Third, it was logical to expect that the success of an actor would have an independent impact on his or her philosophy. Success creates a hierarchy of prestige and reward that fashions a mini class system within the profession. This would be measured in two ways, first by asking for the activists' average income from acting over the previous five years, and second by inquiring as to whether they considered themselves to be leading or character actors. Both higher income and a status as a leading actor, according to my initial expectations, should be associated with conservative beliefs and values.

Finally, Lipset, Trow, and Coleman found that the general political philosophy of the printers correlated highly with their union ideologies. This is a somewhat different expectation, in regard to personal and professional background and success, than the first three parts of the theory. There, the assumption is that beliefs and values formed in a person's life experience play a role in causing his or her philosophical choices. But there is no assumption here that political ideology causes union ideology. Most likely, both are the consequence of the same formative experiences. It is possible, or even likely, that more detailed research would conclude that each is the manifestation, in slightly different arenas, of the same set of ideals.[22]

Be that as it may, the hypothesis here is that they are related. Not wishing to waste time in a lengthy interview by trying to measure and correlate these activists' opinions on national issues, I simply asked them if they considered themselves to be liberal, conservative, or middle-of-the-road in national politics.

Table 8.4 presents a summary of all the hypothesized variables and their actual statistical relationship to membership in the progressive and conservative categories. Gammas are used because the nominal

Table 8.4. Background Variables and Union Ideology

Variables	Relationship to Ideology (Gamma)
Personal background	
Religious background (omitting "other")	− .66
Father's political party	.38
Union family	.29
Father's occupation	− .16
Actor's education	− .11
Professional experience	
Balance of career	− .81
Preference	− .81
Acting school	.65
First job	− .62
City where started	− .60
Unemployed	.19
Years in SAG	.15
Success	
Leading or character	− .55
Income	.09
Political ideology	.93

variables render correlation coefficients meaningless. The statistics reveal that although some of the expected associations are present, many are not. In particular, using .50 as a threshold, with the exception of religion the personal background variables perform poorly. (This is family religious background, not the denomination of the actor—actors are not typically devout). In other words, my theory seemed to give too much weight to these actors' experiences before they entered their profession.

On the other hand, five of the variables measuring aspects of professional experience show a robust association with ideology. The indicators of the medium in which the actors have spent the balance of their careers, and the medium they prefer, are especially strong. (I should note here that these associations are not quite as clear as they appear because of missing data. Some actors stated that they had no preference, or maintained that their career was so varied that it was impossible to identify one predominating medium. The reported statistics are for those who answered the questions unambiguously.) The variables measuring the medium of first job, and the city where the actor started, are also strong. The former variable washes out, however, when the latter is controlled.

Perhaps surprisingly, the primary "success" variable, that for income, shows no relationship to ideology. Moreover, the "type of actor" variable, which appears so strong, washes out when several of the other variables are controlled. Just as social-class background seems to have little determining effect on unionist ideology in SAG, so also does the social "class" that the actor attains in the profession appear to bear no relationship to his or her belief system. In this way, at least, actors in the 1980s are different from printers in the 1950s.

Just as Lipset and his colleagues discovered, however, the larger political philosophy of these activists is strongly related to their union ideology. Twenty out of twenty-four self-described political liberals are union progressives; nine out of nine political conservatives are union conservatives. Rather curiously, the self-described political middle-of-the-roaders are not evenly split between the two ideologies, but are predominantly conservative in their union beliefs. The conservative faction thus appears to contain a greater span of political diversity within its own ranks than does the progressive.

Following the canons of social science, I attempted to control every one of these variables by checking to see if it could be an artifact of any of the others. Tables 8.5 through 8.10 illustrate the relationships that stand independently when all possible controls have been exhausted.

These relationships are very strong when taken one at a time, and when combined are amazingly so. For example, of the nine actors in the sample who both began in New York and prefer stage acting, every one is a progressive; of the eleven who both began in Los Angeles and

Table 8.5. Union Ideology by Religion

Ideology	Religion				
	Protestant	Catholic	Jewish	Other	
Progressive	5	7	9	4	25
	20	28	36	16	
	27.8	53.8	81.8	50	
	10	14	18	8	
Conservative	13	6	2	4	25
	52	24	8	16	
	72.2	46.2	18.2	50	
	26	12	4	8	
	18	13	11	8	50

Notes: V = .40; G = − .43; $p < .05$. Omitting "Other": V = .44; G = − .66; $p < .01$.

Table 8.6. Union Ideology by Balance of Career

Ideology	Balance of Career			
	Film	TV	Stage	
Progressive	1 6.7 10 3.2	9 60 60 29	5 33.3 83.3 16.1	15
Conservative	9 56.3 90 29	6 37.5 40 19.4	1 6.3 16.7 3.2	16
	10	15	6	31

Notes: V = .56; G = − .81; $p <$ .001.

Table 8.7. Union Ideology by Preference

Ideology	Preference			
	Film	TV	Stage	
Progressive	5 22.7 23.8 11.9	2 9.1 100 4.8	15 68.2 78.9 35.7	22
Conservative	16 80 76.2 38.1	0	4 20 21.1 9.5	20
	21	2	19	42

Notes: V = .58; G = − .81; $p <$ .001.

Table 8.8. Union Ideology by Acting School Attendance

Ideology	Attended Acting School?		
	Yes	No	
Progressive	14 82.4 70 48.3	3 17.6 33.3 10.3	17
Conservative	6 50 30 20.7	6 50 66.7 20.7	12
	20	9	29

Notes: G = .65; $p <$ .05.

Table 8.9. Union Ideology by Where Career Began

Union Ideology	Where Career Began			
	LA	NY	Other	
Progressive	2	12	11	25
	8	48	44	
	12.5	70.6	64.7	
	4	24	22	
Conservative	14	5	6	25
	56	20	24	
	87.5	29.4	35.3	
	28	10	12	
	16	17	17	50

Notes: $V = .52$; $G = -.60$; $p < .001$.

Table 8.10. Union Ideology by Political Ideology

Union Ideology	Political Ideology			
	Liberal	Middle	Conservative	
Progressive	20	4	0	24
	83.3	16.7		
	83.3	28.6		
	42.6	8.5		
Conservative	4	10	9	23
	17.4	43.5	39.1	
	16.7	71.4	100	
	8.5	21.3	19.1	
	24	10	9	47

Notes: $V = .69$; $G = .93$; $p < .001$.

prefer movies, ten are conservatives. Clearly there is something here that needs to be explained.

First, however, a word about the centrists. With a total of only six, there is nothing that can be said about them with confidence. Nonstatistical inspection of individual cases reveals that they have all gone to acting school, and suggests that they tend to have spent the balance of their careers doing television series. Beyond these faint hints, there are no regularities.

Patterns

The evidence from these fifty-six activists reveals that there are definite traits which tend to be associated with differing union political ideologies among actors (see table 8.11).

Plainly, my theory must be modified. If we put aside national political ideology as probably a result of the same forces that make for union philosophy, and not a cause of that philosophy, then it is clear that professional experience has a tremendous impact on an actor's system of beliefs and values. Experience on and preference for the stage are strongly associated with progressivism; experience in and preference for the movies are strongly associated with conservatism. In order to come up with a plausible theory of why this is so, it is necessary to remind ourselves about the different circumstances of working in each medium.

Acting in the theater is a community enterprise. Because plays are done live, they must be performed in sequence, proceeding from first to last scene in logical order. The actors are thus constantly attempting to relate their individual performances to the whole. Similarly, the members of the cast rely upon one another, for an individual failure spoils the overall effect. Further, players have to adapt their performances anew to each night's crowd, and therefore must be constantly sensitive to the reactions of the audience.

Despite this "ensemble" nature of stage acting, however, it is also the medium in which performers have maximum control of their craft. Once the curtain rises, an actor knows that what he or she does is what the audience will see. No director, cutter, or other technician can in-

Table 8.11. Summary of Variables Related to Union Ideology

Rank Order of Importance	What Disposes an Actor to Be Progressive?	What Disposes an Actor to Be Conservative?
1. Political Ideology	Political Liberal	Political Conservative
2. Balance of Career	TV or Stage	Film
2. (Tie) Preference	Stage	Film
4. Religious Background	Jewish	Protestant
5. Attended Acting School?	Yes	No
6. Began Where?	Anywhere but Los Angeles	Los Angeles

terpose. For this reason it is a truism among performers that "stage is the actor's medium."

Stage acting is therefore simultaneously the arena in which performers feel themselves part of a group enterprise and believe themselves to be in control of their own work.

The experience of screen acting is contrary in every respect. Films (and, to a somewhat lesser extent, television series and commercials) are shot with scenes out of sequence, to be reassembled in proper order in the cutting-room. Because of this, actors do not depend much on one another, for even stars in the same film may have separately-shot scenes and thus never meet. In addition, because the camera does not function as an audience, motion-picture actors must respond to their own inner cues, or to their director, in fashioning a performance. Film acting is thus an individual, not an ensemble, profession.

Furthermore, once a performance has been shot, it is beyond the actor's influence. Directors may shoot one scene many times, then pick the one example that fits their own conception of the tone of the story. Editors will cut and splice different shots to create a nuance in or cadence to a scene that no one in the cast intended. Every successful actor has a story of one of his or her greatest performances ending on the cutting-room floor. For this reason actors almost invariably say that "film is the director's medium."

Motion-picture acting is therefore simultaneously the medium in which performers feel that they are working as individuals and believe that final responsibility for their work is out of their hands.

> DAN CALDWELL (on stage): "You must be more in touch with yourself and with your fellow actors . . . because stage is a total ensemble experience where the actor is really in control of his art, and film is not." In film: "You're just a piece. Your performance is not in your own hands on film; but on stage you are totally in control." If a stage actor: "You're more prone to be a bleeding-heart liberal because you are more in touch with yourself and the people that you're working with, because they are there all the time; you're living with them. . . . You're not simply coming in, doing a thing, and leaving."[23]
>
> BERT FREED: "On stage, *you* are responsible." (Whereas in the movies the actor is at the mercy of the director and editor.) "So if you consider yourself an actor, and you are your own artist, and what you're doing is *yours*, the only way it is always yours . . . [is to be on stage]."[24]

Both these gentlemen are progressives. Conservatives, who were usually quite articulate in elucidating their ideas, tended to show an

Fritz Feld

uncharacteristic uncertainty when asked to explain why there might be a link between the movies and conservatism. Most of their comments to me seemed to emphasize the individual pleasure in mastering the variety of roles that are available to the successful film actor.

> FRITZ FELD: "Recognizing the value of the stage, yet, if you are lucky enough to work [in the movies] like I was, to do one thing after another, the creativeness is triumphant; it cannot compare with the stage."

Progressivism is a philosophy that emphasizes community solidarity and attempts by workers to control their own lives. Conservatism is a philosophy that emphasizes individual independence and encourages workers to mind their own business. Is it any wonder that the former is associated with the stage and the latter with the movies?

It might be objected here that no causation can be inferred from the association of ideology with "balance of career," since it is entirely possible that conservatives choose to work in film and progressives to work on stage. Only major stars, however, are free to choose their roles. I hope I have established in this book that the working lives of even successful actors are quite precarious. In such a desperate job market, they must take any opportunity they can get short of outright pornography—and sometimes, when they are young, unknown, and hungry, even that. The stars can choose their parts and thus their medium, but, as a generous estimate, no more than five individuals in this sample fall into that favored category. The other fifty-one have chosen the city in which they wish to live (although even that choice is severely constrained, since by far the most jobs are in the Los Angeles area), but cannot choose the medium in which they work.

To return to the substantive point, the association of a background in acting school with progressivism should not be surprising. After so much socialization into the craft and culture of acting, performers would naturally be expected to be rather touchy about their control of their work. This might very well incline them to militancy in a union, which would translate into progressive ideology. This is a speculative argument, of course, but it fits smoothly with the rest of the evidence.

And what of television? Most acting work is done there, not on the stage or in the movies. This is, however, deceiving. Although most actors work on TV, they would rather be either in a theater or on a film set. Of the fifty-six actors in this sample, only three picked television as their medium of choice. Most performers labor in television to sustain themselves while they wait for offers to work in a more desirable medium.

Given the foregoing interpretation of union ideology, the association of religious background with the two philosophies becomes comprehensible. Decades of historical and sociological scholarship have established that Protestantism is a radically individualistic religion. Protestantism, especially the ascetic type that has historically predominated in the United States, created, in the famous words of Max Weber, "a feeling of unprecedented inner loneliness of the single individual . . . he was forced to follow his path alone. . . . No one could help him." Not surprisingly, this lonely perspective tends to permeate the Protestant's view of secular issues as well. To many Protestants, the prospect of any group action is distasteful. Given the reality of union membership, however, they naturally gravitate toward the individualistic communal life envisioned by conservative ideology.[25]

On the other hand, Jewish association with the communal viewpoint of progressivism is also consistent with our historical understanding. A great deal of scholarship has confirmed the political liberalism of American Jews. The Jews' traditional status as a pariah group has tended to make them identify with underdogs; their philosophical tradition has tended to orient them toward group defense. As Jewish scholar Stephen Isaacs put it in *Jews and American Politics*, "Fear undoubtedly is the greatest single factor accounting for Jews' high level of political activity. . . . The Jews of America are, in the main, a product of the psychic ravages of the Western world's deeply entrenched pattern of Jew-hating. . . . Christianity stresses salvation in the afterlife, whereas Judaism stresses obligation to perform good on earth."[26]

Earlier in this chapter I characterized the progressive creed as "group defense is individual self-preservation." From the evidence of Jewish scholarship, this might just as well be taken as a typically Jewish attitude.

Religious world views, surviving in secularized form, thus seem to reinforce other life experiences in producing different orientations to the labor movement.

At any rate, although the effects of religious background which Lipset and his colleagues discovered among printers in the 1950s are evidently strong among actors in the 1980s, the importance of social class is apparently absent. This should not be surprising. Class is an ambiguous concept which must have only an indirect effect on political ideology. Religious belief, on the other hand, is almost by definition an ideology. When a person becomes an actor he or she leaves class behind, but even the atheists are most likely to retain some version of their early religious world view.

As for the relationship between a Los Angeles background and conservatism, and a start anywhere else and progressivism, I can only appeal to the vague notion of "political culture" and let it go at that.

Modern Times

This has been a case study of ideology among actors, but it has applications to all other unionized workers. My theory is simple. To the extent that a worker's personal background (especially religion) and work experience emphasize an individualist outlook, and to the extent that they do not foster the belief that workers should control the context of their labor, that employee should tend toward a conservative union ideology. To the extent that the worker's personal background and work experience emphasize a communitarian outlook and do foster the notion that workers should control their laboring life, that employee should tend toward a progressive ideology. Holding religion constant, therefore, we should be able to make informed guesses about the balance of ideology in different occupations, depending upon the extent to which each fosters individualism or a reliance upon the group.

All of this would require a good deal of empirical confirmation, of course. Nevertheless, some hypotheses suggest themselves. Other things being equal, coal miners should be more progressive than gold miners. Railroad engineers and airline pilots should be more progressive than truck and cab drivers. Football, basketball, and baseball players should be more progressive than golfers, tennis players, or boxers. Fire fighters should be more progressive than police officers. High-school teachers should be more progressive than college professors. Unions that are similar to the Screen Actors Guild in that they contain large segments of their membership that traditionally work in either individualistic or group-oriented jobs can be expected to harbor a potential for two-party politics. For example, musicians work either in a group (a band or orchestra) or alone. The musicians' union is therefore subject to ideological cleavage. These are my testable predictions.

I cannot explain the Printers. But then, neither could Lipset, Trow, and Coleman.

Time, Alec. Do you ever think about time? It goes, Alec.
Tick, tick, tick. You can almost hear it go by. Before you know
it, it's gone.

Bette Davis to Ronald Reagan, *Dark Victory*, screenplay by Casey
Robinson, based on the play by George Brewer, Jr., and Bertram
Bloch

Chapter Nine

VALEDICTION

These are perilous times for unions. According to the Gallup poll, the
public considers only people who write advertisements, sell insurance,
and peddle cars to be less ethical than labor leaders. Since the mid-
1960s the number of adults who claim that they disapprove of unions
outright has grown from 19 to 27 percent. Meanwhile, as the position
of American industry in the world market has declined, management
has taken advantage of the low esteem in which unions are held to
launch an offensive against them. Some of its measures, such as moving
plants to right-to-work states, are legal. Others, such as firing organizers, are not. All, however, have been effective in causing severe de-
clines in labor's membership. The percentage of the American work
force enrolled in a union peaked at about 35 percent in 1954 and has
declined steadily since then to its current level of under 18 percent.
For over a decade, unions have lost more than half of their NLRB certification elections every year. Things are so bad that top labor leaders
are seriously worried that the movement may soon become irrelevant
to American life.[1]

This would be a tragedy. Although the goals of management and
labor no doubt converge over the long run, in the short run it is in
management's interest to exploit its work force to the maximum. In
the absence of unions this is relatively easy. Of the two things necessary
to wield power, resources and organization, management has both and
atomized workers have neither. The historical record is absolutely clear
that in the absence of protective associations of their own, ordinary
employees are helpless before an ownership that ignores their health,

safety, and quality of life while working them long hours for minimum compensation. If the labor movement were to disappear, we would return to the dark ages of industrial misery that prevailed before the 1930s. The decline of American labor, therefore, should be of concern to every humane person.[2]

Furthermore, much of the present criticism of organized labor is based on false information. The common perception that unionized workers, for example, are less productive than their nonunion counterparts is simply wrong; they are more so. The equally common notion that unions contribute to inflation by extorting unjustifiably high wages is also greatly overstated. One study concluded that of the 68 percent rise in consumer prices between 1975 and 1981, only 2.3 points could be attributed to unions.[3]

Nevertheless, although the current indictment of labor is exaggerated, there is no doubt that its leaders have contributed to their own decline. It is hard to expect public sympathy for a movement when so many of its component parts are mired in corruption and tyranny. Moreover, as the economy has evolved over the last generation, taking jobs from the industrial sector and transferring them to the service sector, unions have been extremely lax in attempting to organize the new white-collar employment that has been replacing the old blue-collar jobs. It's fair to say that much of union leadership, rather than providing solutions to labor's malaise, has been part of the problem.[4]

Something Short of Paradise

At first glance, the Screen Actors Guild would appear to be an exception to this pattern of deterioration. From a few hundred members in the mid-1930s the guild has expanded to over sixty thousand, and is presently adding several thousand recruits a year. While only the Hollywood and New York branches existed for its first fifteen years, there are now twenty-three branches, with four being added just in the past decade. Beginning in 1952, residuals contracts negotiated by SAG's leaders for their constituents have brought in a supplementary income that in 1987 broke the $1 billion mark. Guild claims representatives collect an additional $6 million a year for the membership. With a record of unusual member participation in its government, an almost complete lack of personal corruption among its officers, and a vigorous democratic process, SAG would seem to be a paragon among unions, and the picture of organizational health.[5]

The portrait is deceiving. Outside, historical forces are making the guild's mission of protecting ordinary actors more difficult every year. Inside, factional quarreling is threatening to rip the organization apart. It may be only a matter of time before the Screen Actors Guild follows the rest of American labor down the path of decay and disaster.

The tide of history is probably the more dangerous of these trends because it is out of the control of the leadership. The decline of the studio system and the rise of independent production have greatly multiplied the number of people whom the guild must police in its attempt to enforce its contracts. As more and more producers make films, there are increasing numbers of complaints by actors of abuse and exploitation. As the number of complaints rises, the staff falls farther behind in dealing with them, and larger numbers of the rank and file become more frustrated with the guild's services. The bedrock, unchangeable fact of mass unemployment adds further fuel to the membership's resentment. This means that there is always a large reservoir of disgruntled actors ready to be mobilized by factions or individuals within the guild who want to launch an insurgency. The leadership cannot pacify the membership; the best it can do is hang on.[6]

Further, the trend toward runaway production increases the helplessness felt by the unemployed in Hollywood, adds further strain to SAG's centralized governmental structure, and creates jurisdictional headaches concerning the treatment of actors in foreign countries.

Adding to these problems is a more psychological change. The acquisition of Hollywood's studios by conglomerate corporations has increased the distance between the actor and the boss. Old-time members of the guild unanimously agree that the moguls of a previous era, despite their ruthlessness, had both a paternal affection for the Hollywood community and a weakness for personal appeal. Whatever the disagreement, they could be talked to and sometimes convinced to modify an opinion. Now, however, almost everyone asserts that a hard impersonality has taken over the management of the studios. At contract time, SAG negotiators no longer feel that they are arguing within the family. They report a chilling sense of efficient enmity radiating from the other side of the table.

Meanwhile, as history has intensified the challenges the guild must face, it has simultaneously weakened the organization from within. In the old days the stars ran the guild. Whatever the disadvantages of this system, it ensured that the most important and respected actors were in charge of negotiations. Take, for example, the guild of forty years ago, 1947. Besides president Ronald Reagan, officers included Gene Kelly, William Holden, and George Murphy. On the board, among others, sat Joseph Cotten, Henry Fonda, Glenn Ford, Gregory Peck, Robert Taylor, Claire Trevor, and Jane Wyman. Whether they were negotiating with management, playing union politics in the AFL, or representing their membership to the public, these were people whose names compelled respect. Now, however, almost all the big stars are also producers, and thus ineligible to serve. In the current leadership, probably only Patty Duke, Ed Asner, and Cliff Robertson could be considered of the same magnitude as their counterparts of yesteryear. Those who must run the organization, whatever their estimable qualities, simply don't have the clout with the outside world that their predecessors enjoyed.[7]

In addition, the actor-activists of 1947 faced a much less complicated problem than those of today. They negotiated only one contract, for motion pictures made almost entirely in Hollywood, every three years. The guild now must deal with contracts for films and television series one year, TV commercials the next, and industrial films the next, whereupon the cycle begins again. And, as the technology of amusement mutates, the actors are constantly being faced with new, unorganized media: now SAG's leaders are attempting to fashion a contract for performers in music videos. Moreover, the many independent producers who are located in other states must now be dealt with by the guild's local branches at the same time. For a squad of well-meaning amateurs with no training in law or economics, this is a nearly overwhelming challenge. Although they are assisted by a competent, professional staff with the requisite training, the actors, as the ones who are supposed to make the policy, can easily slip out of their depth.

Thank Your Lucky Stars

If the guild is to prevail in this hostile, complex industry of the 1980s, it must find good leadership. In particular, the qualities that the president brings to the job are becoming ever more important. The chief executive, of course, does not technically dominate the board, which is the actual governing body of the union. Nevertheless, as this book has demonstrated, in the absence of an effective president the guild lacks direction, the board frequently dissolves in factionalism, and the organization as a whole gives the impression of weakness. In a town where perceptions are so important, the impression of weakness quickly turns into its reality.

There is, then, no substitute for leadership at the top. And to appreciate how difficult it is going to be to find volunteers for that top job who possess the proper credentials, consider what it is that the ideal Screen Actors Guild president has to do:

1. Symbolize the organization, embodying the best that actors see in themselves, while representing that best to the outside world.

2. Mobilize and educate the rank and file in speeches and written communications, so that they will support initiatives of the leadership. In the context of today's SAG, this means endorsing the eventual merger plan so that it will receive the mandatory 60 percent referendum vote, and, every third year, explaining the inevitable compromises in the new movie and TV contracts so that there will be a minimum of disappointment.

3. Preside firmly yet fairly at board meetings.

4. Marshall votes at board meetings so that everyone, at some point, feels part of the governing majority.

5. Make policy choices. The president must throw his or her weight behind, for example, different options for spending money—more committees, more travel, more contributions to worthy causes?

6. Help negotiate the contract, or at least be knowledgeable enough about its possible provisions to be able to understand the bargains that are being struck by the staff and the negotiating committee.

7. Heal the factional split in the guild, or at least fashion a workable compromise between progressives and conservatives so that their wrangling will not paralyze it. It would be immensely helpful if the president were able to project a centrist, nonpartisan image so as to be able to work amicably with both sides.

This would be a tall order even for a career politician. For an actor, it mandates at least two requirements. First, future presidents simply must be stars, and preferably superstars. Since presidents don't possess a great deal of formal power, they must use their prestige to inspire support. It is a curious thing, but actors, and even fairly well-known ones, are just as star-struck as the average member of the public. They will follow a glittering name purely on the basis of the name. If the guild is to function effectively, it must be led by someone whose appearance in the room is enough to compel majority assent. Dozens of such people belong to the guild; the problem lies in convincing one of them to make the personal and financial sacrifices necessary to become a leader.

Second, a president must have experience in guild government before being elected. While it is possible to fulfill the first requirement and possibly the second without ever having sat on the board, the remaining prerequisite skills can be learned only through several years of unpaid apprenticeship attending committee meetings, reading reports, and arguing policy. The careers of Ed Asner and Patty Duke illustrate what happens to even capable people when they are plunked down in the middle of guild government without preparation. Their problems should serve as a warning to other stars who may at this moment be considering starting their career in union politics at the top.

To summarize, the guild needs to find a handful of world celebrities who are willing to give up millions of dollars a year and several evenings a week to immerse themselves in tedious and thankless details, purely out of their sense of service to their fellow actors. This may sound like a ludicrously impossible recommendation, but it's been done before.

The Accomplices

The guild would not be in desperate need of leadership, of course, had not factional contention reached such a pitch that it presently threatens the union's survival. The fact is that progressives and conservatives have arrived at a stage in their relationship at which they now seem to hate each other more than they love the guild. It is not my intention to take sides in this argument, both because I am not an actor and because I think that both sides are at fault. But I do want to offer some friendly, constructive criticism to both sides, and suggest a strategy for learning to live with each other.

First, actors should discard the misconception that their own politics are unusually difficult because they are a particularly emotional group of people. This prejudice is common among nonactors, but I was surprised to find it among guild activists. They frequently try to explain the intensity of their own politics by observing that actors, by temperament and training, react emotionally rather than analytically to problems, and that sensible decision-making is therefore beyond their reach. In expressing this opinion, however, I think that they overestimate the level of reason and restraint to be encountered elsewhere in politics. Having read about and observed government in action in the United States Congress and five state legislatures, several national and state regulatory agencies, and four university political science departments, I can testify that stupidity, perversity, and neurosis are everywhere a very large component of human affairs. Granted that actors sometimes do strange and repulsive things, but that does not make them distinctive. If other people can govern themselves in relative peace, so can actors.

The fact that they can, however, does not mean that they will. The people in each of the guild's factions seem to adhere stubbornly to a characteristic approach to its problems. In each case, this approach is becoming self-destructive, but the activists cannot seem to escape from it.

Nine months after he left office, Ed Asner and I had a conversation in which he showed that he had learned a great deal, the hard way, about how to be the president of anything. "The good politician knows what he wants and establishes his priorities . . . [But as president I was] spread so thin in so many different areas. I didn't become a more effective leader within the boardroom, I didn't become an effective politician in sizing up what I wanted to achieve, and narrowing it down, because we were always rushing to plug leaks in the dike."

Failure due to inability to place one's priorities in order might well be the legacy of the entire progressive group in the Screen Actors Guild. The number one priority of almost every progressive is the merger with AFTRA. Yet, as a group they refuse to admit that they can't have everything, insisting on pursuing irrelevant symbolic issues—apartheid, TWA pilot's strike, colorization, People for the American Way—that drive the conservatives to furious opposition.

It is not that these are bad causes. Under other circumstances their pursuit might be worthy and even noble. But at the moment they distract everyone from the concrete problems immediately before the guild, and make the conservatives feel that they must withdraw from it in order to preserve their own integrity. Given the conservatives' skill at fanning discontent, and their access to the media, they can, if provided with sufficient reason, be expected to keep the progressives plugging leaks in the dike indefinitely, and the merger will never go through. Yet the progressives go on and on providing them with reasons.

What would be the consequences of the Screen Actors Guild temporarily suspending its vicarious participation in righting the wrongs of the world? Would the racist regime in South Africa survive, where it would otherwise fall? Would the Ku Klux Klan triumph, where it would otherwise be crushed? Would striking airline pilots lose their struggle with management, where they would otherwise win? To even ask the questions is to underscore the absurd unimportance of the guild's involvement in these issues. And yet to keep their hand in causes such as these, the progressives are willing to risk their union's destruction. In the annals of folly, they deserve at least a small mention.

The conservatives, however, are not exactly blameless either. Let it be said clearly: although right-to-work legislation may not be the death of most unions in most places, it would mean the end of the Screen Actors Guild in any historically recognizable form; the same is true of "financial core" membership. The enormous oversupply of actors ensures that SAG could not survive a withdrawal by a significant percentage of its card-holders. If the guild were to go out on strike during a contract negotiation, producers would simply turn to the various nonmembers to fill their casts. This would break the strike. Six months later SAG would be out of business. Which actors would remain in such a pathetic organization, with all the competition from unencumbered actors in Hollywood? What producer would hire union actors, with all the more compliant talent available?

So in trying to institute right-to-work and financial core status, conservative leaders, whether or not they realize it, are attempting to destroy the guild. And the very unimportance of the issues they are contesting leaves one questioning their judgment. Destroy the union over the inclusion of a few thousand extras? Destroy the union over the interest in other labor unions? Destroy the union over a few expressions of solidarity with liberal political movements? Are these the sorts of issues that justify rebellion and sabotage?

Like the progressives, the conservatives seem mesmerized by symbols. While the status of extras does in a peripheral way have some impact on the distribution of resources, and while the various small (less than 1 percent of the total budget) contributions the progressive-controlled board has made do come out of the members' dues, the real impact of these issues is only at the level of emotion. As a consequence, whereas nations and organizations may have perished over the years because of disputes over the ownership of provinces, or who shall have power, or how justice shall be administered, the Screen Actors Guild may be the first polity to die for words. This may be the real difference between actors' politics and politics everywhere else: actors can't seem to decide what's important.

Moreover, some of the conservative leaders are evidently unable to understand that they are not contributing to honest discussion when they make statements that approach red-baiting. Let this also be said: progressives are neither members of the Communist party nor sympathetic to Communism. Some of them sometimes endorse American policies that other people believe will, if followed, lead to the advance of Communism in the world. But this does not mean that they are Communists, any more than a reluctance to meddle in the affairs of South Africa makes someone a racist.

It is not my impression, however, that the conservatives who make this sort of statement really believe that there are Communists or fellow-travelers in important positions in the guild. Rather, it seems a way for them to vent their frustration with and contempt for the progressive way of looking at the world. As such, it is both irresponsible and foolish. What may seem to the conservatives to be only colorful speech or the authentic expression of concern is heard by the progressives as not only a great personal insult but as an accusation that may have fatal consequences for their careers. Although this is probably an overreaction, given the history of Hollywood it is not certainly so. By their inability to contain themselves on this topic, some conservatives ensure that progressives will react to them not with reason and respect but with hatred and fear. Blinded by personal distaste, they can neither empathize with conservative problems nor bring themselves to listen to conservative arguments. The indirect accusation of Communism is thus not only untrue, but, more important, a blunder.

And so the two factions proceed down a path which neither wants. In the future, having collaborated in the destruction of the guild, the members of each side will blame the other, and both will be right.

Real Life

There is no way to reconcile the ideologies or change the characters of the members of each faction. But there is a way to compromise on issues, and thus save the guild. Activists as a group must learn what Ed

Asner finally came to see—that competent politicians must put their goals in priority and be willing to give up those lower on the list in order to achieve those that are more important. Since progressives and conservatives have what political scientists call different "preference orderings," there is room for them to strike a deal.

What progressives want most of all is the AFTRA merger. What conservatives want most of all is a cessation of the guild's symbolic participation in the affairs of other, nonactor unions and liberal social causes. Therefore, the union can achieve peace if the progressives agree to stop trying to be the moral den mother of the world and the conservatives agree to support (not just refrain from objecting to, but support) the merger. Neither side will be happy with such a compromise, but in the real life of actor politics it will at least ensure that their union survives, progresses, and remains governable. The alternative is chaos.

Such an agreement cannot be tacit. Progressive leaders will have to caucus and commit themselves to the terms of such a bargain. Several of them will then have to meet with conservative leaders to come to a formal, if not written, understanding. Among other things, the leaders will have to agree on how long after the merger goes through can the conservatives expect the progressives to exercise restraint over their universalist impulses. They may also have to set up regular channels of communication, so that the inevitable mistakes, misunderstandings, and personal rebellions will not upset the entire detente.

With the mutual suspicion and disgust at such an intense pitch, it will not be easy to create such an agreement, and still less easy to make it last. But if self-government were easy, it would not require leadership. A few respected actors are going to have to rise above the recriminations and take their colleagues in hand. Otherwise, this book, instead of being an analysis of politics in the Screen Actors Guild, may become its epitaph.

NOTES · SOURCES · INDEX

NOTES

1. A UNION OF SCREEN ACTORS

1. Albert Rees, *The Economics of Trade Unions*, rev. ed. (Chicago: University of Chicago, 1977), pp. 3, 27–28.

2. J. David Greenstone, *Labor in American Politics* (New York: Random House, 1969), pp. 25–26; William M. Leiserson, *American Trade Union Democracy* (New York: Columbia University, 1959), p. 55; Michael Rogin, "Volunteerism: The Political Function of an Anti-Political Doctrine," in *The American Labor Movement*, ed. David Brody (New York: Harper and Row, 1971), pp. 100–118; James O. Morris, *Conflict Within the AFL: A Study of Craft Versus Industrial Unionism, 1901–1938* (Ithaca, New York: Cornell University, 1958), passim.

3. John L. Lewis, "The Mass Production Industries" (1935 speech) in *American Labor: The Twentieth Century*, ed. Jerold S. Auerbach (New York: Bobbs-Merrill, 1969), pp. 307–14; Morris, *Conflict Within the AFL*.

4. For the general history, see Morris, *Conflict Within the AFL*, passim; for a discussion of the dispute over woodworkers, see pp. 21–23.

5. John T. Dunlop, "Structural Changes in the American Labor Movement and the Industrial Relations System," in *Labor and Trade Unionism: An Interdisciplinary Reader*, ed. Walter Galenson and Seymour Martin Lipset (New York: John Wiley, 1960), p. 109.

6. Philip Taft, *Organized Labor in American History* (New York: Harper and Row, 1964), pp. 270, 463.

7. Leiserson, *Trade Union Democracy*, pp. 103–5.

8. Quoted in J. David Edelstein and Malcolm Warner, *Comparative Union Democracy: Organization and Opposition in British and American Unions* (New Brunswick, New Jersey: Transaction Books, 1979), p. xi.

9. Philip Taft, *The Structure and Government of Labor Unions* (Cambridge, Massachusetts: Harvard University, 1962), pp. 35–36; Seymour Martin Lipset, Martin Trow, and James Coleman, *Union Democracy: What Makes Democracy Work in Labor Unions and Other Organizations?* (Garden City, N. Y.: Doubleday, 1956), pp. 465–68. Leiserson, *Trade Union Democracy*, pp. 55–75.

10. Lipset, Trow, and Coleman, *Union Democracy*, passim; J. David Edelstein and Malcolm Warner, "Research Areas In National Union Democracy," *Industrial Relations* 16(2): 199 (May 1977).

11. Paul F. Clark, *The Miners' Fight for Democracy: Arnold Miller and the Reform of the United Mine Workers* (Ithaca, New York: Cornell University, 1981), passim; Edelstein and Warner, "Research Areas" and *Comparative Union Democracy*, passim.

12. Otto Fenichel, "On Acting," *The Psychoanalytic Quarterly* 15: 144, 147 (1946).

13. Ronald Taft, "A Psychological Assessment of Professional Actors and Related Professions," *Genetic Psychology Monographs* 64: 334 (1961).

14. Lorenz Kjerbuhl-Peterson, *Psychology of Acting: A Consideration of its Principles as an Art* (Boston: Expression Company, 1935), p. 234; Christopher Lasch, *The Culture of Narcissism: American Life in An Age of Diminishing Expectations* (New York: W. W. Norton, 1979), pp. 298–300.

15. Hortense Powdermaker, *Hollywood: The Dream Factory; An Anthropologist Looks at the Movie-Makers* (Boston: Little, Brown, 1951), p. 254.

16. Mendel Kohansky, *The Disreputable Profession: The Actor In Society* (Westport, Conn.: Greenwood Press, 1984), passim.

17. Quoted in Robert Cohen, *Acting Professionally: Raw Facts About Careers In Acting*, 3d ed. (New York: Harper and Row, 1983), p. xi; William Schallert repeated this assertion, with the slightly different wording I quote in the text, in a phone conversation with me.

18. David F. Prindle (hereafter referred to as DFP) interview with Joseph Ruskin.

19. *Screen Actor*, August 1984, pp. 55, 109; *Literary Digest*, 15 May 1937, p. 12; Leo C. Rosten, *Hollywood: The Movie Colony, the Movie Makers* (New York: Harcourt, Brace, 1941), p. 349.

20. Kevin Brownlow, *The Parade's Gone By . . .* (Berkeley: University of California, 1968), pp. 344–53; Maurice Yacowar, "An Aesthetic Defense of the Star System In Films," *Quarterly Review of Film Studies* 4(1): 39 (Winter 1979).

21. Yacowar, "Star System"; passim; Benjamin B. Hampton, *History of the American Film Industry From Its Beginnings To 1931* (New York: Dover, 1970), pp. 86–92.

22. Gorham Kindem, "Hollywood's Movie Star System: A Historical Overview," in *The American Movie Industry: The Business of Motion Pictures*, ed. Gorham Kindem (Carbondale: Southern Illinois University, 1982), pp. 86, 90–91; Harold L. Vogel, *Entertainment Industry Economics: A Guide for Financial Analysis* (London: Cambridge University, 1986), p. 114.

23. Mark Litwak, *Reel Power: The Struggle For Influence and Success In The New Hollywood* (New York: William Morrow, 1986), pp. 42–63; Todd Gitlin, *Inside Prime Time* (New York: Pantheon, 1985), pp. 145–48.

2. ACTION

1. Leo C. Rosten, *Hollywood: The Movie Colony, The Movie Makers* (New York: Harcourt, Brace, 1941), p. 4.

2. *Historical Statistics of the United States* (Washington, D. C.: U. S. Department of Commerce, Bureau of the Census, 1975), p. 400; Lewis Jacobs,

The Rise of American Film: A Critical History (New York: Columbia University, 1967), p. 4223.

3. Murray Ross, *Stars and Strikes: Unionization of Hollywood* (New York: Columbia University, 1941), p. 44; Nancy Lynn Schwartz, *The Hollywood Writers' Wars* (New York: Alfred A. Knopf, 1982), pp. 5–6.

4. Ross, *Stars and Strikes*, p. 44.

5. Ross, *Stars and Strikes*, p. 45; Schwartz, *Writers' Wars*, p. 9.

6. DFP interview with Ralph Bellamy.

7. Larry Ceplair and Steven Englund, *The Inquisition In Hollywood: Politics In the Film Community, 1930–1960* (Berkeley: University of California, 1983), passim; Schwartz, *Writers' Wars*, p. 21 and passim.

8. Budd Schulberg, *Moving Pictures: Memories of a Hollywood Prince* (New York: Stein and Day, 1982), pp. 176–77.

9. DFP interview with Lyle Talbot.

10. *Screen Actor*, Summer 1979, p. 6.

11. Ibid., p. 10.

12. Ibid., August 1984, p. 58.

13. Ibid., Summer 1979, p. 10; Gary M. Fink, ed., *Labor Unions* (Westport, Conn.: Greenwood, 1977), pp. 4–6.

14. Louis B. Perry and Richard S. Perry, *A History of the Los Angeles Labor Movement, 1911–1941* (Berkeley: University of California, 1963), pp. 338–40.

15. DFP interview with Ralph Bellamy.

16. *Screen Actor*, July/August 1978, p. 12.

17. The information in Table 2.1 comes from the following: Sol Achaneles and Albert Wolsky, *The Movie Makers* (Secaucus, N. J.: Derbibooks, 1974); Dennis La Beau, ed., *Theatre, Film and Television Biographies Master Index*, 1st ed., Gale Biographical Index Series no. 5 (Detroit: Gale Research Co., 1979); Ann Lloyd and Graham Fuller, *The Illustrated Who's Who of the Cinema* (New York: MacMillan, 1983); David Ragin, *Who's Who in Hollywood 1900–1976* (New Rochelle, N. Y.: Arlington House, 1976); John Stewart, *Filmarama, Volume 2: The Flaming Years, 1920–1929* (Metuchen, N. J.: Scarecrow, 1977); Evelyn Mack Truitt, *Who Was Who On Screen*, 3d ed. (New York: R. R. Bowker, 1983); John T. Weaver, *Forty Years of Screen Credits 1929–1969* (Metuchen, N. J.: Scarecrow, 1970); John T. Weaver, *Twenty Years of Silents 1908–1928* (Metuchen, N. J.: Scarecrow, 1971); *Who Was Who in the Theatre: 1912–1976*, Gale Composite Biographical Dictionary Series no. 3 (Detroit: Gale Research Co., 1978).

18. DFP interviews with Leon Ames, Lyle Talbot; *Screen Actor*, October/November 1960, p. 9; Summer 1979, pp. 6–7.

19. David Niven, *Bring On the Empty Horses* (New York: Dell, 1975), p. 214; Ross, *Stars and Strikes*, pp. 64–88; George Frazier, "Nobody Pushes Bob Around," *Collier's*, 4 June 1949, p. 25; *Screen Actor*, August 1984, p. 53.

20. DFP interview with Lyle Talbot.

21. *Screen Actor*, August 1984, pp. 60–61.

22. DFP interview with Leon Ames; Ken Thomson's obituary, *Daily Variety*, 27 January 1967, p. 32; *Screen Actor*, August 1984, p. 60.

23. Articles of incorporation for the Screen Actors Guild, included in overall minutes, pp. 1–6; DFP interviews with Leon Ames, Laurence Beilenson; Ross, *Stars and Strikes*, p. 149 (Ross gives the date as 12 July 1933, but

this is the date of the first meeting of the corporation, not of the decisive organizational meeting); Fink, *Labor Unions*, p. 336; *Screen Actor*, Summer 1979, p. 3.

24. DFP interviews with Leon Ames, Lyle Talbot; *Screen Actor*, Summer 1979, p. 7.

25. Screen Actors Guild articles of incorporation, minutes, overall pages 1–6; DFP interview with Laurence Beilenson.

26. Screen Actors Guild bylaws, overall minutes pp. 7–10; DFP interview with Laurence Beilenson.

27. Minutes, 12 July 1933, p. 3; DFP interviews with Leon Ames, Laurence Beilenson.

28. For the report on guild finances, see minutes of a special meeting, 7 August 1933, p. 1; DFP interviews with Leon Ames; Ross, *Stars and Strikes*, p. 149.

29. Charlton Heston, Danny Thomas, Frederick O'Neal, and Conrad Nagel, "There's No Business Like—and No History Quite Like the History of the Various Labor Unions in Show Business," *American Labor* 1(5): 57 (September 1968); DFP interview with Laurence Beilenson; Douglas Gomery, "Hollywood, the National Recovery Administration, and the Question of Monopoly Power," in *The American Movie Industry: The Business of Motion Pictures*, ed. Gorham Kindem (Carbondale: Southern Illinois University, 1982), pp. 205–6, 210, 212–13; Louis Nizer, *New Courts of Industry: Self-Regulation Under the Motion Picture Code* (New York: Longacre, 1935), passim; Schwartz, *Writers' Wars*, p. 28.

30. DFP interview with Laurence Beilenson; Nizer, *New Courts*, pp. 164, 199–201.

31. Minutes, special meeting, 4 October 1933, pp. 1–4; DFP interviews with Laurence Beilenson and Lyle Talbot; Ross, *Stars and Strikes*, p. 150; Schwartz, *Writers' Wars*, p. 129.

32. See the minutes of the 18 October 1933 meeting, p. 9, for a copy of the telegram to Roosevelt; Ross, *Stars and Strikes*, p. 151; Schwartz, *Writers' Wars*, p. 29.

33. Nizer, *New Courts*, pp. xvii, 198–201.

34. Robert Osborne Baker, *The International Alliance of Theatrical and Stage Employes and Moving Picture Machine Operators of the United States and Canada* (Lawrence: University of Kansas, 1933), pp. 37–42; Hugh Lovel and Tasile Carter, *Collective Bargaining In The Motion Picture Industry* (Berkeley: University of California, Institute for Industrial Relations, 1955), pp. 15–17; Perry and Perry, *Los Angeles Labor*, p. 321.

35. Perry and Perry, *Los Angeles Labor*, pp. 320–29.

36. Ross, *Stars and Strikes*, p. 192; Perry and Perry, *Los Angeles Labor*, pp. 319–25, 328–29; Lovel and Carter, *Collective Bargaining*, pp. 15–17.

37. DFP interview with Roy Brewer; Florabel Muir, " 'All Right Gentlemen, Do We Get The Money?' The Astonishing Story of Bad Boy Bioff in Movieland," *The Saturday Evening Post*, 27 January 1940, pp. 81–82.

38. Perry and Perry, *Los Angeles Labor*, p. 336; Schwartz, *Writers' Wars*, p. 132; Muir, "Bad Boy Bioff," p. 82.

39. Perry and Perry, *Los Angeles Labor*, pp. 330–31; Ross, *Stars and Strikes*, pp. 192–93.

40. See note 39 above.

41. For evidence of leftist support for the FMPC, see *New Masses*, 11 May 1937, p. 9, and 18 May 1937, pp. 6–7; for evidence of such support within SAG, see minutes of the mass meeting of 2 May 1937, pp. 1–2; for evidence of the way leftists used the events of 1937 in subsequent appeals for support, see Father George H. Dunne, *Hollywood Labor Dispute: A Study in Immorality* (Los Angeles: Conference Publishing Co., n. d.), pp. 239–45.

42. DFP interview with Laurence Beilenson; "Amended Agreement Between Equity and Screen Actors Guild," 15 November 1934—Screen Actors Guild file, Margaret Herrick Library, Academy of Motion Picture Arts and Sciences; "Invitation" to Screen Actors Guild Ball, 13 January 1934, Herrick Library, Screen Actors Guild file; *Screen Actor*, Summer 1979, p. 9; Ross, *Stars and Strikes*, pp. 153–61; Jacobs, *Rise of American Film*, p. 425.

43. DFP interviews with Leon Ames, Laurence Beilenson; *Motion Picture Herald*, 7 November 1936, p. 21.

44. Minutes, 14 April 1937, pp. 1–3; Letter from Ken Thomson to Robert Montgomery, dated 13 April 1937, pp. 454–57 in overall minutes; *Motion Picture Herald*, 10 April 1937, p. 31.

45. I must add here that Laurence Beilenson categorically denies the interpretation of events that follows. It is his contention that the FMPC strike and SAG's recognition were purely coincidental.

46. See Ken Thomson's letter to Robert Montgomery of 13 April 1937 in the overall minutes, pp. 454–57, for a discussion of the alliance between the Painters of the FMPC and SAG; see the minutes of the mass meeting on 2 May 1937 for evidence of leftist support for the FMPC, pp. 1–2; see also the minutes of the special board meeting on 2 May 1937, pp. 1–2; Ross, *Stars and Strikes*, p. 194; *Los Angeles Daily News*, 3 May 1937.

47. DFP interview with Leon Ames; Frazier, "Nobody Pushes Bob Around," p. 25.

48. Herbert Knott Sorrell, *You Don't Choose Your Friends*, unpublished memoirs, UCLA Library Department of Special Collections, box 300/11, pp. 23–24, 26; Muir, "Bad Boy Bioff," p. 82; *Los Angeles Daily News*, May 3 and 5 May 1937.

49. Morrie Ryskind, "It Happened One Night," *The Nation*, 15 May 1937, p. 563; *Los Angeles Daily News*, 6 and 8 May 1937.

50. *Los Angeles Daily News*, 8 May 1937; Ryskind, "It Happened One Night," p. 563.

51. Minutes, special meeting, 9 May 1937, p. 1; Copy of letter from L. B. Mayer and Joseph M. Schenck to SAG board of directors, 9 May 1937, p. 483 in overall minutes; Frazier, "Nobody Pushes Bob Around," pp. 25, 72.

52. Minutes, Annual Meeting of 9 May 1937, p. 1; George Murphy with Victor Lasky, "*Say... Didn't You Used To Be George Murphy?*" (Bartholomew House, 1970) p. 207; *New York Times*, 10 May 1937, p. 8; *Motion Picture Herald*, 22 May 1937, p. 51; *Daily Variety*, 10 May 1937; *Screen Actor*, Summer 1979, p. 10.

53. *Los Angeles Daily News*, 10 and 11 May 1937; Perry and Perry, *Los Angeles Labor*, p. 331.

54. Letter from Melvyn Douglas to SAG board of directors, 17 September 1938, p. 898 in overall minutes; DFP interviews with Ralph Bellamy and The Old Hollywood Leftist; *Daily Variety*, 24 October 1938, p. 252.

55. *Los Angeles Daily News*, 11 May 1937.

56. This agreement is reprinted in *Daily Variety*, 21 May 1937.

57. Minutes, 9 August 1937, p. 3; Pete Martin, "Fighting Bob—The Hollywood Crusader," *Saturday Evening Post*, 7 October 1950, p. 98; Frazier, "Nobody Pushes Bob Around," p. 25; Ross, *Stars and Strikes*, p. 199.

58. Minutes, 23 August 1937, p. 6; Pete Martin, "Fighting Bob," p. 98; Frazier, "Nobody Pushes Bob Around," p. 25.

59. Press release from boards of SAG, Screen Writers Guild, Screen Directors Guild, 15 September 1937, files of Screen Directors Guild, 1937 Chronology file; DFP interview with Laurence Beilenson; Murphy and Lasky, "*George Murphy?*" p. 221; Frazier, "Nobody Pushes Bob Around," p. 25.

60. Minutes, 7 September 1937, passim (I am not absolutely certain that this particular appropriation was the one diverted to Beilenson. I can find no other indefinite appropriation during this period in the minutes, however); DFP interview with Laurence Beilenson; Frazier, "Nobody Pushes Bob Around," p. 25; Martin, "Fighting Bob," p. 98.

61. See the proceedings of the 34th annual convention of the IATSE, 6–9 June 1938, for the text of a petition filed by Kibre and the IA Progressives, complaining of IA government, pp. 336–38; For the Browne administration's official rebuttal, see pp. 338–40; Schwartz, *Writers' Wars*, pp. 113–14; Muir, "Bad Boy Bioff," p. 82.

62. Dalton Trumbo, "The Real Facts Behind the Motion Picture Lockout," text of speech delivered 13 October 1945, from Dalton Trumbo file in Southern California Library for Social Research, p. 2; DFP interview with Laurence Beilenson; Muir, "Bad Boy Bioff," p. 82; Perry and Perry, *Los Angeles Labor*, pp. 332–36; Ross, *Stars and Strikes*, pp. 196–97; *Daily Variety*, 12 November 1937, 6 August and 2 November 1938; Murphy and Lasky, "*George Murphy?*" p. 22.

63. Ephraim Katz, *The Film Encyclopedia* (New York: G. P. Putnam's Sons, 1979), p. 1022; Perry and Perry, *Los Angeles Labor*, p. 334.

64. Proceedings, IATSE 35th convention, 3–6 June 1940, p. 371 (on Padway's appointment); *Business Week*, 29 July 1939, pp. 28–29; Ross, *Stars and Strikes*, p. 192.

65. *Business Week*, 29 July 1939, pp. 28–29, and 9 September 1939, p. 52; Muir, "Bad Boy Bioff," p. 10; Perry and Perry, *Los Angeles Labor*, p. 34.

66. Schwartz, *Writers' Wars*, p. 124.

67. For discussion by the board of this complicated campaign, see the minutes, 16 April, pp. 1–2, 4 July, p. 3, and 14 July, pp. 1–2, all 1939; and Executive Committee Minutes, 5 June, p. 2, 19 June, p. 5, 7 July, p. 5, and 31 July, passim, all 1939; Murray Ross, "The CIO Loses Hollywood," *The Nation*, 7 October 1939, pp. 374–77; Muir, "Bad Boy Bioff," p. 10; *Daily Variety*, 14 June 1938; Schwartz, *Writers' Wars*, pp. 123–25, 129.

68. Fink, *Labor Unions*, p. 13; George Creel, "Closed During Altercations: The Unions Fight for the West Coast, With the Public In Between," *The Saturday Evening Post*, 14 May 1938, pp. 25, 106.

69. Ross, "CIO Loses Hollywood," pp. 374–77; Perry and Perry, *Los Angeles Labor*, pp. 332, 335.

70. For leadership discussions, see Executive Committee Minutes, 24 August 1939, pp. 2–3; and minutes, 28 August 1939, p. 3; Ross, "CIO Loses Hollywood," pp. 376–77; *Los Angeles Times*, 1 September 1939, p. 1.

71. A copy of this written agreement, which was technically between the IATSE and the AAAA, not SAG, is appended to the minutes of 2 September 1939, p. 1275 in overall minutes; Ross, "CIO Loses Hollywood," pp. 376–77; Perry and Perry, *Los Angeles Labor*, p. 335.

72. Ross, "CIO Loses Hollywood," p. 377.

3. REACTION

1. DFP interview with John Dales; *Screen Actor*, Summer 1979, p. 18.

2. DFP interviews with Anthony Caruso, John Dales, Don Dubbins, Friz Feld, John Gavin, Charlton Heston, and Gilbert Perkins; Ronald Reagan and Richard C. Hubler, *Where's The Rest of Me?* (New York: Dell, 1965) pp. 206, 210; *Screen Actor*, Summer 1979, p. 20.

3. *Conditions of Work and Employment For All Screen Players*, pamphlet giving terms of Basic Minimum Contract of 1937 and Modified Agreement of 1938, together known as the Basic Agreement; box 6 of *Miscellaneous Correspondence* in David O. Selznick Collection, University of Texas at Austin.

4. Minutes, 28 August 1944, p. 3; DFP interview with Leon Ames, and phone interview with Jack Dales; *Screen Actor*, Summer 1979, pp. 11, 18; *Daily Variety*, 12 November 1938; also undated article reviewing the year 1939, p. 155, from Screen Actors Guild file in Margaret Herrick Library, Academy of Motion Pictures Arts and Sciences.

5. Minutes, 13 November 1944, p. 1, 18 December 1944, pp. 1–2, 26 March 1945, pp. 2–3, 16 October 1945, p. 2; John Dales's report to annual membership meeting, 23 September 1945, pp. 2872A–72C in overall minutes; *Los Angeles Times*, 9 March 1944, 24 March 1944, pt. 2; *Daily Variety*, 12 November 1938, also undated article reviewing the year 1939, p. 155, from Screen Actors Guild file in Margaret Herrick Library, Academy of Motion Picture Arts and Sciences.

6. Minutes, 26 March 1945, p. 2; 28 May 1945, p. 5; 11 June 1945, p. 2; 16 July 1945, p. 4; see also Dales's report to 23 September 1945 membership meeting, pp. 2872A–72C overall minutes.

7. Minutes, 11 February 1946, pp. 2–3; 4 March 1946, p. 2; 18 March 1946, p. 2; 8 July 1946, p. 2.

8. For President Walsh's analysis of the situation as an effort by the construction unions to eviscerate the IA, see his report to the IA's annual convention, 22–26 July 1946, proceedings, pp. 627–34; for Roy Brewer's discussion of the IA's feeling of vulnerability, see his testimony before the House Committee on Un-American Activities, 16 May 1951, *Communist Infiltration of Hollywood Motion-Picture Industry—Part 1* (Washington, D. C.: U. S. Government Printing Office, 1951), p. 487.

9. Herbert Knott Sorrell, "You Don't Choose Your Friends: The Memoirs of Herbert Knott Sorrell," UCLA Library Department of Special Collections, box 300/11; Richard Schickel, *The Disney Version* (New York: Avon, 1968) pp. 211–13, 215–20; Larry Ceplair and Steven Englund, *The Inquisition In Hollywood: Politics in the Film Community, 1930–1960* (Berkeley: University of California, 1983), pp. 216–17.

10. Sorrell, "Choose Your Friends," pp. 50–51, 76, 86–88; Ceplair and Englund, *Inquisition*, p. 217.

11. For Walsh's account, see his report cited in n. 8 above; For the date of the set decorators vote, see Reagan and Hubler, *Rest of Me?* p. 155.

12. Minutes, 12 March 1945, pp. 1–2; On the IA cooperation with the producers, see the informal minutes of the Producers' Labor Committee by Victor Clarke of MGM in *Jurisdictional Disputes in the Motion-Picture Industry, Hearings before a Special Subcommittee of the Committee On Education and Labor,* House of Representatives, 80th Cong., 1st sess., August and September 1947, vol. 1 (Washington, D. C.: U. S. Government Printing Office, 1948), pp. 910–12.

13. DFP interview with Roy Brewer; Vance King, "Portrait of Roy Brewer," *Hollywood Reporter,* 26 October 1953; *Human Events,* 28 September 1985, p. 14.

14. For examples of historians' portrayal of Brewer as a cynic, see Ceplair and Englund, *Inquisition,* pp. 212–13; and Nancy Lynn Schwartz, *The Hollywood Writers' Wars* (New York: Alfred A. Knopf, 1982), p. 244.

15. DFP interview with Roy Brewer.

16. King, "Portrait"; *Human Events,* 28 September 1985, p. 14.

17. DFP interview with Roy Brewer; Brewer's 1951 HUAC testimony, p. 497; Schwartz, *Writer's Wars,* pp. 223–24; Irving Howe and Lewis Coser, *The American Communist Party: A Critical History (1919–1957)* (Boston: Beacon Press, 1957), pp. 410–11.

18. DFP interview with Roy Brewer; see also Brewer's 1951 HUAC testimony, p. 497.

19. For the IA's view of its trouble with the Carpenters, see Walsh's report to the 1946 convention, pp. 630, 634; DFP interview with Roy Brewer; see also Brewer's 1951 HUAC testimony, passim; for an anecdote revealing of the Carpenters' imperialistic designs, see John Dales's testimony in *Jurisdictional Disputes in the Motion-Picture Industry,* p. 924.

20. See the collected boxes of publicity in the UCLA Library Department of Special Collections, under "Hollywood Studio Strike"; see the same in the Southern California Library for Social Research.

21. DFP interview with Roy Brewer; for the date, see Reagan and Hubler, *Rest of Me?* pp. 169–70.

22. See, for example, minutes, 23 September 1946, p. 1; DFP interview with John Dales; Reagan and Hubler, *Rest of Me?* pp. 167, 170; Ceplair and Englund, *Inquisition,* p. 219; George Murphy with Victor Lasky, *"Say... Didn't You Used To Be George Murphy?"* (Bartholomew House, 1970), p. 284.

23. For the way the extras dispute colored SAG thinking about the CSU and the IA, see the minutes, 1 May 1945, p. 1; special meeting, 20 August 1945, p. 1; special meetings, 14 October 1945, p. 2, and 26 November 1945, pp. 1–3.

24. *Screen Actor,* Summer 1979, p. 16.

25. Murphy and Lasky, *"Murphy?"* pp. 219, 239, 256, 284; Reagan and Hubler, *Rest of Me?* pp. 153, 204, 224.

26. Minutes, 9 September 1946, pp. 2–3; Murphy and Lasky, *"Murphy?"* p. 296; testimony of George Murphy before HUAC, 23 October 1947, *Hearings Regarding the Communist Infiltration of the Motion-Picture Industry* (Washington, D. C.: U. S. Government Printing Office, 1947), p. 211.

27. Minutes, 12 March 1945, pp. 1–2, 30 July 1945, p. 3; special meeting, 14 October 1945, p. 2, 16 October 1945, pp. 1–3, 17 September 1946, p. 1;

Dales's report to 23 September 1945 membership meeting, p. 2872E in overall minutes; DFP interview with Roy Brewer; transcript of conversation between John Dales and Steve Trilling, Warner Brothers executive, about Hollywood Studio Strike, 17 October 1945, file 2734, Warner Brothers Collection, Library of the University of Southern California.

28. Minutes, special meeting, 20 August 1945, p. 4, 18 February 1946, p. 3; DFP interview with Roy Brewer.

29. DFP interviews with John Dales, Roy Brewer; Murphy and Lasky, "*Murphy?*" p. 283; *Los Angeles Daily News*, 12 March 1948; Roy Brewer's testimony before HUAC, 28 October 1947, p. 345.

30. DFP interview with Roy Brewer; for a journalist's account of the LAPD Red Squad, see George Creel, "Closed During Altercations: The Unions Fight for the West Coast, With the Public In Between," *Saturday Evening Post*, 14 May 1938, p. 106; on Jeff Kibre, see Schwartz, *Writers' Wars*, p. 221.

31. On the Communist Party's history, see Howe and Coser, *Communist Party*, pp. 444–53.

32. Minutes, 21 October 1946, and 17 November 1946, pp. 1–2; Jack Dales, "Pragmatic Leadership: Ronald Reagan as President of the Screen Actors Guild," interview with Mitch Tuchman, UCLA Library Department of Special Collections, box 300/181, p. 9; Reagan and Hubler, *Rest of Me?* p. 9.

33. Minutes, 4 November 1946, pp. 2–3; for the testimony of John Dales, who presided over the abortive agreement, see *Jurisdictional Disputes in the Motion-Picture Industry*, pp. 917–19; "Screen Actors Guild Report To The Motion Picture Industry," pp. 3147–47B in overall minutes; DFP interview with Laurence Beilenson.

34. For example, Hayden was a member of a group of eight actors who presented a statement to the board endorsing the CSU position, recorded in the minutes, 11 November 1946, p. 2; testimony of Sterling Hayden before HUAC, 10 April 1951, pp. 142–43, 162; Hayden's testimony in civil lawsuit as reported in *Los Angeles Herald Express*, 9 December 1953.

35. For the petition, see the minutes, 9 December 1946, p. 3; see also the minutes of the special meeting, 16 December 1946, pp. 1–3; Dales, "Pragmatic Leadership," p. 16; *Daily Variety*, 20 December 1946.

36. Hedda Hopper's column, *Los Angeles Times*, 18 May 1947; Dales, "Pragmatic Leadership," p. 16; Sterling Hayden's 1951 HUAC testimony, p. 162.

37. *Daily Variety*, 20 December 1946; *CSU News*, 28 December 1946, from Hollywood Studio Strike file, Southern California Library for Social Research; Schwartz, *Writers' Wars*, pp. 249–50.

38. Results of this vote are in overall minutes, p. 3213; see the *CSU News* of 28 December 1946 for that organization's position on the Interfaith Council's resolution; for the text of the referendum questions, see the *CSU News* of 1 February 1947, pp. 1, 4, both available in Hollywood Studio Strike file, Southern California Library for Social Research.

39. Anne Edwards, *Early Reagan: The Rise to Power* (New York: William Morrow, 1987), p. 321; George Murphy's testimony before HUAC, 23 October 1947, pp. 210, 213; Murphy and Lasky, "*Murphy?*" p. 287; *Los Angeles Times*, 14 January 1954; Reagan and Hubler, *Rest of Me?* pp. 199–200.

40. Ceplair and Englund, *Inquisition*, p. 224; Reagan and Hubler, *Rest of Me?* pp. 146–212 and passim.

41. Minutes, 10 March 1947, pp. 1–3; *New York Times*, 23 March 1947.

42. For the FBI's categorization of Reagan as a person with a record of Communist activity, see an FBI internal document dated 11 April 1946, "Communist Infiltration of the Motion Picture Industry," file no. 100–15732, p. 7; for an account of the Reagans contacting the FBI and requesting an interview, see an FBI internal document dated 4 August 1947, "Communist Infiltration of the Motion Picture Industry," file no. 100–15732, p. 156 (FBI file on Ronald Reagan, obtained under the Freedom of Information Act).

43. FBI internal document dated 4 August 1947, "Communist Infiltration of the Motion Picture Industry," file no. 100–15732, p. 156 (FBI file on Ronald Reagan, obtained under the Freedom of Information Act).

44. *Daily Variety*, 7 February 1944; Ceplair and Englund, *Inquisition*, p. 210; Schwartz, *Writers' Wars*, p. 207.

45. DFP interview with Roy Brewer; King, "Portrait"; *Los Angeles Examiner*, 2 March 1944.

46. *Congressional Record*, 7 March 1944, Appendix, p. A1120.

47. For an example of an investigation having nothing to do with Communism, see *Propaganda in Motion Pictures, Hearing before a Subcommittee of the Committee on Interstate Commerce*, U. S. Senate, 77th Cong., 1st sess., 9–26 September 1941; Walter Goodman, *The Committee: The Extraordinary Career of the House Committee on Un-American Activities* (New York: Farrar, Straus and Giroux, 1968), pp. 102, 202.

48. David Caute, *The Great Fear: The Anti-Communist Purge Under Truman and Eisenhower* (New York: Simon and Schuster, 1978), p. 27; Ceplair and Englund, *Inquisition*, pp. 258–60.

49. Victor Navasky, *Naming Names* (New York: Penguin, 1980), pp. 80–82; Ceplair and Englund, *Inquisition*, pp. 261–62.

50. DFP interview with Professor Howard Suber of UCLA; Navasky, *Naming Names*, p. 85.

51. Ceplair and Englund, *Inquisition*, pp. 261–69.

52. 1947 HUAC hearings, Robert Montgomery's testimony, pp. 203–7; George Murphy's testimony, pp. 208–13; Ronald Reagan's testimony pp. 213–18 (the Reagan quotation is from p. 217).

53. Navasky, *Naming Names*, p. 83; Ceplair and Englund, *Inquisition*, pp. 282–83.

54. Navasky, *Naming Names*, p. 83; Ceplair and Englund, *Inquisition*, pp. 325–31.

55. Howard Suber, "The Anti-Communist Blacklist in the Hollywood Motion Picture Industry" (Ph.D. diss., UCLA, 1968), pp. ix, 2–3; Navasky, *Naming Names*, passim. Court decisions bearing on these issues are: Barsky v. United States, 167 F.2d 241; Lawson v. United States, 176 F.2d 49; McGrain v. Daugherty, 273 U. S. 135, 174 (1927); National Maritime Union of America v. Herzog, 78 F. Supp. 146, 165 (1948), *aff'd*, 334 U. S. 854 (1948); Wilson v. Loew's, Inc., 298 P.2d 152 (Cal. App. 1956), *cert. dismissed*, 355 U. S. 597 (1958).

56. For an example of a serious observer who emphasizes the pervading anxiety in Hollywood long before the blacklist era, see Leo C. Rosten, *Hol-*

lywood: The Movie Colony, The Movie Makers (New York: Harcourt, Brace, and Company, 1941), pp. 40, 45, 74; for an example of the same immediately prior to the blacklist era, see Hortense Powdermaker, *Hollywood: The Dream Factory—An Anthropologist Looks at the Movie-Makers* (Boston: Little, Brown, 1951), pp. 29–39, 36, 37.

57. My definition of "blacklist" comes from *The Random House Dictionary of the English Language*, unabridged ed. (New York: Random House, 1973), p. 154; on the illegality of a blacklist under federal law, see Nicholas S. Falcone, *Labor Law* (New York: John Wiley and Sons, 1962), pp. 198, 205; for its illegality under California law, see *1987 California Labor Code* (Los Angeles: Parker and Sons, 1987), sections 1050 and 1101; see also John Cogley, *Report On Blacklisting*, vol. 1, *Movies* (New York: The Fund for the Republic, 1956), p. 89; for the strategies pursued by the defendants, and the court's rejection of their arguments, see Wilson v. Loew's, Inc., 298 P. 2d 152 (Cal. App. 1956), *cert. dismissed*, 355 U. S. 597 (1958).

58. Suber, "Anti-Communist Blacklist," p. 2; Ceplair and Englund, *Inquisition*, pp. 334, 350–54; all court decisions cited in n. 55.

59. Erik Barnouw, *Tube of Plenty: The Evolution of American Television*, rev. ed. (New York: Oxford, 1982), p. 109; John Cogley, *Report On Blacklisting*, vol. 2, *Radio-Television* (New York: The Fund for the Republic, 1956), pp. 1–2; Ceplair and Englund, *Inquisition*, pp. 387–88.

60. Cogley, *Report On Blacklisting* 2: 22–23.

61. Ceplair and Englund, *Inquisition*, pp. 386–87; the quotation is from Barnouw, *Tube of Plenty*, p. 126.

62. Cogley, *Report On Blacklisting* 1: 78–80.

63. "X," Hollywood Meets Frankenstein," *The Nation*, 28 June 1952, p. 630; Navasky, *Naming Names*, p. 86.

64. DFP interviews with Howard Caine and William Schallert; John Henry Faulk, *Fear On Trial* (Austin: University of Texas, 1983), pp. 159–60; Dales "Pragmatic Leadership," p. 22.

65. Cogley, *Report On Blacklisting* 1: 82–84, 85, 155, 157; Cogley, *Report On Blacklisting* 2: 61; Ceplair and Englund, *Inquisition*, pp. 389–90.

66. Dales, "Pragmatic Leadership," p. 22.

67. Lou Cannon, *Reagan* (New York: Perigee, 1982), p. 84; Garry Wills, *Reagan's America: Innocents at Home* (Garden City, N. Y.: Doubleday, 1987), p. 254.

68. Dales, "Pragmatic Leadership," p. 22.

69. For the list of independent candidates, see the minutes of 20 October 1947, p. 2; the two winners are listed at the beginning of the minutes of 8 December 1947, p. 1.

70. *Daily Variety*, 16 March 1951.

71. Minutes, 19 March 1951, pp. 1–2.

72. *Daily Variety*, 21 March 1951.

73. *Screen Actor*, Summer 1979, p. 14.

74. Minutes, 29 June 1953, p. 3, 31 August 1953, p. 1; *Los Angeles Examiner*, 15 January 1948; *Daily Variety*, 1 July 1953.

75. Faulk, *Fear On Trial*, passim; Ceplain and Englund, *Inquisition*, pp. 418–21.

76. Stefan Kanfer, *A Journal of the Plague Years* (New York: Atheneum, 1973), p. 284; *Daily Variety*, 1 July 1953.

4. UPHEAVAL

1. *Historical Statistics of the United States* (Washington, D. C.: U. S. Department of Commerce, Bureau of the Census, 1975), p. 400; Tino Balio, *United Artists: The Company Built By The Stars* (Madison: University of Wisconsin, 1976), p. 219.

2. Mae D. Huettig, "The Motion Picture Industry Today," in *The American Film Industry*, ed. Tino Balio (Madison: University of Wisconsin, 1976), pp. 235–55.

3. Ibid.

4. Gorham Kindem, "Hollywood's Movie Star System: A Historical Overview," in *The American Movie Industry: The Business of Motion Pictures*, ed. Gorham Kindem (Carbondale: Southern Illinois University, 1982), pp. 84–85; Frank Capra, *The Name Above The Title* (New York: Macmillan, 1971), pp. 164–65.

5. *Screen Actor*, August 1984, p. 52.

6. Gary Edgerton and Cathy Pratt, "The Influence of the Paramount Decision on Network Television In America," *Quarterly Review of Film Studies* 8(3): 9–23 (Summer 1983); Balio, *United Artists*, pp. 225–26.

7. Tino Balio, "Retrenchment, Reappraisal, and Reorganization: 1948 —," in Balio, *American Film Industry*, p. 318; Michael Conant, "The Impact of the Paramount Decrees," ibid., pp. 349, 354; Ernest Borneman, "United States versus Hollywood: The Case Study of an Antitrust Suit," ibid., pp. 332–45; David Gordon, "Why the Movie Majors Are Major," ibid., pp. 458–67; Ronald Reagan and Richard C. Hubler, *Where's The Rest of Me?* (New York: Dell, 1965) p. 332.

8. Balio, "Retrenchment," p. 316.

9. Bosley Crowther, *Hollywood Rajah: The Life and Times of Louis B. Mayer* (New York: Holt, Rinehart and Winston, 1960), p. 301; Dan E. Moldea, *Dark Victory: Ronald Reagan, MCA, and the Mob* (New York: Viking, 1986), pp. 92–93.

10. A. G. Jensen, "The Evolution of Modern Television," in *A Technological History of Motion Pictures and Television*, ed. Raymond Fielding (Berkeley: University of California, 1967), pp. 235–49; Balio, "Retrenchment," p. 315; Christopher H. Sterling and John M. Kittross, *Stay Tuned: A Concise History of American Broadcasting* (Belmont, Calif.: Wadsworth, 1978), pp. 511, 535.

11. Douglas Gomery, "Failed Opportunities: The Integration of the U. S. Motion Picture and Television Industries," *Quarterly Review of Film Studies* 9(3): 220 (Summer 1984); Robert Vianello, "The Rise of the Telefilm and the Networks Hegemony Over the Motion Picture Industry," ibid., pp. 204–18.

12. *Historical Statistics*, p. 400; Conant, "Paramount Decrees," pp. 354–55.

13. Gregory Schubert and James E. Lynch, "Broadcasting Unions: Structure and Impact," in *Broadcasting and Bargaining: Labor Relations in Radio and Television*, ed. Allen E. Koenig (Madison: University of Wisconsin, 1970), p. 43.

14. For discussions in which guild leaders express concern over New York domination, see the minutes, 5 June 1944, p. 1, 7 July 1948, p. 1; on George

Heller, see *Weekly Variety*, 24 May 1950, p. 49; *Hollywood Reporter*, 8 November 1949.

15. DFP interview with John Dales; Reagan and Hubler, *Rest of Me?* p. 251.

16. DFP interview with Howard Caine; Reagan and Hubler, *Rest of Me?* pp. 254–55.

17. *Hollywood Reporter*, 8 November 1949.

18. Minutes, 7 July 1948, p. 1; *Daily Variety*, 20 January 1950; *Los Angeles Daily News*, 12 July 1950; Reagan and Hubler, *Rest of Me?* p. 259.

19. Minutes, 9 August 1948, pp. 2–4, 20 January 1949, p. 1, 15 August 1949, p. 3; special meeting, 24 April 1950, p. 2; *Los Angeles Examiner*, 27 April 1950.

20. For discussions of some of these elections and their outcomes, see the minutes, 24 July 1950, p. 3, 9 April 1951, p. 2, 22 October 1951, p. 1, 12 February 1952, p. 2, 22 September 1952, p. 2; Schubert and Lynch, "Broadcast Unions," pp. 43, 46.

21. Minutes, 26 November 1951, p. 2; DFP interviews with John Dales and Chester Migden.

22. *Los Angeles Times*, 11 May 1959; *Screen Actor*, August 1959, p. 3, November 1959, pp. 5–6, and February 1960, p. 4; *Weekly Variety*, 2 January and 24 October 1974.

23. Minutes, 12 March 1951, p. 3; *Daily Variety*, 29 November 1951.

24. Moldea, *Dark Victory*, p. 14; Ronald Reagan, testimony before federal grand jury on 5 February 1962, pp. 75–76 (I am indebted to David Robb of *Daily Variety* for allowing me to reproduce his copy of this document).

25. Minutes, special meeting, 16 October 1939, pp. 1–2, 1 October 1949, p. 5, 5 March 1962, p. 1 (I am indebted to David Robb of *Daily Variety* for allowing me to reproduce his copy of this last document).

26. Minutes, 5 March 1962, p. 2.

27. Ibid., p. 1; agency report, 16 September 1938, p. 892 in overall minutes; Reagan's testimony, p. 67.

28. Minutes, 21 April 1952, p. 2; special meeting, 12 May 1952, p. 4, 16 June 1952, pp. 1–5, 5 March 1962, p. 1; *Hollywood Reporter*, 13 August 1951; Moldea, *Dark Victory*, pp. 99–100; Reagan's testimony, pp. 73, 74, 84.

29. Minutes, 16 June 1952, p. 1, 30 June 1952, p. 2; Reagan's testimony, pp. 73, 74, 84; *Motion Picture Herald*, 12 July 1952.

30. DFP interview with John Dales; Minutes, 14 July 1952, p. 2; Reagan's testimony, pp. 91–92.

31. Moldea, *Dark Victory*, pp. 108–109, 224.

32. Reagan's testimony, p. 81; Moldea, *Dark Victory*, pp. 106, 132–33, and passim; Henry Denker, *The Kingmaker* (New York: David McKay, 1972); Garry Wills, *Reagan's America: Innocents At Home* (Garden City, N. Y.: Doubleday, 1987), pp. 261, 263, 274.

33. Reagan's testimony, passim; Moldea, *Dark Victory*, pp. 5, 208, and passim; Anne Edwards, *Early Reagan: The Rise To Power* (New York: William Morrow, 1987), p. 439.

34. Reagan's testimony, p. 68; Jack Dales, "Pragmatic Leadership: Ronald Reagan as President of the Screen Actors Guild," interview with Mitch Tuchman, UCLA Library Department of Special Collections, box 300/181, p. 45; Stirling and Kittross, *Stay Tuned*, p. 532.

35. Nick Browne, "The Political Economy of the Television (Super) Text," *Quarterly Review of Film Studies* 9(3): 177–78 (Summer 1984); Vianello, "Rise of the Telefilm," p. 210; Douglas Gomery, "Hollywood's Business," *The Wilson Quarterly* 10(3): 54 (Summer 1986).

36. *Hollywood Reporter*, 21 November 1955.

37. Minutes, 22 March 1948, p. 3, 5 April 1948, p. 1; *Screen Actor*, March 1960, pp. 4–5; Dales, "Pragmatic Leadership," p. 25.

38. Minutes, 1 June 1948, pp. 1–5, 7 July 1948, p. 1; Dales, "Pragmatic Leadership," p. 26; *Screen Actor*, March 1960, p. 5; *Daily Variety*, 4 July 1948; *Motion Picture Herald*, 1 March 1952.

39. *Daily Variety*, 28 December 1956; Vianello, "Rise of the Telefilm," p. 24; *Screen Actor*, March 1960, pp. 7–12.

40. Minutes, 4 January 1960, p. 1, 25 January 1960, p. 1; DFP interviews with Chester Migden and Gilbert Perkins; Dales, "Pragmatic Leadership," pp. 36–37; *Screen Actor*, March 1960, p. 6.

41. John R. Simons, "The Union Approach to Health and Welfare," *Industrial Relations* 4(3): 61–76 (May 1965), passim; Schubert and Lynch, "Broadcasting Unions," p. 43.

42. Minutes, 12 October 1959, p. 3, 25 January 1960, p. 2; DFP interviews with Gilbert Perkins, Chester Migden, and John Dales; *Screen Actor*, October 1959, p. 2, August/September 1960, p. 12.

43. Minutes, 25 January 1960, p. 1; *Screen Actor*, October 1959, p. 2, February 1960, pp. 1–2, March 1960, pp. 6, 9; *Hollywood Reporter*, 10 February 1960; *Film Daily*, 23 February 1960; *Los Angeles Examiner*, 28 February 1960; *Hollywood Citizen-News*, 7 March 1960; DFP interview with Chester Migden; Reagan and Hubler, *Rest of Me?* p. 315.

44. DFP interview with John Dales; memo from Jack Warner to all employees at Warner Brothers Studio, dated 24 February 1960, from University of Southern California Library, Department of Special Collections, file named "Screen Actors Guild Strike—1960;" *Los Angeles Mirror-News*, 7 March 1960; *Los Angeles Examiner*, 28 February 1960; Editorial in *Los Angeles Times*, 19 March 1960; *Screen Actor*, April/May 1960, p. 1.

45. Minutes, 8 February 1960, p. 3; *Los Angeles Times*, 8 March 1960; Reagan and Hubler, *Rest of Me?* pp. 317–18.

46. *Daily Variety*, 4 March 1960.

47. DFP interviews with John Dales and Gilbert Perkins; Hedda Hopper's column in the *Los Angeles Times*, 12 March 1960.

48. DFP interviews with John Dales and William Schallert; Morris Gelman, "The Above-The-Line Unions," *Television* 24(1): 46 (November 1967); *Screen Actor*, April/May 1960, p. 1.

49. Bob Hope quoted in Moldea, *Dark Victory*, p. 142; Mickey Rooney quoted in *Daily Variety*, 29 May 1987, p. 24; DFP interview with Ralph Bellamy; Ronnie Dugger, *On Reagan: The Man & His Presidency* (New York: McGraw-Hill, 1983), p. 330.

50. DFP interviews with Chester Migden, Frank Maxwell, Ralph Bellamy, and John Dales.

51. DFP interviews with Chester Migden and Gilbert Perkins; Dales, "Pragmatic Leadership," p. 17; Charlton Heston, *The Actor's Life: Journals 1956–1976* (New York: E. P. Dutton, 1978), p. 92.

52. *Screen Actor*, August/September 1960, p. 13.

53. Sterling and Kittross, *Stay Tuned*, pp. 515, 535; Erik Barnouw, *Tube of Plenty: The Evolution of American Television*, rev. ed. (New York: Oxford, 1982), p. 198; Huettig, "Motion Picture Industry," p. 250; Todd Gitlin, *Inside Prime Time* (New York: Pantheon, 1985), p. 82; Vianello, "Rise of the Telefilm," p. 920.

54. *Movies International* 1(3): 16 (1966).

55. Bill Davidson, "MCA: The Octopus Devours the World," pt. 1, *SHOW*, February 1962, p. 50.

56. For Dales's review of the history of the MCA waiver to the board, see the minutes, 5 March 1962, pp. 2–3; DFP interview with John Dales; Bill Davidson, "MCA Part 2: A Case Study of Power," *SHOW*, March 1962, p. 71.

57. Reagan's testimony, passim. Once again, I am indebted to David Robb of *Daily Vareity* for giving me access to this material; Robb's own story on Reagan's testimony can be found in *Daily Variety*, 18 April 1984, pp. 35, 212; Davidson, "MCA Part 2," p. 71; Moldea, *Dark Victory*, pp. 167, 203.

58. Reagan's testimony, passim; Reagan and Hubler, *Rest of Me?* p. 325; Moldea, *Dark Victory*, pp. 202–3.

59. DFP interview with John Dales; Moldea, *Dark Victory*, p. 207; Minutes, 6 August 1962, p. 1.

60. *Daily Variety*, 18 April 1984, pp. 35, 212; Moldea, *Dark Victory*, pp. 211, 219; Wills, *Reagan's America*, pp. 261–78; Edwards, *Early Reagan*, pp. 435–40.

5. DEMOCRACY

1. Thomas H. Guback, "Hollywood's International Market," in *The American Film Industry*, ed. Tino Balio (Madison: University of Wisconsin, 1976), p. 401; *Screen Actor*, October/November 1961, p. 13, January 1972, p. 3; *New York Times*, 7 February 1965; *Film Daily*, 11 November 1966; *Weekly Variety*, 12 March 1969; *Hollywood Citizen-News*, 18 March 1970.

2. Todd Gitlin, *Inside Prime Time* (New York: Pantheon, 1985), p. 82; Christopher H. Sterling and John M. Kittross, *Stay Tuned: A Concise History of American Broadcasting* (Belmont, Calif.: Wadsworth, 1978), p. 400.

3. *Screen Actor*, July 1972, p. 49; October 1972, pp. 2, 3, 4.

4. *Screen Actor*, August 1984, p. 108; *Business Week*, 29 July 1972, p. 49; *Movies International* 1(3): 16 (1966).

5. Seymour Martin Lipset, Martin Trow, and James Coleman, *Union Democracy: What Makes Democracy Work in Labor Unions and Other Organizations?* (Garden City, N. Y.: Doubleday, 1956) pp. 2–13; Burton Hall, *Autocracy and Insurgency in Organized Labor* (New Brunswick, N. J.: Transaction, 1972), pp. 1–2 and passim.

6. I am indebted to William Schallert for pointing out to me the "Robin Hood" quality of some of the policies instituted by the conservatives; on business unionism, see Alvin W. Gouldner, "Attitudes of 'Progressive' Trade-Union Leaders," *American Journal of Sociology* 52: 389 (March 1947); William M. Leiserson, *American Trade Union Democracy* (New York: Columbia University, 1959), pp. 46, 61–64, 103, 105; Samuel R. Friedman, *Teamster Rank and File: Power, Bureaucracy, and Rebellion at Work and in a Union* (New York: Columbia University, 1982), pp. 30–31.

7. This and the following paragraph are based on my interviews with Don Dubbins, John Gavin, Frank Maxwell, Kathleen Nolan, Joseph Ruskin, and William Schallert, and also on an official letter from Robert Easton to Joyce Gordon on the deliberations of the guild's Government Review Committee, dated 3 March 1972.

8. DFP interview with Robert Easton; *Daily Variety*, 10 October 1969, 11 November 1969, 3 November 1971.

9. For a statement in defense of SAG's democratic qualities, see the minutes of 3 April 1972, p. 2; for evidence of violence and tyranny in unions, see Paul F. Clark, *The Miners' Fight for Democracy: Arnold Miller and the Reform of the United Mine Workers* (Ithaca, N. Y.: Cornell University, 1981), pp. 1–21; Friedman, *Teamster*, p. 4.

10. John R. Coleman, "The Compulsive Pressures of Democracy in Unionism," in *Labor and Trade Unionism: An Interdisciplinary Reader*, ed. Walter Galenson and Seymour Martin Lipset (New York: John Wiley and Sons, 1960), p. 208; Seymour Martin Lipset, "The Political Process in Trade Unions: A Theoretical Statement," ibid., pp. 224, 238; J. David Edelstein and Malcolm Warner, *Comparative Union Democracy: Organization and Opposition in British and American Unions* (New Brunswick, N. J.: Transaction, 1979), p. 30.

11. Edward S. Mason, "Labor Monopoly and All That," in Galenson and Lipset, *Unionism*, pp. 119–120; *Daily Variety*, 15 December 1971; see also Harald O. Dyrenforth's article on the "debasement" of the acting profession in *Screen Actor*, April/May 1961, and the pro and con letters to the editor in subsequent issues.

12. William Schallert explained the "Preference of Employment" clause to me; DFP interviews with Robert Easton, John Gavin; *Movies International* 1(3): 17 (1966); *Hollywood Reporter*, 29 April 1970; minutes, 27 April 1970, pp. 1–2.

13. DFP interviews with Anthony Caruso, Robert Easton, Bert Freed, and Joseph Ruskin; report of Membership Interest Committee to the SAG board of directors, 7 June 1972; minutes, 8 May 1972, p. 2, 28 August 1972, p. 3 and letter from Don Dubbins in appendix.

14. DFP interview with Chester Migden.

15. DFP interviews with Frank Maxwell and Kent McCord.

16. DFP interviews with Howard Caine and Bert Freed.

17. Ibid.

18. DFP interviews with Howard Caine, Bert Freed, and William Schallert; *Weekly Variety*, 26 April 1972.

19. DFP interviews with Edward Asner and Joseph Ruskin; *Daily Variety*, 7 October 1971.

20. I rely on my own interviews with Heston for my judgment of his motives; the rest of the paragraph is a summary based on many sources.

21. DFP interviews with Bert Freed and Dennis Weaver; *Daily Variety*, 4 November 1971.

22. DFP interview with Bert Freed; *Hollywood Reporter*, 1 October 1971.

23. *Hollywood Reporter*, 1 October 1971.

24. *Daily Variety*, 7 October 1971.

25. DFP interviews with Robert Easton and John Gavin.

26. "An Open Letter to Donald Sutherland from John Gavin," in *Daily Variety* and *Hollywood Reporter*, October 1971.

27. *Daily Variety*, 7 October 1971.

28. *Daily Variety*, 5 October 1971; Charlton Heston, *The Actor's Life: Journals 1956–1976* (New York: E. P. Dutton, 1978), p. 371.

29. DFP interviews with Bert Freed and Charlton Heston; *Daily Variety*, 5 October 1971.

30. Vote totals from Screen Actors Guild files; *Daily Variety*, 4 November 1971.

31. DFP interviews with Kathleen Nolan; minutes, 3 April 1972, pp. 1, 2, 28 August 1972, p. 3, 3 April 1973, p. 3, 30 April 1973, p. 3; *Screen Actor*, January 1973, p. 9; *Daily Variety*, 13 October 1972.

32. Minutes, 15 March 1972, pp. 3–5; Government Review Committee report, Easton to Gordon, 3 March 1972.

33. DFP interviews with Robert Easton and Kent McCord.

34. DFP interview with Robert Easton; Don Dubbins's letter in appendix of minutes, 28 August 1972; Fritz Feld's letter in minutes, 1 October 1973, p. 8.

35. DFP interviews with Gilbert Perkins and Diana Muldaur; minutes, 1 October 1973, p. 8; *Daily Variety*, 15 August 1972, p. 8.

36. DFP interviews with John Dales, Don Dubbins, Fritz Feld, Bert Freed, Frank Maxwell, Kent McCord, Kathleen Nolan, and Dennis Weaver; minutes, 8 May 1972, pp. 5, 8.

37. Report of Membership Relations Committee to board of directors, 7 June 1972; Government Review Committee report, Easton to Gordon, 3 March 1972; minutes, 15 March 1972, pp. 3–5, 3 April 1972, pp. 2–3, 5 May 1972, pp. 2, 4, 28 August 1972 (Dubbins's letter in appendix), 1 October 1973, p. 8; *Daily Variety*, 21 April 1972, 24 May 1972, 5 June 1972, 13 June 1972.

38. DFP interview with Kent McCord; *Hollywood Reporter*, 9 November 1972.

39. DFP interview with Kathleen Nolan; minutes, 9 September 1972, p. 4, 9 October 1972, p. 5, 1 October 1973, p. 6; *Screen Actor*, January 1973, p. 9.

40. DFP interview with Kathleen Nolan.

41. Ibid.

42. DFP interviews with Robert Easton and Kathleen Nolan; see Doqui's reports on the Minorities Committee in *Screen Actor*, January 1973, pp. 12–13, and *Screen Actor News-Letter*, May 1972.

43. DFP interview with Kathleen Nolan.

44. DFP interviews with Bert Freed, Kathleen Nolan, and Dennis Weaver.

45. Ibid.

46. *Daily Variety*, 16 October 1973; also see the Gavin ad in *Daily Variety* of 26 September 1973 and 17 October 1973.

47. *Daily Variety*, 8 November 1973.

48. *Daily Variety* and *Hollywood Reporter* of 19 November 1973.

49. *Hollywood Reporter*, 1 July 1974.

50. DFP interviews with Fritz Feld, Kent McCord, Chester Migden, and Joseph Ruskin.

51. For a discussion of the tedium of long board meetings, see the minutes, 18 January 1977, p. 1; DFP interviews with Anthony Caruso, Jeff Corey, Don Dubbins, Robert Easton, Gilbert Perkins, and Robert Vaughn; *Daily Variety*, 5 September 1979.

52. DFP interviews with Diana Muldaur, Joseph Ruskin, Yale Summers, and Dennis Weaver.

53. DFP interviews with William Schallert and Jessica Walter; *Daily Variety*, 20 August 1974.

54. DFP interviews with John Dales, Don Dubbins, Robert Easton, Frank Maxwell, Chester Migden, and Joseph Ruskin; *Screen Actor*, January 1973, p. 2.

55. DFP interviews with Robert Easton and Kathleen Nolan; *Hollywood Reporter*, 2 September 1975.

56. DFP interview with Kathleen Nolan; on the lack of issues in the campaign, see *Hollywood Reporter*, 2 September 1975.

57. DFP interview with Kathleen Nolan; "Why Kathleen Nolan for National SAG President," 1975 Nolan campaign pamphlet, passim.

58. Vote totals and geographic distribution from SAG files.

59. DFP interview with Kathleen Nolan.

60. Minutes, 24 May 1977, President's Report addendum; DFP interview with Kathleen Nolan; *Screen Actor*, Spring 1980, pp. 20–22; *Hollywood Reporter*, 30 January 1976.

61. Minutes, 15 February 1977, President's Report, 8 March 1977, p. 5, 24 May 1977, President's Report, 16 September 1977, p. 1; DFP interview with Kathleen Nolan; *Screen Actor*, October/November 1978, p. 9; Spring 1979, p. 2; *Los Angeles Times*, 9 November 1979.

62. "Women and Minorities in Television Drama 1969–1978," a research report by George Gerbner and Nancy Signorielli (Philadelphia: University of Pennsylvania, The Annenberg School of Communications, 29 October 1979), passim; DFP interviews with Norma Connolly, Janet MacLachlan, Diana Muldaur, Kathleen Nolan, and Jessica Walter; *Screen Actor*, Fall 1979, pp. 8–16.

63. On the redecorated office, and board members' complaints about lack of consultation in general, see minutes, 19 July 1977, pp. 5–7, 16, 17; DFP interviews with Norma Connolly, Bert Freed, Frank Maxwell, Kathleen Nolan, Joseph Ruskin, Ron Soble, and Yale Summers; *Daily Variety*, 5 January 1977.

64. DFP interviews with Bert Freed, Gilbert Perkins, Joseph Ruskin, William Schallert, and Marie Windsor.

65. My informants on this point would prefer to remain unnamed; for Nolan's charge of a "chauvinist plot" on the board, see *New Times*, 28 October 1977.

66. For boardroom discussions of Nolan's financial habits, see minutes, 4 January 1977, p. 1, 19 July 1977, p. 18, 16 August 1977, "Confidential Addendum"; DFP interviews with Frank Maxwell and Kathleen Nolan; *Daily Variety*, 11 October 1977.

67. *Daily Variety*, 11 October 1977.

68. *Daily Variety*, 11 October 1977, 13 October 1977; *New Times*, 28 October 1977.

69. On the committee investigating Nolan's financial practices, see the minutes, 16 August 1977, "Confidential Addendum," pp. 2–4; annual meeting of national board of directors, 18 and 19 November 1977, p. 14; DFP interviews with Jeff Corey, Kathleen Nolan, and Yale Summers; *Daily Variety*, 21 November 1977.

70. Kathleen Nolan campaign pamphlet, 1977 (from the private collection of Bert Freed).

71. Vote totals are from Screen Actors Guild election records; *Daily Variety*, 8 November 1977.

72. DFP interview with Kathleen Nolan; *Screen Actor*, October/November 1978, p. 9; Spring 1979, pp. 1–3; *Hollywood Reporter*, 46th Anniversary Edition, September 1977, pp. 62–64.

73. DFP interviews with Kim Fellner and Kathleen Nolan.

74. Executive Committee minutes, 13 February 1979, pp. 2–3; minutes, 13 February 1979, pp. 1–2; DFP interview with Kathleen Nolan; *Daily Variety*, 1 March 1979.

75. DFP interview with Kathleen Nolan; *Daily Variety*, 13 September 1979, 7 November 1979; *Hollywood Reporter*, 20 September 1979; *Los Angeles Times*, 28 May 1980.

76. Vote totals from SAG files; DFP interviews with William Schallert and Ron Soble.

77. Friedman, *Teamster*, p. 255.

78. Lipset, "Theoretical Statement," p. 230.

79. Ibid.

80. Ibid.

81. J. David Edelstein and Malcolm Warner, "Research Areas In National Union Democracy," *Industrial Relations* 16(2): 190 (May 1977); John C. Anderson, "A Comparative Analysis of Local Union Democracy," *Industrial Relations* 17(3): 289 (October 1978); Lipset, "Theoretical Statement," p. 230.

82. Figures compiled from various SAG financial documents (I am indebted to William Schallert for bringing this information to my attention).

83. Edelstein and Warner, *Union Democracy*, pp. 107, 115, 186, 232.

84. Ibid., p. 186.

85. Ibid.

86. Ibid.

87. Ibid., pp. 132–133.

88. Lipset, "Theoretical Statement," p. 219.

89. Edelstein and Warner, *Union Democracy*, p. 115.

90. Philip W. Nyden, "Democratizing Organization: A Case Study of a Union Reform Movement," *American Journal of Sociology* 90(6): 1191 (1985).

91. Ibid., p. 1192.

6. POLARIZATION

1. Aljean Harmetz, *Rolling Breaks and Other Movie Business* (New York: Alfred A. Knopf, 1983), pp. 165–171; Todd Gitlin, *Inside Prime Time* (New York: Pantheon, 1985), p. ix; Douglas Gomery, "Hollywood's Business," in *The Wilson Quarterly*, Summer 1986, pp. 55–56; *Wall Street Journal*, 23 September 1985, p. 6; *Newsweek*, 15 September 1986, p. 48; *Daily Variety*, 14 May 1986, p. 1, and 53d Anniversary Issue, 28 October 1986, p. 8.

2. DFP interviews with Bert Freed, Ken Barry, and Chuck Dorsett; Harold L. Vogel, *Entertainment Industry Economics: A Guide for Financial Analysis* (Cambridge: Cambridge University, 1986), p. 61; *Screen Actor*, August 1984, p. 107; *Daily Variety*, 23 January 1986, p. 1, 19 November 1985, p. 1, and 53d Anniversary Issue, p. 44.

3. DFP interview with John Dales, Paul Kreppel, Joseph Ruskin, and William Schallert; Christopher H. Sterling and John M. Kittross, *Stay Tuned: A Concise History of American Broadcasting* (Belmont, Calif.: Wadsworth, 1978), p. 399; *TV Guide*, 10 August 1985, p. 40.

4. DFP interviews with Chester Migden, Joseph Ruskin, and William Schallert.

5. DFP interviews with Kent McCord, Chester Migden, Gilbert Perkins, Rhodes Reason, Joseph Ruskin, and William Schallert; Edith L. Johnson, "Strike! An Historical Perspective," *Premiere* 12(3): 18 (December 1980).

6. DFP interviews with Norma Connolly, Joseph Ruskin, and William Schallert; *Hollywood Reporter*, 28 December 1976.

7. Vogel, *Entertainment Industry Economics*, pp. 179–83; DFP interviews with Frank Maxwell, Joseph Ruskin, and Ron Soble.

8. DFP interviews with Frank Maxwell and Yale Summers; Johnson, "Strike!" p. 18.

9. DFP interviews with Kim Fellner and Kent McCord; Johnson, "Strike!" pp. 15–18, 45; *Screen Actor*, Winter 1980/81, passim; *Daily Variety*, 25 July 1980; *Los Angeles Times*, editorials, 28 July 1980, 30 July 1980.

10. This and the following ten paragraphs are based largely on information obtained from interviews with Norma Connolly, Kim Fellner, Bert Freed, Sumi Haru, Janet MacLachlan, Frank Maxwell, Kent McCord, Chester Migden, Gilbert Perkins, Rhodes Reason, Joseph Ruskin, William Schallert, Ron Soble, Yale Summers, and Jessica Walter; see also the *Los Angeles Herald-Examiner*, 21 July 1980; *Weekly Variety*, 30 July 1980.

11. *New York Times*, 24 October 1980.

12. DFP interviews with Daryl Anderson, Howard Caine, and Paul Kreppel.

13. Ibid.; *Screen Actor*, Winter 1980/81, p. 43.

14. DFP interview with Howard Caine.

15. DFP interviews with Howard Caine and Dean Santoro.

16. DFP interviews with Daryl Anderson, Edward Asner, Howard Caine, Norma Connolly, Paul Kreppel, Joseph Ruskin, and Dean Santoro.

17. Caucus of Artists for Merger "Declaration of Interdependence," from the private files of Howard Caine (I am indebted to Howard Caine for giving me access to this material).

18. *New York Times*, 24 October 1980; *Los Angeles Herald-Examiner*, 20 February 1981.

19. DFP interviews with Daryl Anderson, Edward Asner, Howard Caine, Paul Kreppel, Dean Santoro, and Ron Soble; Marc Cooper, "The War For Control of S. A. G.," *L. A. Weekly*, 12–18 April 1985, p. 20; *Los Angeles Herald-Examiner*, 15 September 1981.

20. DFP interviews with Daryl Anderson, Edward Asner, Howard Caine, and Dean Santoro; *Los Angeles Herald-Examiner*, 21 September 1981.

21. DFP interviews with Edward Asner, Howard Caine, Kent McCord, Dean Santoro, and Ron Soble; *Los Angeles Herald-Examiner*, 15 September 1981.

22. Vote totals from Screen Actors Guild files; DFP interviews with Sumi Haru and Dean Santoro; *Daily Variety*, 21 September 1981; *Hollywood Reporter*, 21 July 1981.

23. DFP interviews with Kathy Connell and Daryl Anderson; *Daily Variety*, 18 August 1981.

24. DFP interviews with Robert Easton and Yale Summers; Charlton Heston, *The Actor's Life: Journals 1956–1976* (New York: E. P. Dutton, 1978), p. 449.

25. Minutes, 9 November 1981, pp. 21–22; *Los Angeles Herald-Examiner*, 15 September 1981; Ronnie Dugger, *On Reagan: The Man & His Presidency* (New York: McGraw-Hill, 1983), p. 329.

26. Minutes, 24 November 1981, p. 9; DFP interviews with Dan Caldwell, Anthony Caruso, Don Dubbins, and Marie Windsor; names of past winners from award replica in lobby of Screen Actors Guild headquarters.

27. DFP interviews with Anthony Caruso and Marie Windsor.

28. Ibid.

29. DFP interviews with Dan Caldwell, Kim Fellner, Chester Migden, Diana Muldaur, and Dean Santoro; *Screen Actor*, Summer 1979, passim; Sally Ogle Davis, "Battling It Out In Hollywood" *New York Times Magazine*, 25 April 1982.

30. Letter from Kim Fellner to SAG Executive Committee, dated 12 November 1981, p. 15719 in overall minutes; DFP interview with Kim Fellner.

31. Ibid.

32. Executive Committee minutes, 9 November 1981, p. 5; minutes, 24 November 1981, "Confidential Addendum," pp. 2–9.

33. DFP interview with Frank Maxwell.

34. The Heston quote is from Cooper, "War," p. 13.

35. DFP interviews with Don Dubbins and Marie Windsor; *Daily Variety*, 23 June 1982, 14 July 1982; *Weekly Variety*, 25 August 1982.

36. DFP interview with Marie Windsor.

37. "Screen Actors Guild/Screen Extras Guild Merger Primer," pamphlet published by the Screen Actors Guild, p. 4; DFP interview with Chester Migden.

38. "Merger Primer," p. 4; DFP interviews with Paul Kreppel, Kent McCord, and Yale Summers.

39. DFP interview with Yale Summers.

40. Screen Actors Guild Constitution, Article XIII, sec. 3, p. 12 (1983 edition); *Daily Variety*, 18 November 1982.

41. Gitlin, *Inside Prime Time*, p. 4.

42. The Winston letter and the second unattributed letter are quoted in Pete Hamill, "What Does Lou Grant Know About El Salvador?" *New York*, 15 March 1982, p. 27; *Los Angeles Herald-Examiner*, 25 February 1982. A general account of this episode, and some of the quotes I have used, are available in Gitlin, *Inside Prime Time*, pp. 5–9.

43. Gloria Ohland, "Behind the Celluloid Curtain: The Ed Asner-SAG Controversy," *L. A. Weekly*, 5–11 March 1982, p. 11; Davis, "Battling It Out In Hollywood"; Hamill, "What Does Lou Grant Know?" p. 24; Cooper, "War," 12–18 April 1985, p. 13; *Daily Variety*, 21 December 1981, 12 February 1982, 22 February 1982; *Los Angeles Herald-Examiner*, 17 February 1982.

44. DFP interview with Charlton Heston; Flyer to SAG members initialed by Morgan Paull, no date, from files of AWAG; "Rebuttal by the Minority," in "The SAG/SEG Merger Issues: Executive Secretary's Report," no date, from files of AWAG; Davis, "Battling It Out In Hollywood," p. 2.

45. *Los Angeles Herald-Examiner*, 25 February 1982.

46. Cooper, "War," p. 16; *Los Angeles Herald-Examiner*, 17 February 1982, 28 February 1982; *Daily Variety*, 22 February 1982, 9 September 1982.

47. Vote totals from Screen Actors Guild files.

48. DFP interviews with Kim Fellner, Morgan Paull, and Yale Summers.

49. This and the following two paragraphs are based upon interviews with Anthony Caruso, Don Dubbins, Don Galloway, Charlton Heston, Morgan Paull, and Marie Windsor.

50. DFP interviews with Morgan Paull and Marie Windsor; *Daily Variety* ad, 9 October 1982, p. 2.

51. Minutes, 26 April 1982, attachment no. 5.

52. Minutes, 26 April 1982, pp. 21–27. The quotation of Bert Freed's statement is from p. 24.

53. DFP interviews with Kim Fellner, Frank Maxwell, and William Schallert; Cooper, "War," p. 13.

54. Vote totals from Screen Actors Guild files; DFP interview with Don Dubbins; *Daily Variety*, 24 August 1982, 5 October 1982, 8 October 1982, 10 November 1983; *Hollywood Reporter*, 10 November 1982, 19 September 1983.

55. Minutes, annual meeting of national board of directors, 9 and 10 December 1983, p. 35; DFP interviews with Daryl Anderson, Frank Maxwell, Kent McCord, Dean Santoro, and Marie Windsor; "Minority Report" in "The SAG/SEG Merger Issues; Executive Secretary's Report," published by the Screen Actors Guild.

56. Antimerger flyers from AWAG files (I am indebted to Marie Windsor for giving me access to these files). Windsor's quotation on legal secretaries is from the "Minority Report" in the "Executive Secretary's Report," p. 4.

57. DFP interview with Gilbert Perkins; *Daily Variety*, 20 March 1984.

58. *Daily Variety*, 4 January 1985, p. 20.

7. WAR

1. DFP interviews with Ada Lynn, Ken Barry, Dan Caldwell, Paul Kreppel, Kent McCord, Jessica Walter, Don Livesay, and Norma Connolly; the quoted passage is from Asner's "Keepers of the Flame," *Screen Actor*, August 1984, p. 115.

2. DFP interviews with Daryl Anderson, Edward Asner, Kathy Connell, Kent McCord, and Dean Santoro.

3. DFP interviews with Daryl Anderson, Kathy Connell, Norma Connolly, William Schallert, and Yale Summers; for former executive secretary Chester Migden's assessment of the cable market, see *Weekly Variety*, 24 August 1983.

4. DFP interviews with Edward Asner, Bert Freed, Kent McCord, Mark McIntire, Ed Nelson, Joseph Ruskin, Dean Santono, and Marie Windsor; for a brief reference to the job of a SAG president, see Charlton Heston, *The Actor's Life: Journals 1956–1976* (New York: E. P. Dutton, 1976), p. 283.

5. DFP interviews with Joseph Rushkin and Dean Santaro.

6. Mark McIntire's résumé.

7. DFP interview with Mark McIntire.

8. Ibid.

9. Ibid.

10. *Daily Variety*, 4 January 1985, p. 20.

11. Ibid.

12. On the motion to prepare a compendium of policies, see the minutes,

November 26 1984, pp. 15–17; on the threat of a suit, see letters from Mark McIntire to national executive secretary Ken Orsatti on AWAG stationary, dated 18 February 1984 and 14 October 1984, from AWAG files; Marc Cooper, "The War for Control of S. A. G.," *L. A. Weekly*, 12–18 April 1985, p. 20; *Daily Variety*, 4 January 1985, p. 20, 23 October 1985, p. 1.

13. DFP interview with Mark McIntire; *Daily Variety*, 27 June 1984.

14. The information in the remainder of this section is largely from the minutes, 19 August 1985, pp. 6–18 and attachment no. 2; *Daily Variety*, 11 April 1985.

15. DFP interviews with Patty Duke, Kent McCord, Joseph Ruskin; Patty Duke and Kenneth Turan, *Call Me Anna: The Autobiography of Patty Duke* (New York: Bantam, 1987), p. 285; *Daily Variety*, 1 and 23 July 1985.

16. Pro-SAG campaign literature from files of Edward Asner and Patty Duke; *TV Guide*, 6 April 1985; *Weekly Variety*, 19 June 1985.

17. On the AIDS policy being supported by McIntire, see the minutes, 4 November 1985, p. 21; *Newsweek*, 26 August 1985, p. 1; *Daily Variety*, 31 October 1985, p. 1.

18. DFP interview with Mark McIntire; *Daily Variety*, 6 November 1985, p. 15.

19. Minutes, 4 November 1985, pp. 21–25.

20. Vote totals from Screen Actors Guild files; *Daily Variety*, 6 November 1985, p. 1.

21. DFP interview with Patty Duke.

22. DFP interviews with Patty Duke and Mark McIntire; *Daily Variety*, 7 November 1985, p. 6, 20 November 1985, p. 1.

23. *Daily Variety*, 9 December 1985, p. 1.

24. DFP interview with Mark Locher.

25. DFP interviews with Anthony Caruso, Norma Connolly, Charlton Heston, and Mark McIntire.

26. DFP interview with Mark McIntire.

27. For a discussion of the purpose and consequences of Palmisano's motion, see minutes, 12 January 1987, p. 30; DFP interview with Mark McIntire and William Schallert; *Daily Variety*, 29 August 1986, p. 1.

28. Patty Duke in *Screen Actor*, Fall 1986, p. 2; *Daily Variety*, 29 May, p. 1, 13 June, p. 6, and 28 July, all 1986.

29. DFP interviews with Charlton Heston, Mark McIntire, and Morgan Paull; *Daily Variety*, 1 August 1986.

30. DFP interviews with Charlton Heston, Mark McIntire, and Morgan Paull.

31. DFP interviews with Frank Maxwell, William Schallert, and two others who would rather not be named.

32. DFP interview with Charlton Heston.

33. *Los Angeles Times*, 3 August 1986; *Daily Variety*, 4 August and 15 September 1986 and 5 January 1987.

34. *Daily Variety*, 30 October 1986, 10 November 1986, 6 January 1987, 2 and 4 February 1987.

35. Minutes, 6 October 1986, p. 4.

36. "Memo To All AWAG Sponsored SAG Board Members, et alia, From Mark McIntire, National SAG Board Member Re: Background On Benefits Derived from the 'Buckley Decision,'" 25 August 1986 (from the files of Mark McIntire); William F. Buckley, "Heston's Right To Advocate," *Los An-*

geles Herald-Examiner, 13 December 1986; *Daily Variety*, 28 August 1986, p. 1.

37. DFP interview with Mark McIntire.

38. For Galloway's letter, see the minutes of the Western Regional Board of Directors, 6 October 1986, p. 23; For Paull's statement, see *Daily Variety*, 28 August 1986, p. 1.

39. *Daily Variety*, 29 August 1986, p. 1.

40. Screen Actors Guild Constitution, Article VIII, sec. 1, p. 10, 1983 printing; *Daily Variety*, 10 September 1986, p. 1.

41. George P. Schultz and John R. Coleman, *Labor Problems: Cases and Readings* (New York: McGraw-Hill, 1959), pp. 461, 467; *Daily Variety*, 3 March 1987, p. 28.

42. For a classic discussion of the theory of the "free rider problem" and its relation to unions, see Mancur Olson, Jr., *The Logic of Collective Action: Public Goods and the Theory of Groups* (New York: Schocken, 1968), pp. 66–97.

43. For four scholarly studies, all coming to the same conclusion, see Henry S. Farber, "Right-to-Work Laws and the Extent of Unionization," *Journal of Labor Economics* 2(3): 319–52 (July 1984); Walter J. Wessels, "Economic Effects of Right To Work Laws," *Journal of Labor Research* 2(1): 55–75 (Spring 1981); Ronald S. Warren, Jr. and Robert P. Strauss, "A Mixed Logit Model of the Relationship between Unionization and Right-To-Work Legislation," *Journal of Political Economy* 87(3): 648–55 (June 1979); Craig Petersen and Keith Lumsden, "The Effect of Right-To-Work Laws on Unionization in the United States," *Journal of Political Economy* 83(6): 1237–48 (Dec. 1975).

44. DFP interview with Mark McIntire; Buckley column in *Los Angeles Herald-Examiner*, 13 December 1986; *Daily Variety*, 10 September 1986, p. 1, 11 February 1987, 27 February 1987, p. 1.

45. *Los Angeles Herald-Examiner*, 21 January 1987.

46. Minutes, 6 October 1986, pp. 4–5; *Daily Variety*, 3 March 1987, p. 28.

47. On the membership censure, see *Daily Variety*, 8 December 1986, p. 1, 14 January 1987, p. 1.

48. *Daily Variety*, 29 December 1986, p. 1.

49. *Daily Variety*, 13 January 1987, p. 49, 14 January 1987, p. 1, 29 January 1987, p. 1.

50. Transcript of meeting on 19 October 1986, quoted in "Investigating Committee Report Re Mark McIntire," as part of printed agenda of Hollywood board, 12 January 1986, p. 2.

51. Ibid., pp. 8, 10; DFP interviews with Mark McIntire, William Schallert.

52. *Daily Variety*, 11 February 1987.

53. *Daily Variety*, 30 March 1987.

54. *Screen Actor*, Fall 1986, p. 15.

8. IDEOLOGY

1. For example: Karl Mannheim, *Ideology and Utopia: An Introduction To the Sociology of Knowledge* (New York: Harcourt, Brace, and World, 1936); Michael Walzer, *The Revolution of the Saints: A Study In The Origins of Radical Politics* (New York: Atheneum, 1969).

2. On the negative view of conservatism, see Alvin W. Gouldner, "Attitudes of 'Progressive' Trade-Union Leaders," *American Journal of Sociology*, March 1947, pp. 389–92. I have encountered the negative view of progressives among several of my informants for this book, although I know of no scholar who endorses it.

3. *Screen Actor*, August 1984, pp. 105–9.

4. Ibid., p. 109.

5. *Screen Actor*, August 1984, pp. 105–9.

6. Seymour Martin Lipset, Martin Trow, and James Coleman, *Union Democracy: What Makes Democracy Work in Labor Unions and Other Organizations?* (Garden City, N. Y.: Doubleday, 1956) pp. 313–27. The quotation is from p. 314.

7. DFP interview with Don Galloway.

8. DFP interview with Don Dubbins.

9. "Screen Actors Guild Special Investigative Committee Report Re: Mark McIntire," 12 January 1987, p. 42.

10. DFP interview with Jessica Walter.

11. *Los Angeles Herald-Examiner*, 15 September 1981 (Ed Asner).

12. DFP interview with Bert Freed.

13. Address by Kathleen Nolan to SAG annual meeting, 11 March 1979, reported in *Screen Actor*, Spring 1979, p. 2.

14. DFP interview with Patty Duke.

15. DFP interview with Dean Santoro.

16. DFP interview with John Gavin.

17. Marc Cooper, "The War For Control of S. A. G.," *L. A. Weekly*, 12–18 April 1986, pp. 13, 19 (Charlton Heston).

18. Marie Windsor, "Ramblings About SAG," unpublished manuscript dated 7 August 1985, p. 1 (from the files of AWAG; I am indebted to Marie Windsor for giving me access to this material).

19. "Special Investigative Committee Report" on McIntire, p. 46.

20. Lipset et al., *Union Democracy*, pp. 373–74.

21. See chap. 5 for a full discussion of this subject.

22. Lipset et al., *Union Democracy*, p. 354.

23. DFP interview with Dan Caldwell.

24. DFP interview with Bert Freed.

25. Max Weber, *The Protestant Ethic And The Spirit of Capitalism* (New York: Charles Scribner's Sons, 1958), p. 104; Bernard C. Hennessy, *Public Opinion*, 3d ed. (North Scituate, Mass.: Duxbury, 1975), p. 180.

26. For a summary statement on the scholarly findings on Jewish liberalism, and a list of citations, see Everett Carll Ladd, Jr., "Jewish Life In The United States: Social and Political Values," in *Jewish Life in the United States: Perspectives from the Social Sciences*, ed. Joseph B. Gittler (New York: New York University, 1981), pp. 123, 146. The quotations are from Stephen D. Isaacs, *Jews and American Politics* (Garden City, N. Y.: Doubleday, 1974), pp. 15, 22.

9. VALEDICTION

1. Michael Goldfield, "Labor In American Politics—Its Current Weakness," *Journal of Politics* 48(1): 3–23 (February 1986); *Wall Street Journal*, 19 September 1986, p. 1; *National Journal*, 1 June 1985, p. 1322, 2 November 1985, pp. 2468–69; *Newsweek*, 5 September 1983, p. 51.

2. As one of many compilations of examples of the horrendous working conditions that prevailed prior to the 1930s, see the first section, "Conditions of Work," in Jerold S. Auerbach, *American Labor: The Twentieth Century* (New York: Bobbs-Merrill, 1969), pp. 5–59.

3. *New Republic*, 25 March 1985, pp. 25–30.

4. Stanley Aronowitz, *Working Class Hero: A New Strategy for Labor* (New York: Pilgrim Press, 1983), p. 125.

5. Information on membership and branches from Screen Actors Guild files; *Daily Variety*, 11 February 1987, p. 1, 2 April 1987, p. 1.

6. DFP interview with Chester Migden.

7. Names obtained from "Intelligence Report to Members of the Screen Actors Guild," vol. 1, no. 1 (31 March 1947), p. 1, and *Screen Actor*, Fall 1986, p. 3.

SOURCES

The following is a discussion of unpublished sources used in the research for this book. Readers who are curious about published sources may peruse the notes.

Screen Actors Guild Documents

The basic documentary source for the historical portions are the guild's minutes going back to 1933. At first, when there was only one branch, these were of two types. The minutes of the board of directors are cited as "minutes" in my footnotes. The minutes of the Executive Committee, consisting of the guild's officers, are cited as such. After the New York branch was created in 1938, the same board continued as the government of the Hollywood branch, but there was in addition a national board consisting of representatives from each branch that met regularly and generated its own minutes. For the later years, therefore, whenever the "minutes" are cited in the notes, they refer to the Hollywood board; when I have reason to cite the national board, I refer to it as such. There is also a national Executive Committee whose minutes get cited now and then in my accounts of the more recent years, as well as a Western Regional Board beginning in the 1980s. Occasionally there are "special" meetings of all these entities, and where they are cited they are designated as such.

The minutes are collected in bound volumes in SAG's headquarters, the pages numbered sequentially from the first meeting to the most recent. They also include other documents, such as letters to or from the board or president. These extra documents are included in the sequential pagination. In my notes I cite page numbers starting from the first page of the particular meeting identified by date, not from the first meeting in 1933. This is because if a scholar were to come into possession of a copy of the minutes of a meeting that occurred, say, in the 1970s, it would obviously do him or her more good to be told that a reference was to a vote on page 3, rather than on page 12106. For the extra documents, however, I cite the page in the "overall minutes" (bound volumes) where they may be found.

Other types of documents used in the research, some of which are cited: Constitution and By-Laws of the Screen Actors Guild, February 1983 edition; "Instructions for Candidates" in the election of 1985; various compilations of rules of procedure for the general membership; a "Merger Primer" containing information on the proposed merger with the Screen Extras Guild; various compilations of important facts about the organization, such as dates of the founding of the various branches, earnings by branch by contract, and so on; official financial reports; copies of contracts with producers; reports to the president from the guild's Government Review Committee; minutes of specific meetings of various standing committees; letters to and from the chairs of various committees; reports to the board by some member; minutes of special investigating committees; reports to the board by those committees; and miscellaneous documents such as organization charts, profiles of the membership, and the like.

Directors Guild of America

Historical files containing material on the late 1930s.

International Alliance of Theatrical
Stage Employes Documents

"Proceedings" of the thirty-second through thirty-eighth conventions (1934–1946), held semiannually. I also obtained several miscellaneous documents, all pertaining to the controversy with the CSU in the 1940s.

Federal Bureau of Investigation Files Obtained
Under The Freedom of Information Act

William Holden
Ronald Reagan
Screen Actors Guild

Archives

1. University of California, Los Angeles (UCLA); Department of Special Collections, University Research Library.
   Eddie Cantor Collection
   Special Collections, files:
     Jack Dales, "Pragmatic Leadership: Ronald Reagan as president of the Screen Actors Guild"
     George Harold Dunne, "Christian Advocacy and Labor Strife in Hollywood"

Hollywood Studio Strike
Herbert Sorrell, "You Don't Choose Your Friends: The Memoirs of Herbert Knott Sorrell"
Herbert Sorrell, "Scrapbooks, Los Angeles, 1945–1947"
2. University of Southern California, Warner Brothers Collection, files:
James Cagney
Boris Karloff
CSU Strike
Robert Montgomery
Ronald Reagan
Screen Actors Guild Strike—1960
Lyle Talbot
3. University of Texas at Austin, Humanities Research Center, David Selznick Collection; "Miscellaneous Correspondence," boxes 6, 167, 277.
4. Southern California Library for Social Research; "Hollywood Studio Strike" files
5. Academy of Motion Picture Arts and Sciences, Margaret Herrick Library, files:
William Bioff
Norma Connolly
Patty Duke
Bert Freed
John Gavin
Don Galloway
Charlton Heston
James Kevin McGuinness
Robert Montgomery
Motion Picture Alliance for the Preservation of American Ideals
Ed Nelson
Morgan Paull
Screen Actors Guild
Ronald Reagan
Joseph Ruskin
William Schallert
Lionel Stander
Yale Summers
Jessica Walter
Dennis Weaver
Marie Windsor

Interviews

The great majority of interviews were formal, sit-down discussions with a tape recorder running. About ten were brief conversations primarily designed to elicit the survey information analyzed in chapter 8. Almost all of these discussions took place during the summers of 1985 and 1986, and the Christmas semester breaks of the same years.

About half of the interviews were one-shot affairs. Some informants, however, seemed to take a personal interest in my work, and made themselves available for follow-up discussions, phone conversations, letters, and so on. I ended up communicating with about a dozen people many times over three years. They also loaned or gave me documents that otherwise would have been unobtainable.

Most of the interviews were with present or former actors who have been deeply involved in the Hollywood branch of the guild's government. These included eight present or past national presidents, two presidents of smaller branches, and dozens of present or past officers and members of the board of directors. There are also a smattering of performers who have participated more indirectly, as in contributing money for campaigns, signing petitions, and the like. I talked to three people in the Dallas branch, one in Phoenix, and two in San Francisco.

In addition to actors I had conversations with guild staff members, officers in three other unions, and journalists for the trade press.

With two exceptions, all informants spoke on the record and raised no objections to being identified. One exception was a longtime progressive activist who has never been a guild officer, and whom I have occasionally cited in chapters 2 and 3 as The Old Hollywood Leftist. The other was a reporter for a trade paper, who was helpful in general but who is not cited in the notes.

The others are the following: Leon Ames, Daryl Anderson, Edward Asner, Dick Bakalyan, Ken Barry, Laurence Beilenson, Ralph Bellamy, Roy Brewer, Howard Caine, Dan Caldwell, Rory Calhoun, Anthony Caruso, Virginia Christine, Noel Conlon, Kathy Connell, Norma Connolly, Jeff Corey, John Dales, Chuck Dorsett, Don Dubbins, Patty Duke, Robert Easton, John Henry Faulk, Fritz Feld, Kim Fellner, Bert Freed, Don Galloway, Beverly Garland, John Gavin, Hugh Gillin, Sumi Haru, Charlton Heston, Leslie Hoffman, Henry Holden, Barrie Howard, Paul Kreppel, Hugh Lampmann, Ron Leibman, Don Livesay, Mark Locher, Ada Lynn, Janet MacLachlan, Frank Maxwell, Kent McCord, Mark McIntire, Chester Migden, Chris Mitchum, Diana Muldaur, Ed Nelson, Kathleen Nolan, Nick Palmisano, Morgan Paull, Gilbert Perkins, Rhodes Reason, David Robb, Joseph Ruskin, Dean Santoro, William Schallert, Ron Soble, Yale Summers, Lyle Talbot, Robert Vaughn, Jessica Walter, Dennis Weaver, and Marie Windsor.

Ann Doran, Katherine Hepburn, Ronald Reagan, and Renee Wedel declined to be interviewed.

Index

Academy of Motion Picture Arts and Sciences: salary-waiver plan of, 17; and NRA codes, 24; Duke, as winner of award from, 197

acting: and working conditions in pre-union Hollywood, 18

—screen, as different from stage, 12–13; and media of employment among activists, 185, 201, 206; interaction of, with Los Angeles and ideology, 200–1; relationship of, to ideological cleavages among actors, 203–5

—stage, as different from screen, 12–13, 203–4; and cultivation of the voice, 18; as possible explanation of SAG founding, 18–21; relationship of, to ideological cleavages among actors, 199, 203–5

acting school: attendance of, and progressive ideology, 199, 201, 206; and centrist activists, 202

activists, SAG: behavior of, 10, 182; emotional maturity of, 10; as good citizens, 10, 182; characteristics of those interviewed, 182–86

actors: attitude toward, in Hollywood, 9; psychology of, 9; precarious nature of profession of, 10–11; mythology and folk-lore of, 10–11, 12, 61; unemployment rate among, 11; four main types of jobs for, 12; stars and non-stars, among, 13–14; conditions of, under old studio system, 70–71; consequences of rise of TV for, 74; hostility to extras of, 147; theory of ideological differences among, first, 197–98; theory of ideological differences among, second, 207–8; as not essentially different from other people in political behavior, 214–15; as over-emphasizing symbolic issues, 216–17

Actors Equity: attempts of, to organize Hollywood, 19; in the experience of SAG founders, 19; and founding of TVA, 75; as target of CAM insurgency, 135; as object of desired merger, in CAM, 194

Actors Working for an Actors Guild (AWAG): founding of, 150–51; early recruiting of, 151; and elections of 1982 and 1983, 152; membership totals of, 152; and election of 1984, 154; members of, feel oppressed on board, 158–59; McIntire becomes chair of, 1983, 159; position of members of, on AFTRA merger, 159;

and contract demands of 1971, 99–100; Gavin keeps progressives off of, 104; Schallert as chair of, 129

—Women's Conference: founded, 107; made national under Nolan, 113–14

—Workshop, 104

Communist Party: in USTG, 35; and CSU, 40; and Sorrell, 40, 45–46; anti-strike policy of, in WWII, 42; adoption of new policy in 1945 by, 46; attempts of, to infiltrate SAG, 47; as target of MPA, 50–51; infiltration of, by LAPD, 52; target of graylists, 56–58; and Sondergaard letter, 60; target of oaths of non-membership, 60; oath of non-membership in, repealed, 111; and controversy on board over McIntire remark, 163–65; and attempts to censure McIntire, 168. *See also* blacklist; Communists; graylist; red-baiting

Communists: in labor unions, 4; and CIO, 35; in CSU, 40; and LAPD harassment of, 46; and 1947 HUAC hearings, 52–53; target of graylists, 56–58; and TVA, 75–76; and Heston's "shadowy constituency" remark, 103; and 1979 *Screen Actor*, 141; and conservative unionists in the 1980s, 144; and Asner, 146–47; and Newman, 162; and political involvement by SAG, 195; misperception of, by conservatives, 217. *See also* blacklist; Communist Party; graylist; red-baiting

Concerned Actors Committee (CAC): founding of, 100; attempts to win power of, 101; slate and platform of, 101; as target of Heston's "shadowy

constituency" remark, 103; as model for CAM, 134; Asner as member of, 136

Conference of Studio Unions (CSU): founding of, 40; and set decorators, 40; Communist influence in, 40, 42, 43, 45; conflict of, with LATSE, 40–49; tactics used by, against IATSE, 43; and abortive 1946 agreement, 47; leader of, at 1946 AFL convention, 47; disintegration of, 49

conglomerate acquisition of studies, 211

Congress of Conservative Contributors, 147

Congress of Industrial Organizations (CIO): and industrial unions, 6; conflict of, with AFL, 6, 35; merger of, with AFL, 6; hypothetical relationship of, to screen actors, 14; and strike of 1937, 30; Communist membership in, 35; SAG threatens to join, 35; harassment of, by LAPD, 46. *See also* AFL-CIO; American Federation of Labor; ideologies; labor unions

Connell, Kathy: on producers' fear of Asner, 156; photo of, 156

Connolly, Norma: membership of, on board of directors, 114; membership of, on 1980 Negotiating Committee, 131; defeat of, for vice-president, 168

Conrad, Robert: opposition of, to SEG merger, 147; as actor-producer, 152

conservative unionists: in labor movement, 4; and outside labor and political involvement, 5, 144; and founding of SAG, 22; in SAG, 1940s, 44; and control of TV, 75–76; control of SAG by, in 1960s, 93–94; resentment by, of